I'm Glad
My Mom died

For Marcus, Dustin, and Scottie

Prologue

IT'S STRANGE HOW WE ALWAYS give big news to loved ones in a coma, as if a coma is just a thing that happens from a lack of something to be excited about in your life.

Mom is in the ICU at the hospital. The doctor told us she has forty-eight hours to live. Grandma, Grandpa, and Dad are out in the waiting room calling relatives and eating vending machine snacks. Grandma says Nutter Butters soothe her anxiety.

I'm standing around Mom's tiny, comatose body with my three older brothers—Marcus (the together one), Dustin (the smart one), and Scott (the sensitive one). I wipe the corners of her crusted-shut eyes with a rag and then it begins.

"Mom," Together leans over and whispers into Mom's ear, "I'm gonna move back to California soon."

We all perk up, excited to see if Mom might suddenly jolt awake. Nothing. Then Smart steps forward.

"Mama. Uh, Mama, Kate and I are getting married."

Again, we all perk up. Still nothing.

Sensitive steps forward.

"Mommy..."

I'm not listening to what Sensitive says to try and get Mom to wake up because I'm too busy working on my own wake-up material.

And now it's my turn. I wait until everyone else goes down to grab some food so that I can be alone with her. I pull the squeaky chair close to her bed and sit down. I smile. I'm about to bring the big guns. Forget weddings, forget moving home. I've got something more important to offer. Something I'm sure Mom cares about more than anything.

"Mommy. I am... so skinny right now. I'm finally down to eighty-nine pounds."

I'm in the ICU with my dying mother and the thing that I'm sure will get her to wake up is the fact that in the days since Mom's been hospitalized, my fear and sadness have morphed into the perfect anorexia-motivation cocktail and, finally, I have achieved Mom's current goal weight for me. Eighty-nine pounds. I'm so sure this fact will work that I lean all the way back in my chair and pompously cross my legs. I wait for her to come to. And wait. And wait.

But she never does. She never comes to. I can't make sense of it. If my weight isn't enough to get Mom to wake up, then nothing will be. And if nothing can wake her up, then that means she's really going to die. And if she's really going to die, what am I supposed to do with myself? My life purpose has always been to make Mom happy, to be who she wants me to be. So without Mom, who am I supposed to be now?

before

1.

THE PRESENT IN FRONT OF me is wrapped in Christmas paper even though it's the end of June. We have so much paper left over from the holidays because Grandpa got the dozen-roll set from Sam's Club even though Mom told him a million times that it wasn't even that good of a deal.

I peel—don't rip—off the paper, because I know Mom likes to save a wrapping paper scrap from every present, and if I rip instead of peel, the paper won't be as intact as she'd like it to be. Dustin says Mom's a hoarder, but Mom says she just likes to preserve the memories of things. So I peel.

I look up at everyone watching. Grandma's there, with her poofy perm and her button nose and her intensity, the same intensity that always comes out when she's watching someone open a present. She's so invested in where gifts come from, the price of them, whether they were on sale or not. She *must* know these things.

Grandpa's watching too, and snapping pictures while he does. I hate having my picture taken, but Grandpa loves taking them. And there's no stopping a grandpa who loves something. Like how Mom tells him to stop eating his heaping bowl of Tillamook Vanilla Bean Ice Cream every night before bed because it won't do any good for his already failing heart, but he won't. He won't stop eating his Tillamook and he won't stop snapping his pictures. I'd almost be mad if I didn't love him so much.

Dad's there, half-asleep like always. Mom keeps nudging him and whispering to him that she's really not convinced his thyroid is normal, then Dad says "my thyroid's fine" in an irritated way and goes back to being half-asleep five seconds later. This is their usual dynamic. Either this or an all-out scream-fight. I prefer this.

Marcus, Dustin, and Scottie are there too. I love all of them for different reasons. Marcus is so responsible, so reliable. I guess this makes sense since he's basically an adult—he's fifteen—but even so, he seems to have a sturdiness to him that I haven't seen in many other adults around me.

I love Dustin even though he seems a bit annoyed by me most of the time. I love that he's good at drawing and history and geography, three things I'm terrible at. I try to compliment him a lot on the things he's good at, but he calls me a brownnoser. I'm not sure what that is exactly, but I can tell it's an insult by the way he says it. Even so, I'm pretty sure he secretly appreciates the compliments.

I love Scottie because he's nostalgic. I learned that word in the Vocabulary Cartoons book Mom reads to us every day, because she homeschools us, and now I try to use it at least once a day so I don't forget it. It really does apply to Scottie. "A sentimentality for the past." That's definitely what he has, even though he's only nine so doesn't have much of a past. Scottie cries at the end of Christmas and the end of birthdays and the end of Halloween and sometimes at the end of a regular day. He cries because he's sad that it's over, and even though it barely *is* over, he's already yearning for it. "Yearning" is another word I learned in Vocabulary Cartoons.

Mom's watching too. Oh, Mom. She's so beautiful. She doesn't think she is, which is probably why she spends an hour doing her hair and makeup every day, even if she's just going to the grocery store. It doesn't make sense to me. I swear she looks better without that stuff. More natural. You can see her skin. Her eyes. Her. Instead she covers it all up. She spreads liquid tan stuff on her face and scrapes pencils along her tear ducts and smears lots of creams on her cheeks and dusts lots of powders on top. She does her hair up all big. She wears shoes with heels so she can be five foot two, because she says four foot eleven—her actual height—just doesn't cut it. It's so much that she doesn't need, that I wish she wouldn't use, but I can see her underneath it. And it's who she is underneath it that is beautiful.

Mom's watching me and I'm watching her and that's how it always is. We're always connected. Intertwined. One. She smiles at me in a pick-up-the-pace kind of way, so I do. I pick up the pace and finish peeling the paper off my gift.

I'm immediately disappointed, if not horrified, when I see what I've received as my present for my sixth birthday. Sure, I like Rugrats, but this two-piece outfit

—a T-shirt and shorts—features Angelica (my least favorite character) surrounded by daisies (I hate flowers on clothes). And there are ruffles around the sleeves and leg holes. If there is one thing I could pinpoint as being directly in opposition to my soul, it's ruffles.

"I love it!" I shout excitedly. "It's my favorite gift ever!"

I throw on my best fake smile. Mom doesn't notice the smile is fake. She thinks I genuinely love the gift. She tells me to put the outfit on for my party while she already starts taking off my pajamas. As she's removing my clothes, it feels more like a rip than a peel.

It's two hours later. I'm standing in my Angelica uniform at Eastgate Park surrounded by my friends, or rather the only other people in my life who are my age. They're all from my primary class at church. Carly Reitzel's there, with her zigzag headband. Madison Thomer's there, with her speech impediment that I wish I had because it's so freaking cool. And Trent Paige is there, talking about pink, which he does excessively and exclusively, much to the dismay of the adults around him. (At first I didn't realize why the adults cared so much about Trent's pink obsession, but then I put two and two together. They think he's gay. And we're Mormon. And for some reason, you can't be gay and be Mormon at the same time.)

The cake and ice cream are rolled out and I'm thrilled. I've been waiting for this moment for two whole weeks, since I first decided what I was going to wish for. The birthday wish is the most power I have in my life right now. It's my best chance at control. I don't take this opportunity for granted. I want to make it count.

Everyone sings "Happy Birthday" off-key, and Madison and Trent and Carly throw in cha-cha-chas after every line—it's so annoying to me. I can tell they all think it's so cool, how they're cha-cha-cha'ing, but I think it takes away from the purity of the birthday song. Why can't they just let a good thing be?

I lock eyes with Mom so she'll know I care about her, that she's my priority. She's not cha-cha-cha'ing. I respect that about her. She gives me one of her big nose-wrinkling smiles that makes me feel like everything's gonna be okay. I smile back at her, trying to take in this moment as fully as I possibly can. I feel my eyes starting to water.

Mom was first diagnosed with stage four breast cancer when I was two years old. I hardly remember it, but there are a few flashes.

There's the flash of Mom knitting me a big green-and-white yarn blanket, saying it was something I could keep with me while she was in the hospital. I hated it, or I hated the way she was giving it to me, or I hated the feeling I got when she was giving it to me—I don't remember what exactly I hated, but there was something in that moment that I absolutely did.

There's the flash of walking across what must have been a hospital lawn, my hand in Grandpa's. We were supposed to be picking dandelions to give to Mom, but instead I picked these brown, pokey, sticklike weeds because I liked them better. Mom kept them in a plastic Crayola cup on our entertainment unit for years. To preserve the memory. (Maybe this is where Scott gets his nostalgic instincts from?)

There's the flash of sitting on the bumpy blue carpet in a corner room in our church building watching as two young and handsome missionaries put their hands on Mom's bald head to give her a priesthood blessing while everyone else in the family sat in cold foldout chairs around the perimeter of the room. One missionary consecrated the olive oil so that it would be all holy or whatever, then poured the oil onto Mom's head, making it even shinier. The other missionary then said the blessing, asking for Mom's life to be extended if it was God's will. Grandma jumped up from her seat and said, "Even if it's not God's will, goddamnit!" which disrupted the Holy Spirit so the missionary had to start the prayer over.

Even though I hardly remember that time in my life, it's not like I have to. The events are talked about so often in the McCurdy household that you didn't even have to be there at all for the experience to be etched into your memory.

Mom loves recounting her cancer story—the chemotherapy, the radiation, the bone marrow transplant, the mastectomy, the breast implant, the stage fourness of it, how she was only thirty-five when she got it—to any churchgoer, neighbor, or fellow Albertsons customer who lends her a listening ear. Even though the facts of it are so sad, I can tell that the story itself gives Mom a deep sense of pride. Of purpose. Like she, Debra McCurdy, was put on this earth to be a cancer survivor and live to tell the tale to any and everyone... at least five to ten times.

Mom reminisces about cancer the way most people reminisce about vacations. She even goes so far as to MC a weekly rewatch of a home video she made shortly after learning of her diagnosis. Every Sunday after church, she has one of the boys pop in the VHS tape since she doesn't know how to work the VCR.

"All right, everyone, shhhhh. Let's be quiet. Let's watch and be grateful for where Mommy is now," Mom says.

Even though Mom says we're watching this video so we can be grateful that she's okay now, there's something about watching this video that just doesn't sit right with me. I can tell how uncomfortable it makes the boys, and it definitely makes me uncomfortable too. I don't think any of us wants to be revisiting memories of our bald, sad, then-dying mom, but none of us express this.

The video starts playing. Mom sings lullabies to all four of us kids while we sit around her on the couch. And much like the video remains the same every time it's played, so too do Mom's comments. Every single time we rewatch this video, Mom comments on how the heaviness was just "too much for Marcus to handle," so he had to keep going off into the hallway to collect himself and come back in again. She says this in a way that lets us know it's the highest compliment. Marcus being distraught about Mom's terminal illness is a testament to what an incredible person he is. Then she comments on what a "stinker" I was, but she says the word "stinker" with such a venomous bite that it might as well be a cuss word. She goes on to say how she can't believe I wouldn't stop singing "Jingle Bells" at the top of my lungs when the mood was clearly so sad. She can't believe how I didn't get that. How could I possibly be so upbeat when my surroundings were so obviously heavy? I was two.

Age is no excuse. I feel tremendous guilt every time we rewatch the home video. How could I not have known better? What a stupid idiot. How could I have not sensed what Mom needed? That she needed all of us to be serious, to be taking the situation as hard as we possibly could, to be devastated. She needed us to be nothing without her.

Even though I know the technicalities of Mom's cancer story—the chemo, the bone marrow transplant, the radiation—are all words that will evoke a big, shocked reaction from whoever hears them, like they can't believe Mom had it so hard, to me they're just technicalities. They mean nothing.

But what *does* mean something to me is the general air in the McCurdy household. The best way I can describe it is that, for as far back as I can remember, the air in the house has felt like a held breath. Like we're all in a holding pattern, waiting for Mom's cancer to come back. Between the constant reenactments of Mom's first bout of cancer and the frequent follow-up visits with doctors, the unspoken mood in the house is heavy. The fragility of Mom's life is the center of mine.

And I think I can do something about that fragility with my birthday wish.

Finally, the "Happy Birthday" song's over. The time has come. My big moment. I shut my eyes and take a deep breath in while I make my wish in my head.

I wish that Mom will stay alive another year.

2.

"One more row of clips and we'll be done," Mom says, speaking of the butterfly clips that she's carefully pinning into my head. I hate this hairstyle, the rows of tightly wound hair fastened into place with painful, scalp-gripping little clips. I'd rather be wearing a baseball cap, but Mom loves this style and says it makes me look pretty, so butterfly clips it is.

"Okay, Mommy," I say, swinging my legs back and forth while I sit on the closed toilet seat lid. The leg swing is a nice touch. Selling it.

The house phone starts ringing.

"Shoot." Mom opens the bathroom door and leans out of it, as far as she can go to grab the phone that hangs from the kitchen wall. She does all of this without letting go of the strand of my hair she's currently working on, so my whole body is leaned all the way over in the same direction that Mom is.

"Hello," she says into the phone as she answers it. "Uh-huh. Uh-huh. WHAT?! Nine p.m.? That's the earliest?! Whatever, guess the kids will have to get through ANOTHER NIGHT without their DAD. That's on you, Mark. That's on you."

Mom slams the phone down.

"That was your father."

"I figured."

"That man, Net, I tell ya. Sometimes I just..." She takes a deep, anxious breath.

"Sometimes you just what?"

"Well I could've married a doctor, a lawyer, or an—"

"Indian chief," I finish for her since I know this catchphrase of hers so well. I asked her once which Indian chief she dated, and she said she didn't mean it literally, that it's just a figure of speech, a way of saying she could have had anyone she wanted back in the day before she had children, which has made her less appealing. I told her I was sorry, and she said it was okay, that she'd much rather have me than a man. Then she told me I was her best friend and kissed me on the forehead and, as an afterthought, said that she actually did go on a few dates with a doctor, though: "Tall and ginger, very financially stable."

Mom keeps clipping my hair.

"Producers too. Movie producers, music producers. Quincy Jones once did a double take when he passed me on a street corner. Honestly, Net, not only could I have married any of those men, but I *should* have. I was destined for a good life. For fame and fortune. You know how much I wanted to be an actress."

"But Grandma and Grandpa wouldn't let you," I say.

"But Grandma and Grandpa wouldn't let me, that's right."

I wonder why Grandma and Grandpa wouldn't let her, but I don't ask. I know better than to ask certain types of questions, the ones that go too deep into specifics. Instead, I just let Mom offer up the information she wants to offer up, while I listen closely and try to take it in exactly the way she wants me to.

"Ow!"

"Sorry, did I clip your ear?"

"Yeah, it's okay."

"It's hard to see from this angle."

Mom starts rubbing my ear. I'm immediately soothed.

"I know."

"I want to give you the life I never had, Net. I want to give you the life I deserved. The life my parents wouldn't let me have."

"Okay." I'm nervous about what's coming next.

"I think you should act. I think you would be a great little actress. Blonde. Blue-eyed. You're what they love in that town."

"In what town?"

"Hollywood."

"Isn't Hollywood far away?"

"An hour and a half. Granted, freeways are involved. I'd have to learn how to drive freeways. But it's a sacrifice I'm willing to make for you, Net. 'Cuz I'm not like my parents. I want what's best for you. Always. You know that, right?"

"Yeah."

Mom pauses the way she does before she's about to say something she thinks is a part of a big moment. She bends around to look me in the eye—still holding my unfinished hair strand.

"So what do you say? You want to act? You want to be Mommy's little actress?"

There's only one right answer.

3.

I DON'T FEEL READY. I know I'm not ready. The kid in front of me hops down off the stage steps in a way that confuses me. He doesn't seem nervous at all. This is just another day for him. He takes a seat next to the dozen or so other children who are already sitting because they've already performed their monologues.

I look around at the boring, white-walled, undecorated room and the rows of kids in metal stackable chairs. I thumb the paper in my hands nervously. I'm next. I got in line last so I would have more time to practice, a decision I now regret because my nerves have had more time to build. I've never felt this way before. Sick to my stomach from nerves.

"Go ahead, Jennette," the man with the black ponytail and goatee deciding my fate tells me.

I nod to him, then step up onstage. I set the piece of paper down so I have more freedom to use my hands for the big gestures Mom instructed me to use, and then I begin my monologue on Jell-O Jigglers.

My voice is shaky as I start out. I can hear it so loud in my head. I try to tune it out, but it just keeps sounding louder. I smile big and hope that Goatee doesn't notice. Finally, I get to the closing line.

"... Because Jell-O Jigglers make me giggle!"

I giggle after the line, just like Mom told me—"high-pitched and cutesy, with a little nose wrinkle at the tail end." I hope the giggle doesn't come across nearly as uncomfortable as I feel with it coming out of me.

Goatee clears his throat—never a good sign. He tells me to try the monologue one more time, but "loosen up a bit, just do it simply like you're talking to your friend... oh, and don't do any of those hand gestures."

I'm conflicted. The hand gestures are exactly what Mom told me to do. If I get to the waiting room and tell her I didn't do the hand gestures, she'll be disappointed. But if I get to the waiting room and tell her I don't have an agent, she'll be even more disappointed.

I do the monologue again, losing the hand gestures, and it feels slightly better, but I can tell Goatee didn't get exactly what he wanted. I disappointed him. I feel awful.

After I finish, Goatee calls out nine names, including mine, and tells the other five kids they can go. I can tell only one of the kids understands that she's just been rejected. The other four waltz out of the room like they're going to get ice cream. I feel bad for her but good for myself. I am a Chosen One.

Goatee tells all of us that Academy Kids would like to represent us for background work, which means we'll stand in the background of scenes for shows and movies. I immediately know that Goatee is trying to make bad news sound good by the way that his face is overly animated.

Once he lets us go to tell our moms in the waiting room, Goatee calls out three kids' names and asks them to stay. I linger, trying to be the last one out of the room so I can hear what's going on with these three special children—these three Even More Chosen Ones. Goatee tells them that they have been selected to be represented as "principal actors," meaning speaking actors. They did so well on their monologues that they are not being represented as human props but rather as genuine, certified, worthy-of-speaking ACTORS.

I feel something uncomfortable brewing inside me. Jealousy mixed with rejection and self-pity. Why am I not good enough to speak?

I get out to the waiting room and run over to Mom, who's balancing her checkbook for the fourth time this week. I tell her that I've been chosen as a background actor, and she seems genuinely happy. I know this is only because she doesn't know that there is a higher tier that I might have been chosen for. I worry about her finding out.

Mom starts filling out the representation paperwork. She points her pen at the dotted line I'm supposed to sign my name on. It's next to a dotted line she's already signed—she has to sign too since she's my guardian.

"What are we signing for?"

"The contract just says that the agent gets twenty percent and we get eighty percent. Fifteen percent of that eighty percent will go into an account called a

Coogan account, which you can access once you're eighteen. That's all the money that most parents let their kids have. But you're lucky. Mommy's not gonna take any of your money except for my salary, plus essentials."

"What are essentials?"

"Why are you giving me the third degree all of the sudden? Don't you trust me?"

I quickly sign.

Goatee comes out to give each of the parents feedback. He comes to Mom first and tells her that I have potential to do principal work.

"Potential?" Mom asks, critically.

"Yes, especially since she's only six, so she's getting an early start."

"But why potential? Why can't she do principal work now?"

"Well, I could tell in her monologue that she was very nervous. She seems quite shy."

"She is shy, but she's getting over it. She'll get over it."

Goatee scratches his arm where there's a tattoo of a tree. He takes a deep breath like he's getting ready to say something he's nervous about saying.

"It's important that Jennette *wants* to act, in order for her to do well," he says.

"Oh, she wants this more than anything," Mom says as she signs on the next page's dotted line.

Mom wants this more than anything, not me. This day was stressful and not fun, and if given the choice, I would choose to never do anything like it again. On the other hand, I *do* want what Mom wants, so she's kind of right.

Goatee smiles at me in a way that I wish I understood. I don't like when grown-ups make faces or sounds that I don't understand. It's frustrating. It makes me feel like I'm missing something.

"Good luck," he says to me with a certain heaviness, and then he walks away.

4.

IT'S THREE A.M. THE FRIDAY after signing with Academy Kids when Mom wakes me up for my first day of background work on a show called *The X Files*. My call time isn't until five a.m., but since Mom's scared of driving freeways for the first time, she wants to get a head start and leave plenty early.

"Look at me, getting over my fear for you," Mom says as we pile into our 1999 Ford Windstar minivan.

We arrive at 20th Century Fox studios an hour early, so we walk around for a bit in the dark. When we pass the giant Luke Skywalker vs. Darth Vader mural on the side of one of the soundstages, Mom squeals with delight, whips out her disposable camera, and snaps a picture of me standing in front of it. I feel embarrassed, like we don't belong here.

By 4:45 a.m., Mom figures it's close enough to my call time to show up, so we check in just outside the soundstage with a short, bald production assistant. He tells us we're early, but we can stop by background crafty before it's time to head to set.

Background crafty is a cool place. It's a tent at the edge of the soundstage with food everywhere. Cereal and candy and jugs of coffee and orange juice and silver trays of breakfast foods—pancakes and waffles and scrambled eggs and bacon.

"And it's free," Mom says excitedly as she wraps various muffins and croissants in napkins and tucks them into her oversized Payless purse to give to my brothers later. There are a bunch of whole eggs sitting in a tray. Mom says they're hard-boiled. I pluck one out to try it. Mom teaches me how to roll the egg on a hard surface to crack the shell, then peel the shell off the egg white. I sprinkle it with salt and pepper and take a big bite. I love it. I grab a bag of Ritz Bits mini cheese sandwiches, too. I could get used to this.

By the time I get to the last bite of the egg, all of the other background kids—there are thirty of us—have shown up, and we're all called to set at once.

We trail behind the bald PA as he guides us to the soundstage where we'll be shooting. As soon as we cross onto the soundstage, I'm in awe. The ceiling is so high, and it's covered with hundreds of lights and poles. There's the smell of fresh wood and the sound of hammers and drills. Many people in cargo pants pass us, some of them with tools hanging off their belts, some of them with clipboards in their hands, some of them whispering urgently into walkie-talkies. There's something magical about this. It feels like so much is happening.

We get to set and the director—a small man with light brown hair long enough to tuck behind his ears—ushers us in, talking quickly and frantically. He looks at me and the other twenty-nine children and tells us excitedly that we will all be playing children who are stuck in a gas chamber and suffocating to death. I nod along, trying to remember each and every word so that I can relay them to Mom on the drive home when she asks. Suffocating to death, got it.

The director tells us all where to stand, and I'm near the back of the blob of children until he asks for the smaller kids to come up front, so I do. He then points to each of us rapidly, one right after the other, and says to give him our best "scared-to-death" face. I'm the ninth or tenth kid he points to, and after I give my face, he tells the cameraman standing next to him to get a close-up of me. I have no idea what this means, but I assume it's good because the director winks at me after he says it.

"One more, even more scared!" the director shouts at me. I widen my eyes a bit, hoping that will work. It does I think, since he says, "Got it, moving on!" and pats me on the back.

The rest of the day consists of segments of set-work and schoolwork, which we are required to do on set, so we go back and forth between the two. Since Mom homeschools me, she pulled my schoolwork for the day and paper-clipped all the worksheets together into a little packet. The twelve-year-old girl seated next to me in the schoolroom keeps elbowing me and telling me we don't have to do any schoolwork if we don't want to because we're background actors, and the studio teachers assigned to background actors don't care how much work gets done because they just want to teach the principal actors. I try my best to ignore her and fill out my page on the state capitals. After our half-hour-or-so schoolwork segments, we're pulled from the classroom by the PA to go do the scene again. The same scene. The whole day, the same scene.

I have no idea why we have to keep doing this one scene so many times, and I figure it's best not to ask questions, but I notice that each time I come back to the set, the camera is in a new position, so I have a feeling it has something to do with that. Oh well, at least every time I'm brought to set, I get to see Mom.

Each time the PA walks us kids back to set, we pass the "background parents holding room," where all the parents are stuffed into a small bungalow. I wave to Mom, who notices me every single time. No matter how engrossed in her *Woman's World* magazine she is, she dog-ears the page, looks up at me, smiles big, and gives me a thumbs-up. We are so connected.

By the end of the day, I'm exhausted. It's been eight and a half hours of being on set and doing schoolwork and walking from the stage to the schoolroom and taking directions and hearing drills and smelling smoke (there was a fog machine on the gas chamber set to enhance the ambiance). It's been a long day and I haven't particularly enjoyed it, but I did like the hard-boiled egg.

"Suffocating to death," Mom says eagerly on our way home, as she recounts everything I told her about the day. "And in a CLOSE-UP. That's gonna really show off how good you are. I bet once this airs, Academy Kids is gonna beg you to be a principal actor. BEG."

Mom shakes her head in disbelief as she taps the steering wheel with excitement. She seems so carefree in this moment. I try to soak in her expression as deeply as I can. I wish she was like this more often.

"You're gonna be a star, Nettie. I just know it. You're gonna be a *star*."

5.

"We have to leave for church in fifteen minutes!" Mom shouts from the other room before I hear the distinct smack of a makeup brush being thrown against the mirror. She must've gotten her eyeliner crooked again.

The church my family goes to is the Garden Grove Sixth Ward of the Church of Jesus Christ of Latter-day Saints. Grandma was baptized a Mormon when she was eight, and then Mom was baptized a Mormon when she was eight—just like I'm gonna be baptized a Mormon when I'm eight, because that's when Joseph Smith said you become accountable for your sins. (Before then, you can sin scot-free.) Even though both Grandma and Mom were baptized, they didn't go to church. I think they wanted the perk of going to heaven without doing the legwork.

But then right after Mom was diagnosed with cancer, we started attending church service.

"I just knew the Lord would help me get better if I was a good and faithful servant," Mom explained to me.

"Oh. So we started going to church when we wanted something from God?" I asked.

"No." Even though Mom was laughing when she said it, she sounded kind of nervous, maybe even a little annoyed. And then she switched the subject to how handsome Tom Cruise looked in the new *Mission: Impossible 2* trailer.

I've never again asked when or why we started going to church. I don't need to know the specifics of why we go to church to know that I love it.

I love the smell of the chapel—pine-scented tile cleaner and a whiff of burlap. I love my primary classes and all the songs about faith and Jesus, like "I Hope They Call Me on a Mission" and "Book of Mormon Stories," and my personal favorite, "Popcorn Popping," which, come to think of it, I'm not sure has anything to do with faith or Jesus. (It's about popcorn popping on an apricot tree.)

But more than anything, I love the escape. Church is a beautiful, peaceful, three-hour weekly reprieve from the place I hate most: home.

Home, like church, is in Garden Grove, California, a town not-so-affectionately referred to by its inhabitants as "Garbage Grove" because, as Dustin puts it before Mom always shuts him up, "There's a lot of white trash here."

We get a good deal on renting the house, since Dad's parents own it, but apparently not good enough since Mom's always complaining about it.

"We shouldn't have to pay anything at all. That's what family's for," she'll vent to me while doing dishes or filing her nails. "If they don't leave the house to your father in their will, I swear..."

We're late on our rent just about every month—Mom's always crying about it. And the payments are often short—Mom's always crying about that too. Sometimes it's just not quite enough even though Mom, Dad, Grandpa, and Grandma all chip in. Grandpa and Grandma moved in with us "temporarily" while Mom was battling cancer but just wound up staying even after she went into remission because it worked out better for everyone.

Mom calls it the "curse of minimum wage." Grandpa works as a ticket-taker at Disneyland, Grandma works as a receptionist at a retirement home, Dad makes cardboard cutouts for Hollywood Video and works in the kitchen design department at Home Depot, and Mom went to beauty school but says having babies sidetracked her career—"plus the hair bleaching fumes are toxic"—so she picks up shifts at Target around the holidays but says her main job is ensuring I make it in Hollywood.

Even though the rent payments are often short and almost always late, we've never been kicked out. And I feel like if anybody but Dad's parents owned the house, we probably would have been kicked out by now. Part of me fantasizes about that.

If we got kicked out, that means we'd have to move somewhere else. And if we'd have to move somewhere else, that means we'd have to pack up the stuff we want to take with us into moving boxes. And if we'd have to pack stuff into moving boxes, that means we'd have to sort through all the stuff in this house and get rid of some of it. And that sounds wonderful.

Our home hasn't always been like this. I've seen pictures from before I was born where it actually looked pretty normal—a humble house with a little clutter, nothing out of the ordinary.

My brothers say it began when Mom got sick; that's when she started not being able to let go of things. That would mean it started when I was two. Since then the problem has only gotten worse.

Our garage is filled floor to ceiling with stuff. Stacks of plastic bins are filled with old papers and receipts and baby clothes and toys and tangled jewelry and journals and Christmas decorations and old candy bar wrappers and expired makeup and empty shampoo bottles and broken mug pieces in Ziploc bags.

The garage has two entrances—the back door and the main garage door. It's nearly impossible to get through the garage if you enter by the back door because there's hardly enough space for a walking path, but even on the off chance that you are able to elbow your way through the path, you won't want to. We have a rat and possum problem, so the only thing you'll see on your sliver of path is dead rats and possums stuck in the traps Dad places every few weeks. The dead rats and possums stink.

Since you can't really walk through the garage, our second fridge is placed strategically at the very front of the garage so that we can open the main garage door and access it easily.

Easily is an overstatement.

Our garage door is the only manual one on the block, and so heavy that it broke its own hinges. The door used to make a loud clicking sound once Dad or Marcus—the only two in the household strong enough to lift it—heaved it up high enough. And once that clicking sound happened, the garage door could stay up on its own.

Well, not anymore. A few years back, after the garage door clicked, it came crashing right back down again and it's never been able to support itself since.

So now going to the garage has become a two-person job. Whoever opens the heavy garage door—typically Marcus—has to hold it up with their entire body to avoid it slamming down on top of them, while the other person—typically me—retrieves whatever needs to be retrieved from the garage.

The times when Marcus and I are asked to retrieve something from the garage are scary. When Marcus holds up the garage door and his face winces underneath the weight of it, and I race to open the overstuffed fridge as quickly as possible and locate the needed food item in the sea of other food items, I feel like I'm Indiana Jones and the boulder is coming and I have to snatch the hidden treasure before the boulder comes crashing down on me.

The bedrooms are bad too. I remember a time when Marcus, Dustin, and Scott slept in their trundle bunk bed and I slept in my nursery, but now our bedrooms are so filled with stuff that you can't even determine where the beds are let alone sleep in them; we don't sleep in the bedrooms anymore. Trifold mats were purchased from Costco for us to sleep on in the living room. I'm pretty sure the mats were meant for kids' gymnastics exercises. I do not like sleeping on mine.

This house is an embarrassment. This house is shameful. I hate this house. I hate how being inside it makes me feel tense and anxious, and all week long I look forward to my three-hour escape into the land of testimonies and pine-scented tile cleaner.

That's why it's so upsetting to me that my family can never get out the door on time, no matter how hard I try to make that happen.

"Come on, everybody, move, move, move!" I shout while I buckle my left shoe.

Dustin and Scottie are just now waking up. They rub the crust out of their eyes as Grandpa clumsily steps over their Costco mat "beds." Grandma and Grandpa sleep on the couch in what used to be my nursery but has since transformed into their bedroom–slash–storage room for more stuff.

"You each have ten minutes to eat breakfast and change and brush your teeth," I say to Dustin and Scott as they head to the kitchen to haphazardly pour themselves cereal—Lucky Charms for Dustin and Count Chocula for Scott. I can tell by their eye rolls that they think I'm bossing them around, but it doesn't feel like bossiness to me. It feels like desperation. I want order. I want peace. I want my three-hour reprieve from this place.

"Did you guys hear me?" I ask to no response. Grandpa stands in the corner of the kitchen, buttering his toast, and the amount of butter he's using stresses me out—a pat that size is costly. Mom always tells me he uses "half a stick of butter every day and we can't afford it, and his diabetes can't afford it either."

"Grandpa, can you use a little less butter? You're gonna upset Mom."

"Huh?" Grandpa calls out. I swear to God he huh's me whenever I ask him something he doesn't want to respond to.

Exasperated, I head out and spread open The White Thing on the gray carpet in the living room. The White Thing is a poorly named thin, white, floral-patterned square that folds out into three ten-inch by ten-inch segments. This trifold square serves as our "table." Apparently, we have a thing for trifolds in our household.

So I splay out The White Thing as Dustin and Scottie walk single file into the living room. They're walking like they're on a tightrope, with just as much focus as tightrope walkers, because they've both overfilled their bowls with milk and cereal to the point that the milk sloshes over the sides of the bowls and lands on the gray carpet. Mom tells them every single day how much she hates when their milk spills on the carpet and how it gives off a sour smell, but no matter how many times she tells them, they just keep overpouring their milk and cereal. Nobody listens around here.

Mom hasn't yet put on her church shoes because she saves putting them on for the last minute since they make her bunions throb, so I know that the second she steps onto the milk-sopped carpet, she'll rip off her tights, fly into hysterics, and demand that we stop at Rite Aid on the way so that she can get a new pair of tights. If we stop at Rite Aid, that will cut into my three-hour-escape. We cannot stop at Rite Aid.

I rush to the towel closet. On my way, I pass the bathroom. I press my ear against the closed door and hear Grandma complaining on the phone with a friend of hers.

"Jean left the price tag on the sweater she got me. She does that whenever she gets something on sale but wants to pretend like she paid full price. It's pretty sneaky of her. Anyway, I went to Mervyn's and saw the sweater there, seventy percent off. She didn't even spend fifteen dollars on me...."

"Grandma, get out! The boys need to get in!" I shout as I bang on the bathroom door.

"Why do you hate me!" Grandma yells. She always does that when she's on the phone with someone. Tries to make herself look like a victim.

I get to the towel closet and grab the little red dish towel with the Christmas lights on it, wet the end of it under the kitchen faucet, and press the wet end into the milk-soaked carpet. I look up and see Dustin and Scottie eating on The White Thing. Scott chews silently and with an even and measured slowness, almost like he's in slow motion. Where is the urgency? Where is the purpose? Dustin chews with his mouth open, loud and chomping. Urgent but not efficient.

I check the clock. 11:12 a.m. Somehow, we have to get out the door and into the van in eight minutes so that we can get to church for the eleven thirty service.

"Hurry it up, slowpokes!" I bark at my brothers while pressing my full body weight into the wet Christmas towel on the milked carpet.

"Shut up, poopsmear," Scottie snaps back at me.

Grandpa steps over me as breadcrumbs spill out of his paper towel–wrapped toast. Grandma crosses in from the other end of the room, wrapped in a towel shabby enough that you can see through it—disgusting. Her perm is clipped into place with a makeshift headwrap made of toilet paper and hair clips.

"You happy, little girl?! I'm out of the bathroom now," she says as she heads to the kitchen.

I ignore Grandma and tell my brothers that the bathroom is free so they can go and brush their teeth while I put their cereal bowls in the sink. Through an act of God we may just make it to church on time.

I'm elated. I lift the wet Christmas towel from the milk spot. I head to the kitchen to re-wet it for round two when Mom crosses through and heads for the living room. Anxiety fills my body. I'm just about to warn Mom, but by the time she's out of the kitchen, I know it's too late.

"What is this?" Mom asks in a tone that makes me know she knows exactly what it is she just stepped in.

I tell Mom I already started to clean it up, so the wetness is mostly just water, but it doesn't matter. Her mood has already switched. She's already ripping off her tights and calling for Dad, saying we're gonna need to stop at Rite Aid so she can get a new pair.

I wonder if there's something different I could have done to get us out the door faster. I wonder if there's something I can do in the future. We all pile into the van and head to Rite Aid. Maybe we'll make it to church in time for "Popcorn Popping."

6.

"Daddy!" I scream as soon as he walks through the door. I run into his belly with my head, the same way I do every time he gets home from work. I take a whiff of his flannel—mmm, freshly chopped wood and a dab of fresh paint, his trademark scent.

"Hi, Net," he says, more blandly than I would hope. I'm always crossing my fingers for a laugh, or a hair rustle, or a hug, but they never come, or at least not yet. I'm still hoping.

"How was work?"

"Fine."

I'm desperate for something else to talk about with him. For some kind of connection. With Mom, it's effortless. Why does everything feel so stuck with him?

"Did you have any fun?" I ask as we walk from the entryway into the living room.

He doesn't answer. A concerned look flashes on his face after he locks eyes with something. I turn my head to see what he's looking at.

Mom. And I can tell immediately by her body language and facial expression—upright posture, lifted chin, gritted teeth, widened eyes—that she's not upset, she's not angry, she's livid. She's about to blow. Oh no. There's gotta be something I can do.

"Mark," she says, smacking her lips to really emphasize the anger. It's now or never, time for me to jump in.

"Love you, Mommy!" I shout. I run toward her. I hug her.

I've got this, I can keep her calm. But before I can think of what to say next...

"Mark Eugene McCurdy," Mom says, her voice rising.

Oh no. Once the "Eugene" comes out, we're almost to the blowup.

"I had to stay late 'cuz I was helping a customer, I couldn't get away," Dad tries explaining. He sounds scared.

"Three hours late, Mark..."

I look over at Dustin and Scottie for help. They're playing *GoldenEye 007* for Nintendo 64. If there is ever a time when they're unreachable, it's when they're playing *GoldenEye 007* for Nintendo 64. Grandma and Grandpa are at work. I'm in this alone.

"Mommy, why don't we watch Jay Leno? You wanna watch Jay Leno? Headlines are on tonight."

"Quiet, Net."

And I'm out. She has spoken. I am silenced. I thought for sure Jay would work. Granted, I'm a bigger fan of Conan, but watching Jay is a family affair in our household. (When I mentioned this in church, Sister Huffmire said Jay's a little risqué and shouldn't I be in bed by eleven thirty p.m. but Mom told me Sister Huffmire's a judger so I can disregard whatever she says.)

I watch Mom closely. Her chest starts heaving. The intensity is growing. Her ears get red. She lunges at Dad. Dad takes a few steps back, causing Mom to trip onto her knees. She starts screaming, "Abuse! Abuse!" Dad grabs her by the wrists to try to calm her down. Mom spits in his face. Somebody wins the round of *007*. A celebratory fist pump flies through the air.

"Deb, I'm a couple hours late, this is not a big deal!" Dad tries yelling through her screams.

"Don't undermine me! DON'T UNDERMINE ME!" Mom frees her wrists and starts slapping him.

"Go, Mom! You've got this!" I cheer her on like I always do as soon as I get past the fear.

"Deb, this is unreasonable. You need help!" Dad pleads. Oh no. Doesn't he know that phrase is a big trigger for her? Anytime he or Grandpa have been in an argument with Mom and said "you need help," it only sets her off worse.

"I DON'T NEED HELP, YOU NEED HELP!" Mom screams. She runs into the kitchen. Dad starts taking off his shoes, thinking dumbly that maybe it's over, maybe Mom's mood has shifted and she's back to normal. How can he not know? How can he never know?

One, two, three, I count out in my mind. Less than ten seconds before she comes back. Four, five, six, seven. She's back and carrying a kitchen knife, the big one that Grandpa uses to chop her vegetables every night.

"GET OUT OF MY HOUSE!" she yells. "GET OUT!"

"Deb, please, you can't keep doing this...."

The last time Mom forced Dad to sleep in his car was a few months back. It's been a longer turnaround than usual—typically he's kicked out once a week or so. And with good reason. Mom says he doesn't help the family enough, he's always late from work, he's probably cheating, he's not interested in his children, he's an absent father, etc. The fact that he's gotten by this long without being kicked out is a miracle. He should just be grateful.

"GET OUT, MARK!"

"Put the knife away, Deb. This is unsafe. This is a danger to your children."

"IT IS NOT. I WOULD NEVER HURT MY BABIES. I WOULD NEVER HURT MY BABIES, AND HOW DARE YOU ACCUSE ME OF THAT!"

Tears are streaming down Mom's cheeks. Her eyes are wide and shaky and terrifying.

"GET OUT!"

She lunges at him again. He backs up.

"Okay, okay. I'm out. I'm leaving."

He slips his shoes back on and hurries out. Mom walks back into the kitchen and puts the knife in a drawer. She falls to her knees and starts sobbing a painful, moaning wail. I crouch down next to her and hug her. Somebody wins the next round of *007*.

7.

I'VE BEEN STANDING ON THIS pile of dirt since my call time this morning at six a.m. It's noon now and the sun is out, beating its peak heat down on me. The principal actors around me get shaded by umbrellas between takes, and they get to sit down in foldable chairs to rest their feet, and they get to sip from cold water bottles freshly plucked from a cooler filled with ice cubes. But not me. I don't get that kind of luxury since I'm just a background actor.

Me and the other background actors stand on our piles of dirt here in the hot desert just outside of Lancaster, umbrella-less and water-bottle-less and sweating through every single one of the layers of our scratchy, must-smelling, Great Depression–era clothes. We're wearing these clothes because we're playing impoverished people in the Great Depression for some short film called *Golden Dreams*. The film shows various vignettes of the history of California and is supposedly going to play at the new Disneyland partner theme park, California Adventure. Mom giddily relayed this information to me on our four thirty a.m. drive here, but the only part that sounded exciting to me was that there's a new Disneyland theme park in store.

The worst part of all of this is the stuff on my teeth. This morning when I went through hair and makeup, they did my hair in two braids and then told me to open my mouth wide. I did as I was told, and the makeup person dripped brown juice-like gunk into my mouth, explaining that she was doing it to make my teeth look rotten. The gunk dried quickly and felt disgusting, what I imagine it'd feel like if I didn't brush for a month. It's felt that way the whole day since, and I hate it. I can't help but run my tongue along the gunk because it's so bothersome and distracting.

"You don't look happy to be here. Try and look happy to be here," Mom says as we both enter the background-designated trailer bathroom. I'd been holding my poop for an hour and couldn't hold it anymore, so I finally asked a person with a walkie-talkie if I could please go, even though Mom tells me I might be labeled difficult for doing so.

"Sorry," I say while I poop and Mom wets a paper towel with water. I'm embarrassed she still insists on wiping my butt. I tried to tell her recently that now that I'm eight, I think I can handle it, but she looked like she was gonna cry and said she needs to do it until I'm at least ten because she doesn't want skid marks on my Pocahontas underwear. I know if I did it there wouldn't be skid marks, but it's Mom's tears I'm more worried about.

"Just stop frowning, okay?" Mom asks, to ensure I've heard her request. "Your eyebrows are all bent in and angry-looking."

Wipe. Wipe. Wipe.

"Okay."

I get back out to my dirt pile and try to look the opposite of how I feel, but it's hard with the sun being so bright. I can't help but squint.

"Where's the sad-looking kid, the one I pointed out earlier? Let's just use her," the director shouts to the assistant director.

The AD points to various children, and the director shakes his head no until the AD points to me.

"Yeah, her." The director nods.

"Come on, come with me," the AD says, taking my hand and walking me toward the director.

The director tells me to sit in an old-timey car, look off slightly to my right, and "do nothing." I nod. After a few takes, he says he got the shot.

The AD walks me to Mom, who's waiting near the background crafty table. He says that I'm done for the day because they used me in a key shot so I can't be in the background anymore.

"A key shot?" Mom asks, clearly excited.

"Yeah. Actually, I have to bring over some fresh paperwork because it's technically a principal role."

Mom's almost shaking with joy. "How did this happen?"

"Well, the little girl we hired wouldn't take direction—she just kept smiling no matter how many times we told her to look sad. But not your daughter. She's got a great sad face," he laughs.

"She does. She does have a great sad face," Mom says, nodding and beaming and seeming to forget that a half hour ago that sad face was the very thing she was trying to get rid of.

"Anyway, we used your daughter for the role instead, so now she's technically a principal performer."

The AD peels off to grab the new paperwork, and Mom turns to me and grabs my hands in hers.

"They used you, Net! They used you!"

Mom gets home and calls Academy Kids immediately to gush about my principal contract. They tell Mom this is great news, that this means I'm establishing a reputation as a kid who cooperates and takes direction, two of the most beneficial traits of a child actor. They tell Mom they're going to look for longer-running background jobs for me—"core background" jobs. These are the kinds of jobs you can't get when you're new to extra work because the extras casting director doesn't know your reputation yet. Mom looks perturbed at the news.

"Core background? That just sounds like a glorified extra. What about principal roles? They just hired her as a principal for *Golden Dreams*, so can't she start auditioning for principal roles?"

"Well not quite yet. We want to get a bit more experience under her belt and then we can reassess."

Mom says all right, but I can tell she doesn't like that answer.

"Reassess my ass," Mom says while she's hanging up the phone. I always worry the person on the other end of the line hasn't yet hung up when Mom's complaining about them, but so far it's luckily never seemed to be an issue.

Mom's a bit tense for the rest of the night, but by the next morning she swings into a good mood when Academy Kids calls to say they got me a part as a "core background performer" for an upcoming pilot. Eight days of work.

"You might be a glorified extra for now, baby," Mom says to me as she brushes her teeth. "But if we keep going, you'll be a bona fide principal performer soon enough."

She spits in the sink.

"I think that's how you use 'bona fide,' I'm not sure."

8.

THE PILOT SHOOT GOES WELL, and while I never get upgraded from glorified extra, there is one event on the shoot that gets me closer to Mom's goal of me becoming a principal performer.

There's a principal actress my age with a mother who takes a liking to Mom. That mother gives Mom the number of her daughter's agent, Barbara Cameron.

"Barbara Cameron, Net! Barbara Freaking Cameron!"

"Yay!"

"Do you know who that is?"

"No."

"She's the mother of several famous kids. Several. Kirk Cameron from *Growing Pains*, Candace Cameron from *Full House*. She's their mom. And she managed them. So then she started managing kids who weren't her own. And now she's one of the biggest youth reps out there. Really cool lady."

Mom calls Barbara immediately to set up an audition for me and my oldest brother Marcus, who she recently convinced to give acting a try despite his initial resistance.

"C'mon, you've got a great smile, such big teeth," she said. "And lots of moles. Young Matt Damon."

I secretly envy Dustin and Scottie. I don't understand why Mom has different expectations of them than she does of Marcus and me. I wish I knew the answer to this, but it feels like one of those things that you just don't talk about as a family. It feels like one of those things that are just silently agreed upon.

Barbara works from home. The audition takes place at her house. When we arrive, Marcus and I are each given monologues that we have a half hour to work on before coming back and performing them. I don't know what movies the monologues are from, but Marcus is playing a high school sophomore whose girlfriend committed suicide and I'm playing a little girl who's trying to convince her parents not to get a divorce.

Mom runs the monologues with us in the car, and then we go back inside one-by-one to do our auditions.

Marcus goes first. He's in there for about a half hour. When he comes out, he's in a good mood. He says Barbara and the other woman in the room were both talkative and laughed a lot.

I walk inside. I'm shaking. I do my monologue once. Barbara and the other woman exchange a look, then ask me to do it again, but just "throw it away." I'm puzzled.

"Be more casual," Barbara clarifies.

I try it again. The other woman shrugs at Barbara. Barbara makes an "eh" face.

"Thank you," they say simultaneously.

I walk out as slowly as I can, hoping I can add an extra few minutes to my exit, since I know Mom will be disappointed if I was only in there for as short as I was. Even with my best slow-walk, I only add on a minute. I get to the car and Mom looks concerned.

"Well?"

"It went okay."

"Were they talkative?"

"Not really..."

"Did they laugh at things you said?"

"Not really..."

"Huh."

On the drive home, I can tell Mom's disappointed. She seems proud and excited about Marcus, but I know how to read her, and I can tell she's forcing it. That pride and excitement in Marcus is overshadowed by her disappointment in me.

* * *

"We like Marcus a lot; we want to take him on as a client. But Jennette—she just... lacks charisma."

The person delivering the news is Laura, the woman who was in the room with Barbara. Laura is Barbara's second-in-command and the only other agent working for the company. She's sharp and quick, a no-nonsense type, with a voice loud enough that I can hear it through the phone as Mom talks to her while stirring our ramen dinner.

"That's great about Marcus, but what if you just sign Jennette and if she hasn't booked anything in six months, you can drop her?" Mom pleads, then gives me a thumbs-up like she's pumped about her own idea.

"We already have a lot of young female talent...." Laura trails off.

"She's a quick learner and she takes direction well," Mom says in a singsongy way, like she's trying to tempt Laura. It's such a mismatched tone for a beggar.

Laura says she's going to check with Barbara and call right back with an answer. Mom turns to me.

"Net, say a quick prayer for Barbara to accept you. And fold your arms for the both of us, since I need mine to stir," she says. I take on proper Mormon prayer form. We both shut our eyes.

"Dear Heavenly Father," I start. "Thank you for this beautiful day and for all of our many blessings—"

"Shit!" Mom says.

My eyes fly open. Mom drops the spoon she was stirring with and starts sucking on her finger. She turns on the faucet to run the cool water over it.

"Burnt my finger," she says to me, explaining. "Go on, sweetie, keep going."

I nod and return to my prayer.

"Please bless that Barbara Cameron accepts me. Please bless that we have a good rest of the night. Please bless that Mommy sleeps well since she struggles with that sometimes. Thank you, Heavenly Father. In the name of Jesus Christ, amen."

"Amen, sweetheart. Good job."

Mom starts pouring the ramen into bowls when the phone rings again. She drops the pot into the sink. It makes a loud thud and some ramen broth splatters onto the counter, but Mom doesn't notice. She's too focused.

"Uh-huh," she says, sounding upbeat. I can't hear Laura on the other end of the phone this time because Mom is pacing back and forth to cope with how antsy she is.

"Uh-huh," she says again, eyeing me. This whole thing is making me very uncomfortable.

"Great, you won't regret this," Mom says as she hangs up the phone. She looks at me for a long time as pure joy fills her eyes.

"What?" I ask.

"Barbara Cameron accepted you. She wants you to take a weekly acting class to get more comfortable with yourself, something like that, but she accepted you."

Mom shakes her head in awe and pride. She breathes a sigh of relief, then pulls me into a hug.

"You're a principal actor now, sweetheart. No more background for my baby."

9.

I HATE ACTING CLASS. I'm two months into the one Barbara Cameron insisted I sign up for if I were to be represented by her. I go every Saturday from eleven a.m. to two thirty p.m. Even though it's a chunk of time away from home, I don't look forward to this class the same way I look forward to church because I find acting even more uncomfortable than being stuck at home.

Each class starts out with a bit of "loosening up." The dozen of us walk around mimicking Miss Lasky. That's Laura's last name. Not only is she Barbara's second-in-command, she's also our acting teacher. She stretches her face out in weird contortions, opening her mouth freakishly wide or bulging her eyes out. I have no idea how this helps us act better, but I know better than to be an annoying kid who asks questions.

"You have to always be 'on' in class," Mom reminds me on every one of our drives home. "Miss Lasky's watching. And the kids who are annoying, don't take direction, ask questions—those are the kids who won't get sent out on auditions. The kids who will get auditions are the ones who shut up and do as they're told."

After the face gymnastics, we pretend to be various animals. Some of the other kids seem to have fun with it, but it makes me feel like an idiot. I don't know how to trumpet like an elephant, purr like a kitten, or grunt like a monkey and frankly, I don't want to. Let's leave the animal sounds to the animals.

Sometimes Miss Lasky has everyone freeze, and then she points to one kid to do the animal sound solo. It's supposed to help with getting over our inhibitions or something.

"Trumpet, Jennette! Trumpet like you mean it!"

I don't mean it, but I try my best. I'm humiliated.

After the dreaded animal sounds, we move on to memorization technique. We're given a scene and we have thirty minutes to memorize our character's lines, then we go one-by-one spewing our lines "cold," the showbiz term for "rapid and without emotion." We're told this technique is important, especially for kids, so that we don't overwork the material and sound too rehearsed in auditions. Apparently, memorizing a thing "cold" so we have it down pat, and then adding in the emotions later is the best way to keep the scene fresh.

Memorizing is the part of class that I dislike the least, maybe because I'm best at it. I usually memorize my lines within fifteen minutes and then just spend the next fifteen going over them to solidify them. I also don't mind saying words without emotions. The emotions are the problem, the words aren't. Forcing emotions into a thing is uncomfortable in the first place, but then putting on those emotions for other people to see feels gross to me. It feels weak and vulnerable and naked. I don't want people to see me like that.

After memorization comes scene work, my least favorite part of the class because it's the part where I have to perform. Each week, in preparation for scene work, we're assigned a scene that we have to memorize and break down. Breaking a scene down is a process where we ask questions about our character and the scene and what's really being said underneath the words on the page. What does my character actually want? What does the character I'm interacting with actually want? How are these things at odds? How does my character feel about the character I'm interacting with? After breaking the scene down, we have to rehearse it enough that it's ready to perform in front of the rest of the class come Saturday.

Each of us gets up one at a time, performs our scene, then goes through our breakdown with Miss Lasky. I wish so much that I didn't have to do this part. I don't like sitting up on the little studio stage, acting out a scene in front of everyone. I don't like to be observed. I like to do the observing.

Miss Lasky said in our first class that no parents were allowed for the scene work portion, but Mom insisted.

"I had stage four metastatic ductal carcinoma—breast cancer—and my bones are weak from the chemo. Sitting in the car for too long pains me, and I'm not supposed to walk around in the hot sun."

"Well, there's a coffee shop right up the street," Miss Lasky said with a tense smile.

"I don't believe in spending two fifty on a cup of joe," Mom said with a tenser one.

And that was that. Mom's been the only parent sitting in on the scene breakdown portion since the beginning of class. I'm glad Mom gets what she wants, to watch me act. But it does add stress to me. I can feel her judgments and see her reactions out of the side of my eye. She mouths my lines as I say them and overanimates her facial expression when she wants me to mimic it. It's difficult to perform while navigating Mom's sideline coaching at the same time.

When class is over, I feel a huge wave of relief wash over me because Mom gives me the rest of the day off. I don't have to look at my scene for next week until tomorrow. For tonight, I'm free.

10.

"I DON'T WANNA SAY THAT word," I tell Mom as we look over my lines for an upcoming audition for *Mad TV*. The sketch is a parody on Kathie Lee Gifford and her two children—I'm trying out to be the parody version of Kathie's daughter.

"It has multiple different meanings. Sometimes it just means happy. It's in Christmas songs, for crying out loud. '*Don we now our gay apparel*,'" Mom sing-talks.

I know Mom partially sympathizes with me or she wouldn't be overexplaining herself the way that she is.

"Do I have to say it?"

"Yes, Net, it's one of your first speaking-role auditions. We've gotta go on all these so Barbara knows you're not difficult. Plus, we need you to book something so she keeps sending you out."

I thumb the pages in front of me.

"Look, we can get ice cream afterward if you do a good job, okay? We've got that coupon Sister Johnson gave out in primary class."

"Okay."

* * *

It's the next day and I'm waiting to go in for my audition. The room is small. The walls are white and there's nothing on them. Fellow auditioners and their mothers sit in foldout chairs or stand with their backs against the walls. All the girls are blond. All the moms are anxious.

A casting person comes out to get me. My mouth is dry the way it always is before auditions, and I have to pee even though I already peed four times. I think it's the sugar-free Red Bulls Mom has me drink before comedy auditions because she says I just don't have comedy energy otherwise.

"Jennette McCurdy," the casting person calls out. I swallow.

"Here!" I say excitedly, the way Mom instructed me to.

"Come on back," the casting person says with a gesture.

Mom swats my butt supportively.

"You've got this, Net. You're better than all these other girls!"

I see one of my competitors look down, sad. Her mother comforts her. I follow the casting director into the casting room, where two men are sitting.

"Whenever you're ready," one of them says.

The casting director says her line, then I say my first of two.

"You're old."

The men burst into laughter. I must've done well. My mouth's still dry. I'm nervous about saying the word. Here comes my next line, the line that the word is in.

"Gelman, you are so gay."

More laughter. I'm done. I go out to meet Mom in the waiting room.

"So what'd they say?" Mom asks while we stand in line at Baskin-Robbins.

"They said I was funny."

"That's right, my baby's funny. And serious, too, when she needs to be. She's got it all. You want Nutty Coconut?"

"Um, no, I think I'll do Cookies 'N Cream."

Mom turns to me, alarmed.

"You don't want Nutty Coconut?"

I'm frozen. I don't know what to say. Mom seems upset that I haven't chosen Nutty Coconut. I pause, waiting to see how she reacts before making my next move. There's a beat where we're both just standing at the ice cream counter looking at each other instead of at the ice cream. Then Mom's posture softens and her eyes well with tears.

"Nutty Coconut's been your favorite for eight months. You're changing. Growing up."

I take her hand in mine.

"Never mind. I want Nutty Coconut."

"You're sure?"

"Positive." I nod.

Mom orders a kids' scoop for us to share and hands the coupon to the teenage employee with so much black makeup around her eyes that she looks like a raccoon. We sit at one of the little booths to enjoy the ice cream together. I'm secretly sick of the coconut flavor but I'm sure to make lots of *mmm*s so Mom thinks I love it. A few bites in, Mom's little gray pager starts buzzing. She got this pager for herself as a Christmas gift so she could know the second Barbara needed to get ahold of her. Like right now.

"It's Barbara! I have a page from Barbara!"

Mom hops up and bounds over to the ice cream counter. I stop eating the ice cream since Mom's not watching me.

"Do you have a phone back there?" Mom asks the employee.

"Yes, but it's for employee use only," Raccoon Eyes says in a monotone.

"My daughter is an actress and she might have just booked her first speaking role on a show called *Mad TV*. Have you heard of *Mad TV*? It's supposedly very funny. The more underground SNL. Is there any way I can use your—"

"Sure, go ahead and use it," the employee says, bored.

Mom reaches across the counter and starts dialing Barbara's number, which she knows by heart. Mom glances over at me with her fingers crossed. I take a bite of the ice cream.

"Ahhhh!!" Mom screams. The employee plugs her ears. "Net, you booked it! You booked *Mad TV*!"

Mom hangs up with Barbara and rushes over to me. She pulls me into a tight squeeze. I love the smell of her warm skin mixed with her Wings perfume. I'm so happy she's happy.

"This is fantastic, Net. Your first speaking role. This is big stuff. Big stuff."

Mom kisses me on the forehead excitedly, then digs her spoon into the ice cream, finishing off the last of the Nutty Coconut. I'm glad I don't have to.

11.

"You look so pretty," I tell Mom.

She stands in front of the bathroom mirror doing her makeup while I brush her hair. She likes when I do this. She says it's comforting. Soothing.

"Thanks, Angel. Karen's gorgeous though. She looks like a beauty queen." Mom puts the cap on her tube of lipstick and rubs her lips together to spread the plum color over both of them. I think her natural color is so much prettier.

"You look like a beauty queen too," I say, partially because I do believe it, but mainly to reassure Mom. She doesn't have many friends her age, and the ones she does have she hardly sees. So the fact that she's meeting up with one of them today for lunch is a big deal.

Karen is Mom's best friend from high school, and after they graduated, they went to beauty school together. Mom's relationship with her seems complicated. One minute she'll say Karen is this amazing person and so wonderful and so sweet, and then the next she'll say that Karen is actually kind of a B-I-T-C-H.

"We're not supposed to say that word."

"I'm just spelling it, Net, plus God would understand if he knew Karen. Did I ever tell you about how she stole my baby's name?" Mom asks while she spritzes herself with perfume.

"Uh-huh," I say while I keep brushing.

Mom looks down. I can tell I hurt her feelings. She's told me this story so many times before, but here she is wanting to tell it to me again. And that's okay. She just wants to be heard.

"But I could hear it again."

"So I had the name all picked out," Mom launches in immediately. "Jason. I thought it was a good name. Sturdy. Not too common, but also not weird like some of these new kids' names. Lagoon or whatever. And you're not supposed to tell anyone 'cuz it's bad luck, you know? You're not supposed to tell anyone the baby name you've chosen."

"Uh-huh..."

"Are you listening, Net? You seem like you spaced out."

"I'm listening."

"So you're not supposed to tell anyone, but I did. I told Karen because I figured she's my best friend and she wanted to know, plus we were pregnant at the same time so we were going through all that stuff together. Well, lo and behold, she pops out her kid first, and what name does she choose? Jason. She stole my name."

"I like the name Marcus better anyway," I tell her. "It's more unique."

"Oh I know it is, but it's just the principle."

"Oh I know," I agree.

Mom takes a deep breath and brushes her eyelashes with a third coat of mascara.

"Anyway, I don't trust her as far as I can throw her, but she's still a good friend."

This logic confuses me so I just say, "Uh-huh."

"Not my best friend though," Mom continues. "You're my best friend, Net. You're Mommy's best friend."

I beam. I'm so happy to be her best friend. To be the closest person in the world to her. This is my purpose. I feel whole.

"Why'd ya quit brushing?"

I return to the task.

12.

"WELL, THIS MORNING IS GOING to hell in a handbasket!" Mom shouts as she chucks a dish into the sink. I flinch at the sound but head to the kitchen regardless. Someone's gotta help Mom, and most everyone else is still asleep.

"Maybe if somebody else did the damned dishes for once!" she shouts again, slamming down a mug. The handle breaks off it. She throws the mug pieces into a Ziploc bag, to preserve the memory.

"I'll do them, Mommy," I say carefully, not wanting to aggravate her any further.

"Oh no, not you, sweetie," Mom says, reaching out to stroke my hair with her dish-soapy hands. "I don't want you to get prune fingers. That won't do you any good. Who's gonna wanna cast a little girl with prune fingers?"

"Okay."

"Mark! Can you take Jennette to dance?! I need to finish the dishes so I can take her to acting class!"

Dad heads toward us from the living room. He steps over a sleeping Dustin and Scottie on their Costco mats.

"Huh?" he asks once he finally gets into the kitchen.

"Jennette's dance class, can you take her?"

"Sure," he says plainly.

"Try not to be too enthusiastic," Mom says.

"Sorry."

"Well don't apologize for everything. Just hurry. You have to leave in twenty to get her there on time."

Mom signed me up for a rigorous schedule of dance classes after I had an audition for a Paula Abdul dance special and did terribly. All the other girls at the audition were doing splits and twirling three and four times in a row, but I didn't know how to do any of that. We were taught a minute of choreography and, even though I'm good at memorizing lines, the two types of memorizing are clearly unrelated because I couldn't remember one move. Mom told me she never wanted me to be humiliated like that again, so she signed me up for fourteen dance classes a week—two each of jazz, ballet, lyrical, musical theater, and hip-hop, plus one of stretching and three of tap—and told me two background jobs a month will cover the costs.

I actually like dance. A lot. I like moving my body, it gets me out of my head. And I like most of the girls I dance with—they've been nice and welcoming to me. I secretly like being away from Mom, too—she doesn't watch me dance the way she watches me act. Maybe it's because she didn't want to be a dancer growing up, she wanted to be an actress, and maybe Mom only sits in when I'm being the thing she wanted to be. I don't know. Regardless, even though I would never mention it to her, it feels good that she's not around. It's a relief. I don't have to worry about constantly being monitored.

Dad has taken me to dance class a few times before. I'm excited because when Mom takes me, I never know if she's gonna yell at someone or complain to the dance studio owner that my part in the ballet isn't big enough or whatever. Dad doesn't do stuff like that. He doesn't even seem aware of stuff like that. He just kinda... exists.

"Do you wanna bike to dance class?" Dad asks me.

"Yes!" I say, honestly thrilled. I think about asking Mom, but then I don't because I don't want to give her a chance to say no.

Dad and I don't get much time together since he works his two jobs at Home Depot and Hollywood Video. He usually gets home late and goes right into the back room to get some sleep. Even though the room is full of stuff, there's a sliver of bed stuff-less enough for one person to sleep on, so that's where Dad goes. He also goes back there because Mom says there's no way she's sleeping in the same bed—or even the same room—as someone who disgusts her so much. So since Mom's in the living room on the couch or a Costco mat with us, it makes sense that Dad's in the farthest room possible.

On top of that, I'm busy with my acting career and schoolwork (even though Mom homeschools us, we still have to turn in samples once a month to the state to prove we're learning things) and now dance classes too.

The few times we do spend together stick out since they don't happen that often. Like when Dad was able to come to my eighth birthday party at the public swimming pool—the first birthday party of mine he'd been to in a few years due to his work schedule. He gave me a birthday card, which he had never done before. He spelled my name wrong on the envelope. People spell my name wrong all the time, and I usually don't think much of it, but that time it made me sad. I opened the card to see what he wrote inside. That's the more important part anyway. "Love, Dad" was all he wrote underneath the poem in the card. I was even more sad, but it's the thought that counts, and the fact that he had the thought meant something to me. Until on our way home I heard Mom say, "Did you get her a birthday card like I told you to? You should be nurturing a relationship with her, like a FATHER does." So it was really Mom's thought all along.

The other times we spend together are a bit more routine, like when Dad gets off work a little early and watches a rerun of *MacGyver* or *Gilligan's Island* with us, or when he makes a stew on Sunday after church. Each time he makes one it's apparently a different stew—beef, corn chowder, chili, split pea—but I swear they all taste like lentil. These times with Dad are decent but never anything special. I wish I felt connected to Dad the way I feel connected to Mom. Being around Mom can be tiring, sure, but at least I know what to do to make her happy. Around Dad, I never really know. It's less work, but it's also less rewarding.

But today I'm excited that he's pitched this idea to go bike riding. I know he loves riding his bike, the one he inherited from his dad when he died.

"A bike is no home," Mom complained. "Guess we'll have to wait 'til Grandma Faye passes too, though that doesn't seem to be anytime soon. Eighty-two and her health is better than ever." Then she clicked her tongue the way she often does when she's annoyed.

I like riding my bike too, the one that my aunt Linda sent me for my seventh birthday but that I can still fit on if I hunch over a bit. Maybe today Dad and I can make a good memory together. Maybe today we can have a fun time.

So we pile onto our bikes and ride to the Dance Factory in Los Alamitos, the next town over from us. We stop at the park on Orangewood and do a quick round of monkey bars. Dad's smiling like he's having a good time. And I know I'm having one. This is good.

We get to the Dance Factory ten minutes late for my class. They don't allow you to enter past fifteen, but I'm allowed in with nothing more than a stink eye from the teacher. I'll take it.

Class goes by quickly and we're released into the waiting room to greet our parents. I see Dad sitting on the bench with his legs crossed the way Mom doesn't like, eating a Clif Bar.

"Where'd you get that?" I ask, fearing that I already know the answer.

"The snack table at the front of the studio."

"Mom says no snacks from the snack table 'cuz they're too expensive."

"It was a buck."

"Exactly."

"Yesterday was payday," Dad says with a wave of his hand, and then leads me outside to our bikes.

We hop on and ride home, past the empty Los Alamitos High School and Polly's Pies. Dad takes a right turn into an outdoor shopping center and pedals up to a smoothie shop.

"Where are we going?"

"Let's get smoothies."

"Smoothies are expe—"

"Payday," Dad reminds me.

Somewhere in the middle of the smoothie-maker blending the strawberry-banana smoothie Dad and I are gonna split, my stomach drops with a realization. In all the excitement and bonding with Dad, I forgot. I forgot I had acting class. I forgot that we would never make it in time if we rode bikes.

But now I remember. In the middle of a painfully loud blender blending up various fruits, I remember. I look at Dad.

"A little extra lemon juice, if you can," he says over the counter as he eyes the lemon in the smoothie-maker's hand.

I wonder if Dad knows. If he purposely had us take our bikes and stop for smoothies because he knows that I hate acting class. Maybe he wants to help me. Maybe he wants to save me.

"Eeeeeven more lemon," he reiterates.

I decide that I'm crazy for thinking this way. Dad's clearly more focused on the amount of lemon in his smoothie than he is on my well-being.

I debate reminding him of acting class, that we need to hurry and even still I'll be late. But then I decide not to. Why should I? I'm enjoying my time with Dad despite the disconnect. I'm enjoying the ease, so I say nothing.

We finish up the smoothie and pedal back slowly. We stop at the park again and ride on the swings. By the time we get home it's 11:05. Mom's pacing in the front yard, jangling her keys like it's a threat.

"WHERE HAVE YOU BEEN?!" she screams.

Bud, our nosey neighbor, pokes his head over the fence. I wonder if he's gonna threaten to call social services again, like he did the last time Mom was screaming on the front lawn. I pray Mom keeps her voice down so he doesn't.

"We stopped for a smoothie," Dad says with a shrug, slow on the uptake.

"YOU STOPPED FOR A SMOOTHIE??" Mom's furious.

I wave at Bud to let him know at least someone can see him watching. He ducks down below the fence.

"Yeah..." Dad says, trying to figure out why Mom's upset.

Mom storms into the house and slams the door shut behind her. Dad follows after her, and I trail behind him.

"Deb, come on..."

Mom's in the kitchen by now, opening and closing appliance doors—first the fridge, then the oven, then the microwave. I don't know why she's doing this, what she's looking for, but there's a wildness to her gestures that scares me.

"I told you Jennette had acting class. But she MISSED IT NOW. They were doing a scene from *I Am Sam* this week. *I AM SAM*, Mark. Jennette would've KILLED that."

Mom kicks in a cupboard door. Her foot gets stuck in the wood. She yanks her foot out. The wood is fragmented and splintery.

"I'm sorry," Dad says.

"I guess she doesn't have to act that one since it's her REAL LIFE. A WISE LITTLE GIRL with a RETARDED DAD."

13.

THERE'S A LOT OF TALK about big breaks in Hollywood, but so far I haven't experienced that. Instead, I've experienced a bunch of little breaks that trickle in just as I'm almost positive I won't catch one again. Mom says Hollywood's like a bad boyfriend.

"They keep stringing you along without making any type of formal commitment."

I'm not exactly sure what this means, but it sounds right.

So far, my little breaks since *Mad TV* have been these:

- A commercial for Dental Land. The dentist's office we shot the commercial in was in a Westfield Shopping Mall, so we got to spend the lunch break walking around the mall, and Mom got me a grab bag from Sanrio Surprises for being "by far the best actor of the group." We were all just sitting down for the commercial, so I'm not sure what gave Mom the idea that I was a better actor than everyone else, but I'll take the compliment if it gets me a Sanrio grab bag.
- A low-budget independent movie called *Shadow Fury*. Mom complained because I wasn't even paid a principal's salary. "My baby deserves a proper salary when she spends Halloween crouched over a fake dying man with sugar blood running down her arms." In the scene, my fake dad gets shot and I hear the gunshot from upstairs, come downstairs, and cradle his head while he dies in my arms. The sugar blood was not the worst part of it, despite how sticky and uncomfortable it was. The worst part by far was the mic pack. The budget was so low that they didn't have a proper waistband for the mic pack so they just duct-taped it to my body. At the end of the night, I cried while they peeled the duct tape off me, but we got home in

time to catch the two thirty a.m. rerun of Conan O'Brien, and Mom smeared aloe vera gel on my body while we watched it, so it wasn't all bad.

- A role in an episode of *Malcolm in the Middle*. This one was particularly exciting because it was my first guest-star role instead of co-star. Co-star roles are usually fifteen lines or less and credited at the end of the episode; guest-star roles are typically more significant and credited at the beginning. The episode was about the mom character dreaming of having girls instead of boys. I played the female Dewey aka Daisy. They put hard wax behind my ears to make them poke out more because they said the trademark of Dewey is that he has big ears that poke out and that I have small ones. The wax was bulky and made the backs of my ears really sore, but I liked the studio where we shot the episode and the producer was very kind to me. I thought Frankie Muniz was nice to look at and I liked when he said hi to me in the hallways. I felt like I was being pretty discreet about my feelings until Mom snapped at me. "Don't even think about it. He's way too old for you. And more important, not Mormon."
- A Sprint PCS commercial—my first national commercial, which means... residuals! Enough residuals to pay for the oak bunk bed I bought for myself. Mom did as she'd promised and cleared the space in Grandma and Grandpa's room for my bed. She wound up filling the top bunk with stacks of papers and old toys and books and things, though, which was a little frustrating since I had initially wanted to sleep on the top bunk. Mom said it was too risky anyway and that she never would've let me. "We can't risk you falling out and cracking your head open, like when Dustin fell out of the stroller at Knott's Berry Farm! I've never forgiven myself for that and I'd never forgive myself for this. Even though they did give us some free boysenberry punch, which was nice."

Aside from the little breaks, there have been a lot of sub–little breaks, or hints at little breaks. I get callbacks for around 75 percent of the roles I audition for, which Barbara says is a good sign even if I'm not booking.

"She's clearly doing something right," Barbara says to Mom on the phone. (Barbara has started taking Mom's calls instead of Laura. Moving on up!)

"Just not right enough," Mom always adds.

"She'll get there. I'm telling you, she'll get there," Barbara says. "You've just gotta be a little patient."

Mom hangs up, exasperated.

"Heavenly Father, please grant me patience. And be quick."

14.

"Okay, Jennette, we're gonna have a quick conversation with the director and then we'll come and get you," the casting director tells me. I nod. My leg starts bouncing nervously. I can't get it to stop.

I'm sitting in a room waiting to go in for my fourth callback for *Princess Paradise Park*, the current hot family drama film to audition for if you're an actress between seven and ten years old. Apparently thousands of girls auditioned, but the role is now down to me and one other girl. It's the closest I've been to a project this big.

I have my seventeen pages of lines down pat thanks to Mom's help. Sometimes when we're running errands together, she'll just say "Go!" and I'll know what that means because, even though I've had a few other auditions over this monthlong audition process for *Princess*, this is the audition that's the most demanding, and the role I'm closest to getting. This is the one Mom cares about the most.

"Barbara says since it's a studio film, the role would make you a star," Mom tells me every time I get another callback. "You'd just get offers from then on. No more auditioning."

No more auditioning does sound good. As I'm sitting here waiting to go in, I start fantasizing about how good it would be to not have to do the thing that cripples me with nervousness. To not have the constant nagging pressure of being chosen, and the sadness that comes with not being chosen. I'm in the middle of my fantasy when I hear Him, loud and clear in my mind.

"Jennette, I, the spirit of the Holy Ghost, command you to cross your name out on the sign-in sheet, go to the restroom, touch your underwear band five times in a row, twirl on one foot, unlock and relock the bathroom door five times, come back, and re-sign in on the sign-in sheet."

I'm elated. He has spoken. The Holy Ghost, aka my Still Small Voice, has finally spoken to me. I've been waiting for Him to speak to me since my eighth birthday when I had my baptism.

The Gift of the Holy Ghost was definitely the gift I was most excited for. A friend from church did get me some gooey slime, though, which was a close second.

The Holy Ghost is a great guy up in heaven who helps out Heavenly Father and Jesus. He's kind of like them, in spirit and attitude, but he's different, too, because he lives in each and every one of us Mormons. And every day we can talk to him whenever we want to, and he can talk to us, guiding us to do what is right, which is whatever he tells us to do. We're so lucky.

My first few weeks of having The Gift of the Holy Ghost were underwhelming. Maybe even disappointing, but I never told that to anybody at church. Whenever anyone asked me if I'd been communicating with my Still Small Voice, the Holy Ghost in me, I'd say yes, we'd been having all sorts of great conversations. And then they'd ask what the conversations had been like, what I'd been learning, and I'd say that I couldn't tell them because the conversations were private.

But that's not the truth. The truth is that I happily would have told any and everyone what my conversations with the Holy Ghost had been like if I'd had them. But I hadn't had any. And I didn't know why. I'd prayed privately every morning, afternoon, and night, on my knees even, to hear the Holy Ghost. Even though Mormons aren't accountable for our sins until we're eight years old, so I knew I hadn't had a ton of time to really screw things up, I wondered if somehow I had.

Why haven't I heard the Holy Ghost? I'd ask in my prayers. *Is there something I've done wrong that has made me not deserve him? Is it my impure thoughts about Frankie Muniz? Please forgive me and send me The Gift of the Holy Ghost, whenever you get around to it. I know you're busy, but I'm desperate here. I want to hear what he sounds like and what he tells me to do. Thanks.*

My prayers didn't work for a long time. Months. But now, today, at my final callback for *Princess Paradise Park*, here He is.

Okay, Holy Ghost, and why do you want me to do these things? I ask in my mind.

"To ensure that you do well at your *Princess Paradise Park* callback. If you do what I tell you to do, you will eventually book the role. When this happens, your mother will be happy and all of your family's problems will be solved."

Wow. I love how direct he is. I jump up out of my seat to accomplish the list of tasks he ordered me to do.

"Where are you going?" Mom asks me.

"I have to pee," I tell her as I cross my name out on the sign-in sheet. She follows me into the bathroom and then into the stall. I touch my underwear band five times.

"What are you doing, Net?" Mom asks me, looking concerned.

"The Holy Ghost talked to me!" I tell her excitedly, sure this will assuage her worries. I twirl on my left foot.

"Uh-huh," Mom says.

"He talked to me!" I tell her again. She must've not heard me or she'd be just as excited as I am. I unlock and relock the bathroom door five times while she watches.

"Why are you looking at me like that?" I ask her.

She pauses and looks a little sad. "Nothing."

We head back into the waiting room and I re-sign in.

Thank you, Holy Ghost. Thank you.

15.

"Your eyelashes are invisible, okay? You think Dakota Fanning doesn't tint hers?"

Mom is tinting my eyelashes with the over-the-counter brown eyelash tint she picks up from Rite Aid once a month or so, during the same trip where she picks up the L'Oréal blond highlights, the three-dollar tube of clear mascara, and the store-brand version of Crest Whitestrips. It's the "maintenance trip" as she calls it—the trip dedicated solely to the enhancement of my "natural beauty."

Mom calls it "natural beauty," what I have. She says my eyelashes are long, but so light that it looks like I don't have any. She says that my hair has golden highlights, but only toward the bottom and that it's important I have some golden highlights around my face, too, to frame it. She says that my hair is very thick, which is good, but that it has a mind of its own, which is bad, and that it needs to be tamed. She says I have a good smile but my teeth aren't quite white enough. Each "good" thing Mom says about my "natural beauty" is followed up by its downside, which serves as the justification for its need to be enhanced by a little good old-fashioned store-bought beauty. And since it seems like every single "naturally beautiful" thing about me comes with a downside that needs to be enhanced by store-bought beauty, I'm beginning to wonder if I'm really naturally beautiful at all, or if Mom's use of the term "naturally beautiful" goes in the same place where others would just use the term "ugly."

"Ow!"

"Ow what?" Mom asks, because there are a variety of things that could be *ow*ing me right now.

Little paper eye patches are tucked up under my eyes, just on the lash line to the point where they could be poking my eyeballs, which could be *ow*-worthy. (Mom tucks them nice and tight and keeps them in place with Vaseline because she doesn't want the brown eyelash tint to drip on my skin and tint it.)

What feels like one thousand sheets of foil are folded into all the layers of my hair. There are so many layers and so much foil that my hair is extending outward nearly horizontally around me. There are two potential *ow*s with this—the foils could be tugging at my roots and causing pain, or the fumes from the bleach could be burning my eyes.

The knockoff Crest Whitestrips are cupping my teeth and even though they're only supposed to stay on for fifteen minutes, Mom keeps them on for forty-five, for good measure.

Even though I try and spit out the nasty whitening juice periodically, sometimes it leaks from my teeth onto my gums and not only turns them white, but stings badly, which could also be an *ow*.

"Da dye is n y eye," I say as best as I can with the strips on my teeth.

"Spit, then say it again," Mom urges me.

I do as she says.

"The dye is in my eye!"

"Shit. Shit shit shit. Why didn't you tell me?! This stuff could make you go blind. Lean back!"

I throw my head back. It bangs on the back of the toilet seat. I *ow* again. Mom starts squirting eye drops into my eye. A cocktail of tears and eye drops trickles down my cheeks. I try to sit up again but my hair catches on the toilet flusher. Mom starts unhooking it. I feel trapped.

My appearance has always been of great importance to Mom. Even before I started acting.

Some of my earliest memories are of me wearing giant pastry-puff dresses. The dresses scratched and irritated my skin, and the look of them felt silly and over-the-top to me. Mom would always tell me I looked so pretty, even though every time she told me I looked pretty I shrieked as loud as I could that I wasn't pretty, I was "hampsome." I was too little to be able to say "handsome" properly, but old enough to know that I wanted to be called what my brothers were called, not some stupid, lesser term designated for the girls.

Acting only made Mom's obsession with my appearance worse, especially after I couldn't get an audition for the lead role in the film *Because of Winn-Dixie*.

"Get me Meredith Fine! Get me Meredith Fine!" Mom screamed into the phone at Coast to Coast Talent Group's scared young receptionist. We switched to Meredith a few months back after Mom said Barbara Cameron is old news and that this new agency, Coast to Coast, represented the cream-of-the-crop young talent. Meredith is head of talent at the agency.

"Yeah, Meredith, it's Debra McCurdy. How could you not submit Jennette for *Because of Winn-Dixie*?! How?! She's perfect for that role. You just don't care about her enough or prioritize her, that's what it is," Mom cried.

"Debra. Deb—"

"I bet you submitted Taylor Dooley!"

"Debra, you need to calm down and stop lobbing these wild accusations at me. I submitted Jennette for the role, but they didn't want to see her because they're looking for an ethereal beauty, and Jennette reads more homely."

Mom looked stunned then hung up the phone and started wailing like somebody died. It was the first time I wished that I was prettier and didn't care about being hampsome.

16.

"Are you sure I should wear this?"

I'm looking down at the outfit that's sprawled out for me on our torn couch, the same outfit I've worn on every audition since the *Winn-Dixie* situation: a fuzzy pink shirt with a rhinestone heart in the center of it, black faux-leather skorts, and black gogo boots.

"Yes, I'm sure."

"But I feel like a streetwalker in it," I tell Mom as my hot curlers rattle. These curlers are also a post-*Winn-Dixie* development.

Mom lets out a big laugh.

"How do you know what that is?"

"From when you had me watch *Taxi Driver*."

"Oh, that's right," Mom remembers. "Jodie Foster's an—"

"Unrivaled child performer," I finish for her, since she says the same thing every time Jodie Foster's name comes up.

"That's right, baby. Unrivaled. Unrivaled except for you."

I nod along and look down at the outfit again. I dread putting it on. It makes me feel embarrassed and not like myself.

"Are you sure this is what I should wear?"

"Yes, the outfit makes you look very pretty. Not streetwalker pretty, but very pretty."

"But is pretty the—?"

"ARMS," Mom orders, cutting me off. I raise my arms. She pulls off my shirt and starts changing me into the outfit.

I was just going to ask if pretty should be the goal. I'm trying out for a hermaphrodite on *Grey's Anatomy*. I didn't know what that was until I asked Mom and she said it's when a person is both a girl and a boy. If I'm supposed to be part-boy, I don't know if a rhinestone shirt is the best article of clothing to communicate that.

Despite the outfit, I get a callback the same day. Afterward, the casting director comes out and asks to speak with Mom.

"We'd like to bring Jennette in for a final callback. Just her and one other girl."

Mom nods along, violently excited.

"But can you change her into a different outfit? Something a bit more... androgynous?"

"Well, we live really far away—Garden Grove. Do you know where it is? No one knows where it is. It's far. We'd have to take the 101 to the 110 to the 405. We could just take the 5, but traffic's always bumper-to-bumper on that freeway. Not enough lanes—"

"Greg?" the casting director calls out to her assistant, interrupting Mom. Greg hurries over. "Would you mind lending your flannel shirt to Jennette for her callback?"

Greg takes off his flannel shirt. He's wearing it over a plain tee. The casting director takes it and hands it to Mom.

"There you go. Problem solved."

"Oh, thank you so much. I'm so happy we don't have to take the 5!"

Mom takes my hand and we walk into the bathroom together. She changes me into the flannel. It's an odd combo because I'm still wearing the skorts and gogo boots on the bottom. I guess in a way it is part-girl and part-boy. Maybe it's spot-on?

The final callback goes well—I don't think I could've done the lines any better—but we're in the van on the way home when Meredith calls and tells Mom that I didn't get the part.

"What!? Why not?!" Mom veers aggressively.

"They said she's too pretty."

Mom hangs up the phone. There's no swearing, no screaming, no crying. There's almost a joy to her. I'm shocked. I've never seen Mom be happy I didn't get a role, ever... but I've also never been too pretty for a role, ever. And now I am. I'm too pretty to play a ten-year-old androgynous hermaphrodite.

17.

"Deb, I think Jennette's got OCD," Grandpa says heavily. He doesn't know I can hear; he thinks I'm asleep on my Costco mat while he and Mom watch Jay Leno. But I'm not asleep. I just don't like Jay Leno very much, so I rest my eyes while I wait for Conan to come on.

"Oh please." I can tell by Mom's tone that she waves her hand dismissively while she says it.

"You oughta take her to a therapist," Grandpa says.

"Come on. Jennette is not some troubled girl with tics."

"I don't know, I see her doin' all her little rituals constantly. And she looks so frantic when she's doin' 'em. Makes me feel bad."

"Dad, please, she's fine. You're just a worrier. Now let's watch. Kevin Eubanks is so charming. Look at that smile."

Grandpa pauses to watch. I hear the crowd laugh two separate times. Then he speaks again.

"Maybe we should take her to a doctor, just to check. She might need some professional help."

"She does not," Mom says sternly. "Jennette's perfect, all right? She does not need help."

They go back to watching Jay. I keep my eyes shut and think about what Mom said. That I'm perfect. I know this is important for her to believe, even though I'm not sure why. I'm not allowed to have any problems.

Then I think about what Grandpa said. That he thinks I've got OCD because of my rituals. Frankly, I wish Grandpa would have just asked me about my rituals because then I could have explained to him that it's not OCD, it's the Holy Ghost. I wonder if he would have believed me. And then I wonder if I even believe myself.

Are my rituals coming from the Holy Ghost? If they were coming from the Holy Ghost, wouldn't I have booked *Princess Paradise Park* like He said I would, back two years ago when I first heard Him? Instead, the movie lost funding. Would the Holy Ghost have let the movie lose funding? Is it possible that this voice in my head isn't the Holy Ghost, and that instead it's OCD? Would Mom be able to handle that? Would she be okay if I wasn't perfect?

The commercial break starts. Grandpa gets up to get a bowl of ice cream and Mom gets up to pee.

Holy Ghost? I ask internally. *Are you the Holy Ghost, or are you OCD?*

"Of course I'm the Holy Ghost," the Still Small Voice answers back in my mind.

So that settles it. I asked him directly, and He answered me right back. There you have it. That voice in my mind is the Holy Ghost after all.

"Now squint your eyes five times fast, fold your tongue, then tighten your butt cheeks for fifty-five seconds," my Still Small Voice tells me. So I do.

I know he means well, but sometimes my Still Small Voice can get a little loud. And sometimes, as much as I hate to say it, I wish my Still Small Voice would shut up.

18.

I'M SCREAMING AT THE TOP of my lungs. Hysterical. I'm yelling that my stuffed animals are gonna kill me, I know they're gonna kill me. I'm rolling around on the floor, bruising my sides as I thrash around, bumping into couch legs and edges of dressers. I'm screaming, screaming, screaming until...

"And cut!" Mom says intensely, the same way she does whenever we finish practicing my sides (scenes selected by a casting director) for an audition.

"Wow, Net," Mom says while she looks at me with a fierceness that almost scares me. "Where did you learn to act like that?"

"I don't know," I say, even though I do. I know exactly where I learned to act like that.

But I know better than to tell Mom that I got my character inspiration from her erratic and violent behavior. That would only invoke more erratic and violent behavior. I want her calm. I want her steady. I want her happy.

"Well, wherever you learned it from, whatever TV show or movie it was, it's working. That was the performance of a lifetime," Mom says, shaking her head in disbelief. "I don't want to burn you out, I want you to save that magic, keep it bottled up, so let's not run this one again."

I nod. I will save that magic.

My audition for the little girl with bipolar disorder in an episode of *Strong Medicine* comes the next day.

Mom heads to the east lot even though I gently tell her three times that, per the directions attached to the sides, I'm pretty sure we're supposed to go to the west one.

"Come on, we'll be really quick," Mom says to the bland-faced east lot security guard. "She has an audition at two ten and we don't wanna run late. It's a bad first impression."

"The east lot is only for series regulars and producers, people who are here every day."

"Is there any way to make an exception? I'm a cancer survivor, stage four, and sometimes my bones—"

"Fine," the guard interrupts Mom. It's embarrassing when Mom rattles off her cancer story to people we don't know who don't seem to care, but I've gotta say, sometimes it's pretty effective.

We park then run to the proper bungalow, and Mom signs me in while I pace the hallway nervously.

"Don't be nervous, Net," Mom says as she walks over to me. "You've got this."

I believe her. I always believe her. My body language shifts immediately. Mom has a way of doing that to me. Just as she can set my body on edge and make me rigid with fear or anxiety, she can also calm me down. She has that kind of power. I wish she'd use it this way more often.

The audition goes well and I get a callback for later that day. Mom and I go to the local mall to walk around and kill some time, then we head back to the callback around six p.m. I'm the only one there for my role. Everybody else there is an adult, and they're trying out for other guest and co-star roles in the episode.

My name is called quickly, so I go into the room and do the lines. I scream and kick and roll around intensely. I get lost in it. There's a part of me that almost feels good doing it. Like this has been waiting to come out for a long time. Like I've been stuffing this down, shoving it down, and finally here it is. This is how I really feel. Like screaming.

The director stares at me and says he's blown away and doesn't know what to say. I'm proud. I did a good job kicking and screaming.

I leave the casting office. The grown-ups in the seats lining either side of the hallway all start clapping. I wonder what's going on, then I realize they must've heard me through the walls. They're clapping for me. Mom's sitting at the end of the hallway. Tears are welled in her eyes. She's so happy. And in this moment, so am I. Yes, it's nice to make Mom feel good, but it's also nice to feel good at something. Even if that thing makes you very uncomfortable at times. Even if that thing puts a lot of pressure on you. Even if that thing is very stressful. Sometimes it's just nice to feel good at something.

19.

"Use that clip, that one right there, where she's got the fire in her eyes," Mom says, pointing to the big monitor in front of the editor.

We're standing in a small dark room with padded, soundproof walls. It's just Mom, me, and the deeply-in-need-of-a-shave editor who's editing together my demo reel. A demo reel is a thing actors make to show their on-camera work. Usually the goal is to show some variety, good performance moments, and anytime you shared the screen with a big actor. The demo reel is then used for multiple reasons: it can be sent to casting directors to try to get you good auditions, it can be sent to producers or directors to try to get you job offers instead of having to audition, or in my case, it can be sent to managers to try to get represented by them.

Mom wants me to get a manager because she thinks it'll take my career to the next level.

"We're so close to a big break, we just need a little extra support," Mom says regularly. "We need a demo reel that'll really impress Susan Curtis."

Susan Curtis is the talent manager Mom's determined to get me signed with. Mom's heard she's the best in town for young performers.

So here we are today, in a building owned by a company that makes demo reels, sorting through clips of my performances, including *Strong Medicine*. (I booked the role. Mom said I didn't do as good on set as I did in the callback.)

The demo reel gets finished up in a few days and sent off to Susan. We get a call a couple days later that she wants to represent me.

"Yes, baby, yes!" Mom screams, so excited. "Even with an under-performance, you still impressed. Imagine how impressed she'd have been if she'd seen your callback!"

So I do. I imagine it. And I feel bad. I was better in the callback than I was on the day of filming. I failed. I wish Mom would stop bringing it up, but I know she's just trying to get me to be better. I know she means well. She just wants me to stop messing up and not doing as well as I could. She just wants me to be as impressive as I can be. She's just being a good mom.

20.

"Chug the Gatorade, chug it!" Mom yells at me like a boxing coach to their fighter.

I chug. The red Gatorade trickles down both sides of my mouth.

"But don't get it on your shirt!"

I lean forward to avoid spilling on my shirt.

"Keep chugging!"

I do.

"Okay, that should be good, baby."

I set the drink in the car cupholder and take a few deep breaths. Chugging Gatorade is exhausting.

"That should definitely help bring your fever down. Good girl, Net. Good girl."

It's been a week since signing with Susan. I have a fever of 103 and a cold so bad it sounds like I'm pinching my nose when I talk, but Mom says it'll look noncommittal if we cancel the first audition I got since signing, so here we are.

At least the audition is at Universal Studios, my favorite studio to audition at. There's something so romantic about walking to the bungalow where your audition is and passing Steven Spielberg's bungalow or seeing the Universal Studios tram drive by. It's the feeling of opportunity.

I'm auditioning for a network crime show called *Karen Sisco*, for the role of an eleven-year-old homeless child named Josie Boyle. Mom debated wiping dirt on my cheeks for the audition, but ultimately decided against it because "that's too over-the-top." I'm relieved with her decision.

The bungalow waiting room is so crowded with girls auditioning that the door is pushed open and little girls are sitting on the bungalow steps running their lines. The *Karen Sisco* casting director must really want to pick the right homeless child.

During the hour or so that I'm waiting to get called in, Mom continuously gives me Ricola cough drops and pulls me into the restroom to run lines or chug some Gatorade and Tylenol. My eyes are hot with sickness at this point and my body feels so sleepy and heavy. I just want to curl up in a ball. But I can't right now. There's work to do.

Finally, my name is called and I go into the crammed casting office to audition. There's a part in the sides where my character has to snort, and I have so much snot built up in my nose that it catches and makes this long, disgusting, sinus-infected snort-noise. The casting director doesn't seem to notice. She says I did a great job.

I go in for a callback the next day, still sick. This time, instead of in the bungalow, I audition in a more spacious room in one of the nice buildings near the soundstages. It's just the casting director again, and she doesn't videotape me, which means there will have to be another callback. Casting directors rarely choose the actor for a role unless it's a very small one. They typically do the narrowing down process, and then the producers and director decide on the person for the part.

I get called in for a second callback a couple days later, on Friday. Luckily, my fever's almost gone by now. Only 99.6, I'll take it. The director, a British man in a baseball cap and a button-down shirt, watches me. The snort goes by without too much snot, and the rest of the lines go well. He tells me I did a good job, gives me some direction on a few of the lines, and has me do it again. He tells me I take direction well. I leave and report all of this to Mom.

My third callback, fourth audition all around, comes the following Tuesday. I've never had so many auditions for a one-episode role on a TV show, but apparently this role has been very tricky to cast and they want to make sure they cast the right girl since it's a demanding guest lead (upgrade from guest star) opposite Carla Gugino and Robert Forster. Mom found this information out from Susan, which made Mom repeatedly say what a good decision it was to sign with her.

"She knows things. She just knows things."

I'm nervous at this fourth audition. I almost wish I were still sick, because there was less room for nerves when I was sick. Sickness takes the edge off. It's down to me and two other girls. They both have bigger credits than me, which Mom whispers anxiously to me every thirty seconds, as if there's anything I can do about it.

"Andrea Bowen's on *Desperate Housewives*. That show's doing very well. Though I'm not sure why. Pretty hokey, if you ask me."

I'm the last girl called in. I see the director again, and there's a camera in the room this time. He says they're gonna tape the audition for the producers. I nod.

"You're quiet, huh?" he asks.

I can't bring myself to respond. I'm petrified.

"Guess so," he says with a good-natured laugh. "Don't worry about it. Just have fun."

I'm a little confused by the direction, since the scenes in the sides are (1) my character witnessing the homeless man who takes care of her getting shot; (2) my character sitting with Robert Forster's character, telling him how she wants nothing to do with the father who abandoned her as a baby; and (3) my character sitting with her father, telling him she wants nothing to do with him since he abandoned her as a baby.

Where is the fun? I don't see any fun here.

The six-minute audition goes by in a blur. The director tells me I'm good and that he thinks I'll make it in this business. I say thanks and leave the audition. That night, we get the call I booked the role. Mom jumps up and down. So do I.

"My baby's homeless! My baby's got edge! My baby's homeless!"

21.

"Do it in bold letters," Mom says over my shoulder while she dries a plate with a dishrag and watches me type.

I drag the mouse over the three words and click on the B tool at the top of the page to make them bold, then I whip my head around to gauge Mom's reaction.

"Yeah, that's good." Mom nods in agreement with herself. "I'm gonna make Scottie some SpaghettiOs. Print it out when you're done so I can take a look."

Mom heads into the kitchen and I turn my attention back to the Microsoft Word document on the computer screen in front of me. Both of these things—the computer screen and Microsoft Word—are fairly new developments in the McCurdy household. Marcus built the computer in his computer-building class at high school and I bought all the add-ons with the check from my co-star appearance on *CSI*, where I played a murderer's sister. The part was emotionally draining, but after Mom said I could buy Microsoft Word and The Sims with the part of my paycheck she wasn't using for bills, it was worth it.

I'm typing up my own résumé. This makes me feel proud. Capable. Competent. How many other eleven-year-olds are typing up their own résumés? I feel ahead.

However, those three words Mom just suggested I make bold cause me a deep pang of dread in my gut. I look at the words for a long beat.

Those three words get top billing in the Special Skills portion of my résumé. They come before pogo sticking, hula hooping, jump roping (including double Dutch), piano, dance (jazz, tap, lyrical, hip-hop), flexibility, and twelfth-grade reading ability—all special skills that Mom thinks will either give me a leg up for having, or that will lead me to miss an opportunity for not having, like the time I missed out on a Chef Boyardee commercial by not being able to pogo stick. Mom immediately bought a pogo stick from Pic 'N' Save and had me practice an hour a day for two weeks until I could get to one thousand jumps without falling off the pogo stick. Yes, I'm really good at pogo sticking.

But none of those special skills are as important as this three-word one. The one that Mom designated top billing to, the one that she wanted in bold...

Crying on cue.

Crying on cue is *the* skill you want in child acting. Everything else pales in comparison. If you can bring the tears on command, you're a real player. A real contender. And on a good day, I can bring the tears on command.

"You're like a female Haley Joel Osment," Mom tells me regularly. "He's the only other kid these days who can bring the tears. Well, I suppose Dakota Fanning, but she's more of a weller. The tears don't actually fall. You want the tears trickling down the cheeks for the camera."

The first time I cried on cue was in acting class. Miss Lasky told us to take an object from home and think of a sad story to go with that object, and then come to class the next week with the object and tell the story onstage.

I brought in a stapler. Dustin and Scottie draw a lot, and they staple their drawings into little packets to categorize them. So I made up a story about our house burning down and my brothers dying in the fire and the only thing that remained was their stapler. If I really wanted to bring the waterworks, I would have thought of Mom dying, but thinking of Mom dying is off-limits. Even though she's been in remission for years, her health is still fragile enough that I don't want to jinx anything, since her life is in my hands with my annual birthday wish. That's a responsibility I don't take lightly and one I would never want to undermine for the sake of a teary monologue. My brothers' lives, on the other hand, are perfectly okay to exploit for artistic growth.

As I was on the little acting class stage telling the story, my eyes welled with tears to the point that my vision was blurry. But the tears weren't falling. I was sort of feeling the sadness from the monologue, but sort of feeling the frustration of the tears not falling. Miss Lasky walked onto the stage with thunderous steps and leaned three inches from my face so our noses were nearly touching. I was scared. I didn't know what was coming next. Then she lifted up her hand and snapped her fingers right in front of my eyes. The suddenness of the gesture scared my body into a jolt, and with the jolt, the tears fell. Miss Lasky beamed. I did too. Underneath the tears, I beamed.

From that point on, if an audition required crying on cue, I felt nearly positive I would book the job. Word of mouth spread. It got to the point where Susan would phone Mom and proudly announce, "I got another call from a casting director saying, 'So tell me about the kid who cries.'"

Granted, crying on cue was not fun for me. It was one of the more miserable experiences of my life, sitting in a cold casting office imagining tragic events that harm my beloved family. Any given event could last me four to six auditions' worth of tears, but eventually I'd become immune to the event—Mom referred to this as being "all cried out"—so we'd have to switch to a new event. The stapler story became Dustin dying of meningitis; he'd actually had a bad case of it a few years back, so Mom would say, "Imagine if the spinal tap went wrong!" Dustin dying of meningitis became Marcus dying of appendicitis and then Scott dying of pneumonia and then Grandpa dying of old age. ("Imagine he's in the hospital bed clutching the sock doll you made him when you were six.")

The time I brought the most tears was for an audition for a bit part in *Hollywood Homicide*, a feature film starring Harrison Ford and Josh Hartnett. The part was for a little girl sitting in the back of a van with her tourist family, driving down Hollywood Boulevard when Josh Hartnett hijacks the car and starts driving it, causing the family to fly into hysterics.

I don't know what was going on that particular day, but my tear ducts were especially filled. All I had to do was plop down in the casting office and think of Grandpa clutching his sock doll and BAM!, the tears spilled. An absurd amount. This wasn't crying, this was sobbing. My body convulsed with me. I was hysterical.

"Wow," the casting director said as soon as I was finished. She had curly reddish-brown hair and a voice like butter. She was very nice.

"I mean, you have the part, but I kinda wanna see you do it again, just to see it again," said the guy with gray hair and a brown leather jacket sitting to the casting director's side.

And so I did it again. I had become the Cirque du Soleil performer of crying on cue. People wanted to see me do it over and over, like I was climbing silks or contorting in aerial hoops. Crying on cue was truly my Special Skill.

22.

EMILY'S DAD HAS JUST been murdered and her mom is a suspect. A crying-on-cue audition for yet another network police procedural, *Without a Trace*, has just come through. The audition scene is a scene where Emily gets called in for an interrogation and starts getting overwhelmed and then the tears fall.

I'm sitting in the waiting room mustering up all my sadness when something shifts in me. It feels strange. I don't know how to describe it, but I know, my gut knows, that the tears aren't gonna come. I feel detached, disconnected, and then irritated.

I tug on Mom's arm. She dog-ears the diet section in her current issue of *Woman's World*. The diet section is her favorite, even though I'm not sure why. Mom's very petite, four foot eleven "and a whopping ninety-two pounds!" as she often announces with proud irony, knowing her pound count is far from whopping. She sets the magazine down on her lap and leans closer to me so I can whisper in her ear.

"Mommy, I don't think I'm gonna be able to cry."

Mom looks at me, puzzled at first, then her confusion turns to intensity. I can tell immediately that she's switched into pep-talk mode, a role she switches into more often than is necessary because it makes her feel necessary. She furrows her eyebrows and tightens her lips. There's a childishness to this expression of hers, like she's a kid pretending to be an adult.

"Of course you will. You're Emily. You *are* Emily."

Mom often says this when she's "getting me into character." She'll say, "You ARE Emily." Or Kelli. Or Sadie. Or whoever I'm supposed to be that day.

But today, right now, I don't feel like being Emily. I don't want to be Emily. This has never happened before, but it's happening now and it's scaring me. A part of me is resisting my mind forcing this emotional trauma on itself. A part of me is saying, "No. It's too painful. I'm not doing this."

That part of me is foolish. That part of me doesn't realize that this is my Special Skill, that this is good for me, for my family, for Mom. The more I can cry on cue, the more jobs I can book; the more jobs I can book, the happier Mom will be. I take a deep breath, then smile up at Mom.

"You're right. I'm Emily," I say half to convince Mom, half to convince myself.

The part of me that doesn't want to cry on cue is not convinced. That part of me screams that I'm not Emily, that I'm Jennette, and that I, Jennette, deserve to be listened to. What I want and what I need deserves to be listened to.

Mom finds the fold in her magazine, but just before she goes to reopen it, she leans over once more.

"You're gonna book this one, Emily."

But I don't. The audition doesn't go well. My heart isn't in it. I don't "feel my words." And worst of all, I do not cry on cue. I tank.

We're on the way home, in bumper-to-bumper traffic on the 101 South. I'm sitting in my booster seat since I'm still small enough to be required to sit in it. I try to work on my history homework but I'm unable to focus because I'm too upset at myself over the audition.

I was in my head during it because that scary part of me decided to try and speak up. That part of me that doesn't want to be doing this.

"I don't want to act anymore," I say before I even realize I've said it.

Mom looks at me in the rearview mirror. A mixture of shock and disappointment fills her eyes. I immediately regret saying anything.

"Don't be silly, you love acting. It's your favorite thing in the world," Mom says in a way that makes it sound like a threat.

I look out the window. The part of me that wants to please her thinks maybe she's right, maybe it is my favorite thing and I just don't know it, I just don't realize it. But the part of me that doesn't want to cry on cue, that doesn't want to act, that doesn't care about pleasing Mom and just wants to please me, that part of me screams at me to speak up. My face gets hot, compelling me to say something.

"No, I really don't want to. I don't like it. It makes me uncomfortable."

Mom's face looks like she just ate a lemon. It contorts in a way that terrifies me. I know what's coming next.

"You can't quit!" she sobs. "This was our chance! This was ouuuuur chaaaaance!"

She bangs on the steering wheel, accidentally hitting the horn. Mascara trickles down her cheeks. She's hysterical, like I was in the *Hollywood Homicide* audition. Her hysteria frightens me and demands to be taken care of.

"Never mind," I say loudly so Mom can hear it through her sobs.

Her crying stops immediately, except for one leftover sniffle, but as soon as that sniffle is over, it's complete silence. I'm not the only one who can cry on cue.

"Never mind," I repeat. "Let's just forget I said anything. Sorry."

I suggest we listen to Mom's current favorite album, Phil Collins's ... *But Seriously*. She smiles at the suggestion and puts it in the CD player. She flips to "Another Day in Paradise," and the song starts blasting through the speakers. Mom sings along. She eyes me in the rearview mirror.

"Come on! Why aren't you singin' along, Net?!" she asks giddily, her mood having switched.

So I start singing along. And I throw on my best fake smile to go with it. Maybe I wasn't able to bring the tears for *Without a Trace*, but I was able to bring the smile for Mom on our drive home. Either way, it's performing.

23.

"A LITTLE GIRL SHOULDN'T HAVE to worry about her entire family," Grandpa says to me one afternoon.

He can tell I'm stressed. I've been pacing back and forth on our front lawn for a half hour while I try to memorize my lines for an upcoming audition for a low-budget movie called *My Daughter's Tears*. Could there be a film title more perfectly suited to my Special Skill? Mom won't let me read the script because she says there's too much "adult content," which is honestly a relief because I'm struggling enough as it is to try and memorize these fourteen pages by my audition tomorrow, and with a Russian accent no less. The character I'm trying out for, the daughter whose tears the title is based upon, is Russian. Mom booked me an appointment with an accent coach, but I still don't have my *r*'s quite right.

I'm not allowed to go outside alone. Mom says I might get kidnapped and abused and murdered like Samantha Runnion—the girl who was kidnapped three weeks before her sixth birthday and lived just five minutes away from us—so whenever I go outside, someone has to join me. Today it's Grandpa. He's been watering the lawn while I've been memorizing.

"What?" I ask, not because I didn't hear what he said, but because I'm confused. Of course a little girl should worry about her entire family. That's what little girls do.

"I just..." He steps closer to me. "I just think... you deserve to be a kid."

My eyes well with tears, and not from me forcing them to. This is a natural welling. I can't remember the last time I cried naturally. I'm taken off guard. I shuffle my feet.

"Come here, give Papa a hug."

I step forward and wrap my arms around his big belly. He pats my back with his free hand.

"Love you, Poppy Seed," I say to him.

"Love you too, hun."

Papa goes to bring his other arm around me to a get a proper hug going, but he forgets he's holding a hose and the water squirts on me.

"Woops!"

He sets the hose down on the lawn and lets the water run into the grass, then he envelops me in his big Papa hug. It feels so nice and cozy, even though he kind of smells like beef jerky.

"You know, I was gonna give you a little present once you finished memorizing your lines, but maybe I oughta go ahead and give it to you now."

"Okay!" I'm excited. Who doesn't love presents?

Grandpa reaches into his back pocket and digs around. Crumpled-up receipts spill out onto the grass. Finally, he pulls out a little car antenna topper. It's Mike Wazowski, the main monster character from *Monsters, Inc.* This kind of free movie merch is among the perks he receives as a Disneyland employee.

I take Mike into my palm. He's squishy and made of Styrofoam.

"I love how funny-lookin' he is," Grandpa says. "Idn't he funny-lookin'?"

"Yeah."

"He makes me laugh. I was hoping he'd make you laugh too."

"Thanks, Poppy Seed."

"'Course," he says with a nod. "You know, I hope you remember to have fun. Life should be fun for a kid."

Grandpa bends down, picks up the hose and starts watering the grass again. I look down at Mike, running my thumb over his rubbery skin while I think about what Grandpa said.

Fun isn't a thing I'm particularly familiar with. Life's a serious thing. There's a lot going on in this place. Being prepared and working hard and doing well are far more important than fun.

I tuck Mike Wazowski into my pocket and go back to my Russian accent.

24.

I'M LOOKING DOWN AT THE papers in front of me. The stack of 110 freshly printed papers filled with size 12 Courier New font. This is *Henry Road*, my first screenplay.

I printed the screenplay out because I can't wait to show it to Mom. I know she could use a pick-me-up since she's in the hospital right now. It can't be easy for Mom, to be in the hospital as often as she is—typically several times a year. Even though sometimes the reason she's in the hospital is unrelated to her cancer (like this time when she's there for her diverticulitis—or diverticulosis, I'm never sure which one it is), the fear is always there... the fear that maybe when she's having an exam or a test or a surgery, the doctor will find a recurrence of her cancer.

Grandpa drives me to the hospital in his beat-up, dark-blue Buick with the Bush/Cheney bumper sticker. I sit in the back seat thumbing my pages.

"Be careful you don't get a paper cut, hun," Grandpa tells me while he drives through a light that's in the middle of turning red.

We get to the hospital. I've been to a lot of hospitals for Mom's various health conditions, but I've never been to this one. This one's small, boutique-seeming. It's less daunting than they usually are, and less mazelike, so we find our way to Mom's room quickly.

She's resting, but when she hears my footsteps, her eyes flutter open and she beams. "Hi, Net!" Her smile makes me smile.

"Hi, Nonny Mommy!"

I sit down in the chair next to her bed and take her hand in mine. I notice that our wrists are the same size.

"What did you bring with you?" Mom asks, gesturing to the stack of papers tucked under my other arm.

I can hardly contain my excitement. There's a wheeled food table that's rolled up to Mom's bed—much more luxurious than the white folding mat we eat on at home. The food tray on top of it—the turkey, green beans, mashed potatoes, side of chicken noodle soup, and crackers—are uneaten. I shove the food over a bit to make a clearing and then I plop my pages on top of the table proudly.

"It's my screenplay. *Henry Road.*"

"You wrote a screenplay?" Mom asks. I'm sure she's impressed. But then a concerned look crosses her face.

"Have you been going outside every day for twenty minutes to get your vitamin D?"

"Of course," I say, reassuring her.

"And you've been going to your dance classes?"

"Yep."

She thumbs the cover page, but not with the pride I have when I thumb it. Her thumbing has a sadness to it.

"What?" I ask.

"It's just..." Mom looks down and smiles wistfully. This is one of her most rehearsed-looking expressions to me. I've never once seen her do this expression and felt like it was really coming from her in that moment. It always feels forced.

"It's just what?" I ask.

"It's just... I hope you don't like writing more than you like acting. You're so good at acting. So, so good at it."

Suddenly I'm embarrassed I gave Mom my screenplay. I'm ashamed. How could I be so stupid? She would never support this.

"Of course I don't like writing more than acting. I could never."

Hearing the words come out of my mouth, I think I sound fake, with the feigned innocence of the characters on the *Leave It to Beaver* reruns that Grandma insists on watching even though I hate them so much.

Mom doesn't notice that I'm lying, even though it feels so obvious in my bones that I am. I absolutely prefer writing to acting. Through writing, I feel power for maybe the first time in my life. I don't have to say somebody else's words. I can write my own. I can be myself for once. I like the privacy of it. Nobody's watching. Nobody's judging. Nobody's weighing in. No casting directors or agents or managers or directors or Mom. Just me and the page. Writing is the opposite of performing to me. Performing feels inherently fake. Writing feels inherently real.

"Well good," Mom says as she eyes me, as if she's deciding whether or not she can trust my response. "Writers dress frumpy and get fat, you know? I would never want your little actress's peach butt to turn into a big, giant writer's watermelon butt."

Duly noted. Me writing makes Mom unhappy. Me acting makes Mom happy. I pick up the pages from the food table and tuck them back under my arm.

As an afterthought, Mom asks what the screenplay is about.

"It's the story of a ten-year-old boy and his best friend as they try and pair their single parents together."

"Hm," Mom says with a long look out the window. "They already did that in *The Parent Trap*."

25.

I WAKE UP AT EIGHT a.m. on my Costco mat. My bunk bed is now overwrought with stuff, so I'm back to sleeping on the mat. I'm wearing my Revlon Run/Walk 2002 tee. I like the design. It's got a lot of purple in it, which I'm into right now.

I can't let Mom know I'm into purple, since Mom prefers pink. She would be heartbroken if I suddenly announce that I've switched my favorite color to one that isn't also hers. It is an honor that Mom cares about me so much that something like me having my own favorite color would devastate her. True love.

Last year's Revlon Run/Walk tee was mostly silver, and the year before that it was mostly blue. I know about all the Run/Walk tee colors for the past seven years because that's how long my family has been attending the annual Run/Walk. We started attending the Revlon Run/Walks after Mom went into remission for her stage four metastatic ductal carcinoma, a term I am well acquainted with because, in addition to our weekly VHS viewing, Mom often has me recite it to casting directors.

"Everyone loves the story of somebody overcoming adversity. If you mention my ductal carcinoma, you'll get the sympathy vote."

Mom's cancer rarely seems to come up organically in my auditions for the *Suite Life of Zack & Cody* and the *King of Queens*, but on shows like *ER*, I can wedge it in a little more naturally, especially if there's a character in the episode who has cancer.

"You know, my mother had stage four ductal carcinoma, so I really relate to the material."

Mom always says that we go to the Revlon Run/Walks to support women with breast cancer, which is so noble of her. Dustin once said under his breath that he thought Mom went more for the free cancer merch than the cause itself, but Dustin is a "troublemaker" and also Mom's least favorite child, which she even told him directly, so obviously Dustin doesn't know the first thing about Mom or her intentions.

I'm rocking my oversized cancer tee and planning what poem I'll write for Mom this weekend. Since Mom's not a fan of me writing screenplays, I've taken an indefinite hiatus from those, but she is very supportive of me writing quick little poems about how much I love her, so I keep up with writing this way now.

I'm trying to figure out what to rhyme with the word "mommy" when I realize my chest is kind of sore. More specifically, the nipple area of the right side of my chest. I reach my right hand up to touch the sore area and there I feel it... A LUMP. Terror immediately fills my body. This can't be happening. First Mom and now me? The room starts spinning. I weigh my options—I can go wake Mom to tell her now, but that seems burdensome. Or I can let her sleep until eleven a.m., when I usually wake her up with her morning cup of tea. "I'd wake up earlier if I wasn't up so late stressing about money," Mom always says. "Maybe if your father got a job that PAID THE BILLS for once so I wouldn't have to depend on a CHILD..."

I don't know which to pick, so I do what any sensible, cancer-ridden tween deciding when to tell their mom does—I eeny meeny miny moe it.

"Oh, Sweetie." Mom half laughs as she runs her fingers back and forth along my puffy, lumped nipple on the right, and then over my smooth, flat nipple on the left to compare. "That's not cancer."

"Then what is it?"

"You're just getting boobies."

Oh. No. The only thing worse than a cancer diagnosis is a growing-up diagnosis. I am horrified of growing up. First, I'm small for my age, which is a benefit in showbiz because I can book roles for characters younger than me. I can work longer hours on set and have to take fewer breaks by law. Logistics aside, I'm more cooperative and can take direction better than those seven-year-old scumbags.

Mom is constantly reminding me how good it is that I look so young for my age. "You'll book more, baby. You'll book a lot more."

If I start to grow up, Mom won't love me as much. She often weeps and holds me really tight and says she just wants me to stay small and young. It breaks my heart when she does this. I wish I could stop time. I wish I could stay a child. I feel guilty that I can't. I feel guilty with every inch I grow. I feel guilty whenever we see one of my aunts or uncles and they comment on how much I'm "growing up." I can see Mom's eyebrow twitch whenever they say that. I can see how much it pains her.

I'm determined to not grow up. I'll do anything to stop it from happening.

"Well, is there anything I could do to stop the boobies from coming in?" I ask Mom nervously.

Mom breaks into a laugh-exhale, the kind where her eyes wrinkle up. I know this expression well, the way I know all of Mom's expressions well. I have learned them inside and out so that I can behave accordingly at all times.

No one else in the family seems to understand Mom's emotions. Everyone else walks around clueless, never knowing which Mom they're going to get. But I always know. I've spent my whole life studying her so that I can always know, because I always want to do whatever I can in any given moment to keep or make Mom happy. I know the difference between Mom being irritated and outraged. I know the difference between when she's upset at Dad or when she's upset at Grandma (clenched jaw means Dad, tight eyebrow means Grandma). I know the difference between when she's a little happy (kisses me on the forehead) and a lot happy (sings Phil Collins). And right now, in this moment, where she laugh-exhales and her eyes wrinkle up, I know that she's not only a lot happy, but a special, particular kind of happy.

Mom is grateful-happy.

This is my favorite way to see her, because I am directly the source of it. I've seen Mom be grateful-happy when I book roles and when I side with her when she's in the middle of an argument with anyone else in the house. Mom is grateful-happy when she feels seen, valued, and nurtured.

"What can I do to stop the boobies from coming?" I repeat, leaning further into my question now that I know it satisfies Mommy so much.

Mom looks down, the way she does when she's about to tell me a secret, like the time she told me Grandma has false teeth or the time she said she finds Dad boring. I know something juicy is coming. Something special, something just the two of us will know. Something that will cement and validate our wonderful best friendship, the way only secrets can.

"Well, sweetheart, if you really want to know how to stay small, there's this secret thing you can do... it's called calorie restriction."

* * *

I take to calorie restriction quickly and I'm quite good at it. I'm desperate to impress Mom. She's a great teacher because she's been calorie restricting for so long, she tells me.

"Once when I was falling asleep as a child, I heard my mom and dad talking in the other room. They said my brother could eat anything and his metabolism would work it right off, but that anything I ate turned to fat. Those words got to me, Net, they really did. I've been restricting ever since."

Now that I think about it, it does make sense to me that Mom's been restricting. She only has hot tea every morning for breakfast, nothing in it, and a plate of steamed vegetables every night for dinner, nothing on them. I rarely see her eat lunch, and if she does, it's a salad with no dressing or half of a chocolate chip Chewy Granola Bar. I'm in good hands.

I start shrinking by the week as Mom and I team up to count our calories every night and plan our meals for the next day. We're keeping me on a one-thousand-calorie diet, but I have the smart idea that if I only eat half my food, I'll only be receiving half the calories, which means that I will be shrinking twice as fast. I proudly show my half-eaten portions to Mom after every meal. She beams. Each Sunday, she weighs me and measures my thighs with a measuring tape. After a few weeks of our routine, she provides me with a stack of diet books that I finish quickly. I learn the value of eating water-dense fruits and vegetables like jicama and watermelon. I learn how helpful cayenne and chili peppers are for increasing your metabolism. I learn that coffee is an appetite suppressant, so I start drinking decaf—black—alongside Mom. Drinking coffee in any form is technically against the church's rules.

"Well it's decaf so I'm sure God would make an exception," Mom says, and I nod like I agree, even though I'm pretty sure the God I've learned about doesn't make exceptions.

The thinner I get, the stricter I get with what I'll ingest, because it seems like my body is trying to hold on to whatever I eat.

I notice that most foods add a little body weight to me, four-tenths of a pound or so. I know this because I weigh myself five times a day. Five is my lucky number, so this amount of daily weigh-ins seems appropriate. I also want to make sure that I'm staying on top of every single shift in my body so that I can make proper adjustments and be on track for my weekly weighing session with Mom.

My favorite foods are sugar-free Popsicles, applesauce, and unsweetened iced tea, because these are the foods that don't seem to add weight to me. Popsicles and applesauce add nothing, and iced tea is peed right out. These are stress-free foods for me. Safe foods. Comfort foods. Whoever said mac 'n' cheese and fried chicken were comfort foods was out of their mind. These are the real comfort foods.

Mommy and I continue our mission, and I am thrilled. Every day feels to me like the montage of the twins in *The Parent Trap*, where Mom and I give each other Eskimo kisses and do silly hand jives in between our weekly weigh-ins and daily calorie counts. (I watched the film after Mom suggested my screenplay *Henry Road* was a rip-off. She was right.) Calorie restriction has brought me and Mom closer than we already were, which is really saying something because we were already so close. Calorie restriction is wonderful!

We're about six months into our calorie-restricting plan and you can really see the difference. I'm down three sizes and am now wearing a kids' size 7 slim. The Holy Spirit tells me to touch the word "slim" on my clothing tags five times every day because that ritual, along with my restriction, will keep me small. Thanks, Holy Spirit!

Overall, things are going well. But today is an exception.

Today I am anxious, because I'm sitting in the waiting room at my doctor's office waiting to be called back. And waiting to be called back means waiting to be weighed. And I'm terrified of being weighed on a scale that isn't my own. What if the numbers are off? What if I weigh more on this one?

Mom seems to sense that I'm nervous, so she holds my hand while we wait. And wait. And wait. Until finally... "McCurdy, Jennette," the doctor's assistant calls out. My heart starts pounding so intensely, I'm sure everyone in the room can hear it. My face feels hot. Time blurs while I walk through the waiting room door and into the hallway. Mom starts taking off my corduroy Children's Place jacket, knowing it adds extra weight. We're in this together. The nurse tells me I can leave my shoes on, but Mom tells me to take them off. Always looking out! I kick off my shoes and step on the scale. Mom and I lock eyes.

"Sixty-one pounds," the nurse says as she scribbles on her clipboard paper.

As I hear the words come out of her mouth, they feel morphed and warped. I am crushed. The scale at home said fifty-nine. I immediately try to read Mom's expression. It's even, which means disappointment. I am even more crushed. We are escorted to room 5, my lucky number not seeming so lucky in this moment. I step up the little stepping stool and sit on the teddy bear paper on the patients' table. It's rough and pokey. The assistant asks a few more questions, then closes the door behind her. I open my mouth to say something, but Mom speaks before I can.

"We'll talk about it later."

A few minutes pass, and Dr. Tran comes in. I'm disappointed it's Dr. Tran instead of Dr. Pelman because Mom seems in a much better mood when it's Dr. Pelman. (If it wasn't against the gospel, I'd think Mom has a crush on him, but I know better because lust is a sin and Mom would never engage in a sin.) Dr. Tran keeps her eyes on her clipboard.

"Debbie, could I speak with you privately for a minute?"

Mom steps outside with Dr. Tran. The doors are thin enough and Mom talks loud enough that I can completely hear them.

"So... I wanted to speak with you about Jennette's weight," Dr. Tran starts. "It's significantly lower than what's normal for her age."

"Huh," Mom says, sounding a little anxious. "She's eating normally. I haven't noticed any changes."

That's not true. Mom *has* noticed the changes because she's the one who wanted the changes in the first place.

"Well..." Dr. Tran takes a big breath in. "Sometimes when young girls have anorexia, they're very secretive about their food habits."

This is the first time I've heard the word "anorexia." It sounds like a dinosaur. Dr. Tran continues on.

"I suggest you keep a close eye on Jennette's eating behaviors."

"Oh, I will, Dr. Tran. I certainly will," Mom assures her.

I'm confused. Mom already keeps an eye on my eating behaviors. She's as involved in them as I am, if not more so. Mom not only knows everything about how and what I eat, but she encourages and supports my habits. What's going on? What does this even mean?

A few months later, I hear the word "anorexia" again in the parking lot of my dance studio after class. I'm on the bench out front, waiting for Mom to arrive while I learn some sides for an audition to play Val Kilmer's daughter in an upcoming movie.

Mom's always twenty to forty-five minutes late picking me up, which makes sense because she's so busy with other things, like calling bill collectors to ask for holds and stopping by the Westminster Mall to pick up Hallmark thank-you cards for every casting director I've read for in the past six months. ("They might not remember your read, but they'll remember a thank-you card with pretty cursive writing on the front!")

I notice Anjelica Gutierrez's mom has been loitering near her minivan, even though Anjelica's last class was the same last class as mine and the Gutierrezes usually leave right on time. Then I see Mom's copper Ford Windstar minivan make the left turn onto the street of the studio and pull into the parking lot. I grab my dance bag and start to head to the car, but Mrs. Gutierrez beats me to it. She approaches Mom's passenger window and asks her to roll it down.

"Hi, Deb, I just wanted to talk to you real quick about Jennette. I notice she's losing a lot of weight. It seems like she might have anorexia. I wanted to see if you're working on getting her help. Another girl in class struggled with it, and her mom gave me the name of a specialist—"

"Let's talk about this some other time," Mom interrupts Mrs. Gutierrez in the way that tells me "some other time" is never going to come. I pull open the car door and jump in. And with that, we're on our way home.

"Mom?" I ask once we're stopped at a red light.

"Yeah, sweetheart?"

"What's anorexia?"

"Oh, don't worry about it, Angel. People are just being dramatic." The light turns green. She steps on the gas.

"Did you learn your lines?"

"Yeah."

"Great. Great. You've got a good shot at this one, Net. I can feel it. Val's blonde, you're blonde, you're a shoo-in."

"Uh-huh."

"An absolute shoo-in."

I look out the window, then go back to learning my lines. I'm excited for the sugar-free Popsicle I'll have when I get home.

26.

TODAY IS THE DAY I enter Beehives, the church's program for girls twelve to thirteen years old. Upon entering the program, you're assigned a "role" and the role I've just been assigned is assistant secretary—a position that doesn't even exist.

"But Madison's already secretary," I tell Sister Smith, my teacher. "So what am I supposed to do?"

"Well, you can help her out."

I look down at my fingernails to hide my disappointment. Makaylah Lindsey leans over to talk to me.

"The girls who get the good positions are the ones who are for sure always gonna be active."

I hate Makaylah. I know she was adopted and I should feel bad for her and all that, but I don't. I just plain hate her. She continues on.

"They gave you your position because they think you'll probably eventually become inactive."

"Inactive" is all but a cuss word in the Mormon church. Active members are those who regularly attend service, inactive ones are those who have "fallen off," or stopped attending even though they're still on the church's records. Whenever an inactive member is brought up in a conversation in church, the member's name is said with a nose scrunch and a whispery tone, like it's something shameful and pathetic.

"We're not gonna go inactive."

"We'll see." Makaylah shrugs.

Even though I hate Makaylah and I desperately want her to be wrong, I fear that she might be right. If I really think about it, there are already a few signs.

For as far back as I can remember, my family has never fit the bill of "First-Rate Mormons." In every Latter-day Saints ward, there are the kinds of

Mormons who have perfect attendance in seminary and are off-book for their Third Nephi verses. The kinds of Mormons who are trusted to bring the chicken potpie to the potluck, those clearly capable of that level of responsibility. These are the First-Rate Mormons.

And then there are the kinds of Mormons who skimp on tithing and always show up twenty minutes late to service. The "just go ahead and bring the salad" kinds of Mormons—those who can't be trusted with any more responsibility than some bagged iceberg lettuce with the stale croutons already mixed in. These are the Second-Rate Mormons.

We, the McCurdys, are Second-Rate Mormons. I've known this for a while. There's a certain pity that First-Rates view Second-Rates with, and I've sensed that pity in side-eyes from Sister Huffmire and Sister Meeks, who are both First-Rates.

Everybody knows that Second-Rates are much more likely than First-Rates to go inactive, but still, I didn't think our fate was by any means sealed. I was sure we could reverse our Second-Rate status with some Mormon milestone, like Marcus serving a mission or us never skipping service.

But now that Makaylah's brought it up and I'm thinking it through, I'm coming to terms with the fact that maybe those Mormon milestones won't happen after all.

Marcus has been old enough to go on his mission for several years, but he hasn't gone. And even though there's no age restriction for going on one, men are 70 percent less likely to go if they don't go within that first year that they're able, according to the Mormon magazine *Ensign* (the only magazine besides *Woman's World* that's in Mom's regular rotation). Mom says it's Marcus's girlfriend Elizabeth's fault, and that she's got the devil in her, but I'm not so sure. Elizabeth seems fine to me.

We've also started skipping service some weeks, usually around the release of episodes of shows that I've had guest-star roles on. It first started after *Law and Order: SVU*, when Sister Salazar asked Mom if she thought it was "in line with the Gospel" for me to be portraying a nine-year-old rape victim. Mom had a brilliant defense about how she thinks the value of a TV starlet being Mormon outweighs the roles that that starlet plays. Sister Salazar let it go for awhile, until I was in an episode of a show where I played a child who murders another child. Ever since then, every time an episode of a show I'm on airs, we skip a week or two of church to "avoid the judgers," as Mom says. Regardless of the reasoning, we're skipping service. And skipping service is the opposite of a Mormon milestone required to turn us into First-Rates.

"Mom?" I ask when we're back at home, folding laundry together.

"Yes, sweetheart?"

"Are we gonna become inactive Mormons?"

"Of course not. Why would you even ask that, Net?"

"Makaylah said the reason I got assigned assistant secretary is because they think we'll probably go inactive."

"Oh, please. What does Makaylah Lindsey know? She's adopted."

27.

"Net! Shower time!" Mom shouts from another room.

My whole body freezes. Oh no. Not shower time.

I've dreaded showers for a while, five years or so. Whenever it was that I started to feel uncomfortable that Mom still showers me.

She doesn't mean to make me uncomfortable, I don't think. She says she has to shower me because I wouldn't know how to shampoo and condition my own hair. She says maybe if it wasn't so long or such a specific texture that she wouldn't have to, but because it is those things, and since she was a professional hairstylist, it just makes sense for her to do it.

Mom showers me with Scottie sometimes. He's almost sixteen at this point. I get really embarrassed when she showers us together. I can tell he does too. We usually just look away from each other and Scott distracts himself by drawing Pokémon in the fogged glass. He does a pretty good Charizard. When she showers us together, Mom says it's because she's got too much to do. Scott asked if he could shower himself once. Mom sobbed and said she didn't want him to grow up so he never asked again after that.

Whether or not Scott's there with me, Mom gives me a breast and "front butt" exam, which is what she calls my private parts. She says she wants to make sure I don't have any mysterious lumps or bumps because those could be cancer. I say okay because I definitely don't want cancer, and since Mom's had it and all, she would know if I do.

I usually just try and think of Disneyland when Mom's doing the exams. I think of the next time Grandpa will sign us in. I think of the parade and the fireworks and the characters all happy and everything.

By the time the exams are done, a huge wave of relief washes over my whole body and I usually realize that's the first time I've felt my body since the exam started. It's weird... when the exams are happening, I feel like I'm outside of myself. Like my body is a shell I'm disconnected from and I'm living entirely in my thoughts. My Main Street, Fantasyland, Mr. Toad's Wild Ride thoughts. (Actually, I usually don't think of Mr. Toad's Wild Ride because as much as people love it, I think that ride's mediocre.)

"Net?!" Mom calls out again.

My body's still frozen. I swallow and force a response up my throat.

"I'm ready!"

She's showering me alone tonight. I know because I have an audition for *House* tomorrow, and I've noticed this pattern that whenever I have an audition, Mom showers me alone. I think it's because she wants to make sure she gets the shampooing and conditioning just right so that my hair will look perfectly glossy for the casting director. Mom says this business is shallow and that glossy hair can be the difference between getting a callback or not.

My breathing is shaky as I set down my schoolwork and get up off the couch. My hands are clammy. I try and focus on the relief I'll feel as soon as the exams are done and I know the shower's just about over. I try and focus on that lightness. That feeling that everything's better and rosier for the rest of the night. I'm trying. I'm trying. I'm trying.

I get to the bathroom. Mom won't let me turn on the faucet because she says it's tricky to twist the handles and get the right temperature, so I wait for her. While I wait, I take off my pants, then my underwear, then my shirt. I step into the shower and hear the drip of the leaking faucet. I study the mold on it. It's white and blue and crusty. I hear Mom's footsteps as she approaches the bathroom. I'm off to Fantasyland.

28.

I'M SITTING IN THE BACK seat of the Ford Windstar. We're driving to the Art Supply Warehouse to visit Dustin on his shift. Dustin seems to hate this, but Mom loves it. I think she enjoys knowing people who work at the place she's visiting. I think it makes her feel like a VIP. Her posture and energy shift completely whenever she walks into Best Buy to visit Marcus, or the ticket stand at Disneyland to visit Grandpa. She gets this aura like she owns the place. I love seeing Mom so confident.

As we drive over, Mom's on the phone with a bill collector, asking for an extension, when she turns to me excitedly.

"Susan's calling!"

I know why Susan's calling. Yesterday I screen-tested for a show called *iCarly*, a new Nickelodeon show about young teenagers who create a web show together. And next week I'm supposed to screen-test for a show called *Californication*, a new Showtime show about a man who mistreats women. By the time you get to the screen test for a TV show, they already have the contracts all written up, and apparently it's good when you're testing for more than one show at the same time, because your manager can use that as "leverage" to get you the best deal possible. (Mom loves saying the word "leverage" on calls with Susan. She says it makes her sound "in the know.") There's also this weird rule that whichever show tests you first gets first choice on whether to pick you or not. They get a designated amount of time to decide if they for sure want you, then if they haven't decided by that point, the other network gets first choice.

I had my screen test for *iCarly* yesterday, so they have first choice as to whether they want me. Susan calling right now means Nickelodeon has made up their mind.

As excited as Mom is to talk to Susan, she finishes up with the bill collector first, like she always does.

"I'm not gonna drop the call after I've been waiting on hold for an hour."

Mom weeps her way through an extension, but by the time she hangs up with Brandon at Sprint PCS, her tears are dry. While she dials Susan, she thrusts her hand back behind her and toward me. I'm sitting in my booster seat. (I'm fourteen and still in the booster.) I have to lunge forward as far as I can to grip her hand, and since the seat belt is pulled through the booster seat, the length of the belt is shortened so it locks sooner. The second I lean forward to grab Mom's hand, the belt makes the clicking sound of it locking. I'm trying to reach her hand but I can't. *Click, click, click.*

"Hi, can I speak with Susan? It's Debbie McCurdy."

Click, click. Mom's hand wags around, trying to find mine. Our fingers almost graze. "Okay, yeah, I think I can figure out how to put it on speaker."

Mom presses buttons aimlessly on her phone until something works, and Susan's voice starts blaring from the phone speaker.

"She booked *iCarly*! She booked *iCarly*!"

Mom's hand flies forward to accompany her woohoo in what can only be described as a questionable fist pump. Whatever it is, it takes her hand away from mine and my whole body feels that. But just for a second. Because then it hits me. I've booked my first series regular role.

Mom pulls into the Art Supply Warehouse parking lot while we both scream at the top of our lungs. She pulls into a reserved-for-handicapped space—she's thrilled she has a handicapped card since her diverticulitis diagnosis. I unbuckle my seat belt as quickly as I can.

I jump into Mom's arms. She squeezes me. I'm elated. Everything's going to be different now. Everything's going to be better. Mom will finally be happy. Her dream has come true.

29.

"Ooh, a fruit basket!"

Mom unwinds the twist tie and starts peeling off the cellophane wrapping.

"Pineapple's really high in sugar, but you can have some of this cantaloupe and honeydew."

"Okay!"

Mom yanks two cantaloupe skewers out of the basket. Just as she's about to pass mine to me, she has a second thought and places it back.

"We can split one," she says.

We start chewing on our flower-shaped cantaloupe pieces as we look around at the other baskets on my dressing room table. There's a basket of teas from Coast to Coast, an at-home spa basket from Susan, and a meat and cheese basket from Nickelodeon.

"We can take that one home for Grandpa and the boys," Mom tells me.

This is the first difference I notice about being a series regular. You get a lot of baskets. I never got one basket in all my years as a guest star. (Although when I did my guest spot on *Karen Sisco*, Robert Forster did give me a silver pen with my name engraved on it, and he gave Mom a silver shoehorn. What a guy.)

Today is our first day back to work after being officially picked up for a first season order. After you shoot the pilot of a TV show, the network executives watch all the pilots and pick about a third of them to actually get made into a series. We were part of the lucky third, and, even cooler than that, we got the highest episode order of all the picked-up shows. Most of them got ten- or thirteen-episode pickups. We got twenty. Mom says this is probably because of my outstanding performance as Sam Puckett, a zinger-slinging, rough-around-the-edges tomboy with a heart of gold who, ironically compared to my experience with it, loves food.

"You ready to run lines, Angel?" Mom asks.

"Sure," I say, even though I'm never ready. I still get nervous to practice lines with Mom. I thought my being cast as a series regular might help her lighten up a bit, but it hasn't. She's still so critical. It's stressful.

I take a deep breath in to get ready for my first line when there's a loud knock at my dressing room door.

"Answer it," Mom tells me as she slaps her thigh, exasperated to be interrupted the second before we started.

I pull open the purple door and on the carpet in front of me is yet another basket. This one's filled with movie theater snacks: Milk Duds and Twizzlers and a few packets of popcorn. In the middle of the basket is a hundred-dollar gift card to ArcLight, the fanciest movie theater I've ever seen, the one just up the street from Nickelodeon Studios, where we shoot the show. Mom and I almost saw a movie at ArcLight the week that we shot the pilot, but Mom said there was no chance in hell she was paying $13.75 for a movie ticket. "I don't care how surrounded their sound is."

This gift card is the highest-dollar-amount gift card I've ever seen. I almost can't believe it.

"It's from Miranda," I tell Mom, shocked. "A hundred dollars to ArcLight."

Miranda is my co-star on *iCarly*. She plays the titular role of Carly Shay—a sweet, feminine teenage girl who, with her best friends Sam and Freddie (played by my other co-star, Nathan), starts a web series. Mom says they didn't flesh out Miranda's character very well. "Poor thing gets all the exposition. She's a pretty girl, but it's a shame her character has no personality."

I look back down at the basket. I'm really surprised that another child actor would be so nice to me. Usually there's such a sense of competition. This gesture is the opposite of that. I'm touched. I reach into the basket.

"You're not getting anywhere near those Milk Duds but that's very nice of her. Now let's practice your lines."

30.

"What about this?" Mom asks as she holds up a TY plush panda bear. We're in Hallmark Greeting Cards at the Westminster Mall. Since Miranda got a gift for me to celebrate the start of the season, we're picking one out for her, too. Mom wags the panda around.

"It's a cute little panda, plus it rhymes with her name. Miranda. Panda. Cute, right?"

"Yeah, it's really cute. Maybe we could just keep looking around to make sure that's the absolute best gift."

"Well, I think this with the fuzzy journal and we're good, right?" Mom asks.

"Sure. Right."

I swallow. We're not good. Miranda got me a very expensive gift card to a very fancy movie theater. That is a *cool* gift. A TY stuffed animal and a fuzzy journal is *not* a cool gift.

I used to think these were cool gifts, up until a few months ago. Up until a few months ago, I thought my rainbow bell-bottoms from the Children's Place and my quiz books from Limited Too were cool. But since meeting Miranda, my cool radar has shifted.

The first time I met her was at my screen test for *iCarly*. She was leaning against a wall, sipping Coke from a glass bottle and texting on her Sidekick. Whoa. Coke and a Sidekick. This girl knows what's up.

We talked briefly at the screen test, but not much more than introductions because we were rushed into the room to do our scenes together for the long table of executives.

We didn't talk a ton during the shooting of the pilot, either. I felt shy, and it seemed to me like she did too. We ran our lines between takes and said an enthusiastic "Bye! See you tomorrow!" at the end of each day, but there wasn't much else in between.

I studied her from afar though. Miranda seemed to have an independence I didn't have, and it fascinated me. She walked alone to pick up food from a different nearby restaurant each day—alone! What's that like? Then I'd always hear when she came walking back into the studio because she'd be playing Gwen Stefani or Avril Lavigne from her Sidekick. I knew of these artists, but Mom didn't allow me to listen to them because she said their music might make me wanna "do bad things."

On set, Miranda said cuss words like "shit" and "ass," and she took the Lord's name in vain at least fifty times a day. Mom warned me not to get too close to Miranda because she doesn't believe in God. (Nathan is okay for me to get close to, Mom says, because he does. "Southern Baptists are no Mormons, but at least we've got Jesus in common.")

Even though Mom said not to get close to Miranda, I really wanted to. I wanted some of her coolness to rub off on me. And she seemed nice, too, which is hard to be if you're cool. I had my fingers crossed that somehow, despite our mutual shyness, a friendship between us would develop.

But then, unfortunately, it didn't seem likely. Each day that passed where we didn't exchange phone numbers, I felt like we were getting further away from a potential friendship. Until, on the last day of shooting the pilot, just as Miranda was leaving set, she turned back and said, "Hey, Jennette, do you have AIM?"

"Not really," I said, thinking she was talking about throwing things. I've never had good aim.

"You don't have AOL Instant Messenger?" She seemed shocked.

"Ohhhh, AIM," I said, hoping that I sounded convincing, like I knew what it was even though I still didn't. "Yeah, I have it."

"Cool. Add me."

"Cool." And I felt it.

As soon as I got home that day, I had Marcus sign me up for an account. Over AIM, our friendship blossomed. Miranda and I spent hours talking every day on it. Sometimes if Mom walked past and asked me what I was doing, I'd tell her I was talking to Miranda, but most of the time I'd shrink the AIM text bubble, lie, and say I was doing schoolwork. She didn't question me. She'd leave the room and then I'd pull the text bubble back up and start laughing.

Even though in person Miranda seemed shy and quiet, she had a distinct and hilarious personality through her written words. So many of the things she said made me laugh. Her way of observing things—people, habits, human nature. I loved her. And I was so excited we were becoming friends.

But now Mom's lame gifts were going to ruin it.

Back at work, I set the gift bag down and knock three times on Miranda's door, then I rush back to my dressing room. I didn't want to see her reaction when she opened the stuffed animal and fuzzy journal. I was too embarrassed.

Miranda doesn't mention the gifts at first, not for almost our entire workday. I'm scared our friendship may be over.

But then as we're walking toward the parking lot with our moms at the end of the day, she turns to me and, through nervous laughter, says:

"Thanks for the stuffed animal. It's really cute."

"You're welcome."

"And the journal too. I'm excited to get back to journaling."

"Awesome."

She smiles at me. I can tell she's just being nice. But I appreciate the kindness.

"See you on AIM later," she says with a wave.

"Okay," I say excitedly. A little too excitedly. Even if she didn't like her panda and fuzzy journal, even if she was just being nice when she said thanks for them, she still wants to be friends. I'm so glad I have AIM.

31.

I'M STANDING BEHIND THE CURTAIN in the dressing room of the soundstage that we shoot the show on. My arms are folded across my body. My foot is tapping anxiously. I don't want to come out from behind the curtain.

"Come on out, Net, they'll just get one picture and then you'll be good to go."

"Okay."

I step out. I feel my cheeks blush with embarrassment. I hate this feeling, the feeling of so much of my body being exposed. It feels sexual to me. I'm ashamed.

"You look great," the wardrobe assistant who's always sewing yell-says from across the room without looking up from her sewing machine.

I worry that "great" means "sexual." I fold my arms across my body to try and cover it up more. I hunch my shoulders over like a little cave to protect me. I don't want to look sexual. I want to look like a child.

"I'll definitely push for the one-piece, but thank you for humoring me and trying on the bikini," the head of wardrobe says while she pulls her hair up into a bun and pins it into place with chopsticks.

"Sure," I say, unable to look at her, or at Mom, who sits on the stairs in the opposite corner of the room.

"Set your arms down, Angel; try and look more comfortable," Mom tells me.

I set them down. I'm no more comfortable.

"Shoulders back." Mom does the gesture herself, to lead by example.

I pull my shoulders back the way she loves and I hate. I don't like puffing out my chest. I'm not proud of my chest and the little nipple buds on it, and the only reason for puffing out something is if you're proud of it. I hate this. I want to be done with this wardrobe fitting. I asked if I could please just try on one-pieces with board shorts, the way that I feel most comfortable in a bathing suit. Being covered up. But our wardrobe designer said that The Creator explicitly asked for bikinis, and so she had to at least have me try on one or two of them so he had the option.

"Okay, take a few steps toward me so I can get a picture," our wardrobe designer tells me as she pulls her Polaroid camera up to her eyes.

I take a few steps forward. She snaps the photo.

"What do you say, want to try on the last bikini?" she asks me like she's tempting me. It confuses me when people throw a spin on the delivery of something to overcompensate for the fact that the thing they're delivering is unpleasant.

"Can I just... um... can I not?" I ask. "Can I leave it at the one I just tried?"

"Well, he wants options," the wardrobe designer says, pulling an overexaggerated "you know him" kind of expression that doesn't resonate. Because I don't know him. Not really. I've only met him a few times. He seems effusive and boisterous to me, but Mom says she's heard rumblings from crew members that he's got a "hair-trigger temper" and to "be sure not to get on his bad side."

I pick my nails.

"Come on, Net, just one more," Mom urges me.

"Okay," I say.

I try on the last bikini. It's blue with a green stripe around the edges of it. There are ties on the bottoms. I hate the way the ties trickle down my legs. I feel sick to my stomach. I look at myself in the dressing room mirror.

I'm small. I know I'm small. But I worry that my body is fighting the smallness. That it's trying to develop. To grow. I feel like I'm barely hanging on to my childlike body and the innocence that comes with it. I'm terrified of being looked at like a sexual being. It's disgusting. I'm not that. I'm this. I'm a child.

I step out of the dressing room. The wardrobe designer snaps my picture.

"You look great," the ever-sewing wardrobe assistant calls out again without looking up.

32.

OUR LIPS ARE TOUCHING. HE'S moving his mouth around a bit, but I can't move mine. I'm frozen. His eyes are closed. Mine aren't. Mine are wide open, staring at him. It's so odd, staring at a person while your faces are touching. I don't like it. I can smell his hair gel.

"Move your head around a bit more, Jennette!" The Creator yells from off-camera.

Sometimes, even when the camera's rolling, producers or directors shout things off-camera. So long as they're not overlapping a line of dialogue, the editor can just take out the yelling in postproduction.

I try to do as The Creator tells me, I honestly try, but I can't bring myself to do it. My body is stiff. Unflinching. My body is rejecting my mind. My mind is saying who cares that this is your first kiss, that your first kiss is on-camera. Get it over with. Do what you're told. My body is saying no, I don't want this. I don't want my first kiss to be like this. I want my first kiss to be a real first kiss, not a kiss for a TV show.

I disdain the part of me that's romantic. I'm embarrassed by it. Mom's been very clear about how boys are a waste of time and will only disappoint me, and how I should just focus on my career, which I get. So I try to force it away. But as much as I try to force it away, that romantic part of me is there. And it's been there for a while.

I wonder about boys sometimes. What it would be like to love one. I wonder if one will ever love me. I fantasize about watching the Disneyland fireworks together, about holding hands, about resting my head on his chest, about laughing together. I used to wonder about kissing. How it would work. It's a thing you can't practice ahead of time. It just happens at some point. Do you just go with it? Is it difficult? What do lips taste like? These are all questions that now, in this moment, I have the answers to.

You try to just go with it, and if you're Nathan, my co-star, it seems like you can. But if you're me, you can't. If you're me, you're just thinking about every single little thing that's happening, and your mind is racing, and you can't wait for it to be over with. It is difficult. Lips taste like Blistex chapstick.

I start to wonder if all of this would be different if I loved the person. Maybe that's the secret ingredient. The missing piece. Maybe if I were kissing somebody I loved, it would be magical and incredible and not this terrifying rush of anxiety.

"Cut!" The Creator yells off-camera, his mouth full of something. I hear his footsteps as he pads over to us, carrying a paper plate piled with cheese slices and unwrapped mini candy bars. The crew parts like the Red Sea, letting The Creator pass by them and walk up to us.

The Creator looks me right in the eye but doesn't say anything for four or five seconds. I almost start to laugh, thinking he might be messing with me for fun like he does sometimes, but then I recognize that there is a deep anger in him. This is no time for laughter. Finally, he speaks.

"Jennette. More. Head. Movement."

He turns and walks away.

"WHY AREN'T WE ROLLING!" he shouts.

The cameras roll. We start the scene. I don't even know the words coming out of my mouth, but I trust that they must be the words that were written on the page because nobody's stopping me and saying I'm speaking gibberish. It's an out-of-body experience, doing the scene leading up to the kiss. My heart is pounding. My hands are clammy. Here it comes here it comes here it comes.

We lean in. Our lips touch. Lips feel nasty. They're like little gross fleshy piles of flesh. It's disgusting to be a person.

Shoot, I'm supposed to move my head. I start moving it. Back and forth. Back and forth. I sway it around. It doesn't feel natural so I'm sure it doesn't look natural. Nathan, as his character, Freddie, finally breaks away.

"Cut!" The Creator shouts. I can tell by his tone that he isn't happy. He looks to the assistant director.

"Do we have time for another?!"

"Not really, sir, we've gotta head to scene J if we're gonna wrap on time."

"Fine," he says angrily. "That was not ideal but FINE, we'll move on. I'll be at crafty!"

The Creator storms off, heading to crafty for his chips or his bagel or his minestrone soup. I watch him go. I'm sad I didn't please him.

"Hey, we're done," Nathan says kindly, knowing how nervous I was to do my first kiss on-screen with him.

"Yeah," I say with a nervous half laugh. "We're done."

Just like that, my first kiss is over with. And my second kiss, and my third kiss, and my fourth and fifth and sixth and seventh, technically, since we did seven takes.

33.

"Make sure you smile a lot. With teeth. When you do your no-teeth smile it looks kind of forlorn," Mom tells me as she changes lanes on the 405.

We're on our way to a lunch meeting with The Creator. I'm nervous because Mom says a lot is at stake. She thinks this could be an "I'm thinking of giving you a spin-off" lunch date, since it's very common for him to write spin-off shows for characters of his current shows. I've thought about telling Mom I think we might be disappointed if we put that expectation on it, but I haven't said a word. She does well when she has something in my life to look forward to.

"And don't forget to act really interested in whatever he says. Really engaged," Mom tells me. "Try and make your eyes a little wider if you can, it'll help 'em pop."

I nod along.

"One of us should bring up my cancer, too, to really get him on our side. I can take that if you'd like..."

"Sure."

"Great. Great great great," Mom says excitedly.

We get to lunch right on time. The Creator's already there, sunglasses on even though he's indoors. He lifts them up when he sees us. He stands up from the booth, hugs Mom first, and then hugs me into a tight squeeze, picking me up off the ground.

"McCurdy Curds," he says, finally setting me down as he repositions his sunglasses. "My favorite little actress."

Mom beams.

"You know, I work with a lot of young actresses. A lot of them are pretty, some of them are funny, but none of them are as talented as you."

Mom's face looks like it's gonna rip if she smiles any bigger. I smile too, with my teeth like Mom specified.

"Thank you."

"I mean it," The Creator continues on, spooning some of the tuna tartar he already ordered onto his appetizer plate. "You act circles around them. You could win an Oscar someday."

"Thank you."

This is how conversations with The Creator usually start. He'll heap the compliments on, while undercutting other talent that he works with. I appreciate the compliments. The Creator's approval means a lot to me. He's the reason I'm a series regular on a television show. He's the reason my family and I don't have to worry about money anymore. But at the same time, I wonder if he's trying to pit me and his other talent against one another. I wonder if he says the same sorts of things to each of his talent so that we each stay in line and think we're in his good favor.

I wonder this because, now that we've worked on an entire season of television together, I've had plenty of time to get familiar with The Creator's ways. To understand him.

I feel like The Creator has two distinct sides. One is generous and over-the-top complimentary. He can make anyone feel like the most important person in the world. I've seen him do this when he made the entire crew give our production designer a five-minute standing ovation for the jail set he built in two days, or when he gave a speech thanking our stunt coordinator. The coordinator cried with gratitude. The Creator knows how to make someone feel important.

The other side is mean-spirited, controlling, and terrifying. The Creator can tear you down and humiliate you. I've seen him do this when he fired a six-year-old on the spot for messing up a few lines on a rehearsal day. And when a boom operator accidentally dropped the boom into a shot and The Creator stomped over to him and screamed in his face that he was responsible for ruining a magical take and he hoped that he would regret it for the rest of his life. I've seen The Creator make grown men and women cry with his insults and degradation —he'll call people idiots, buffoons, stupid, dumb, sloppy, careless, retarded, and spineless. The Creator knows how to make someone feel worthless.

That's why I've learned with time that, as much as I want the compliments to mean something to me, I can't let them, because tomorrow he might be screaming insults in my face that will hurt me just as much as the compliments raise me up. I feel that I always need to be on guard around him. Catering to him emotionally. I feel similarly around The Creator as I feel around Mom—on edge, desperate to please, terrified of stepping out of line. Put both of them together in the same room and I'm overwhelmed.

The Creator orders main courses for us to share—something with lobster, a pasta with meat, and a flatbread. I know Mom won't approve of me eating any of these foods, but I know The Creator will be offended if I don't eat them, and he will comment on me not trusting him or thinking he has bad taste, so I pick at the food as convincingly as I can, hoping The Creator will believe I'm eating and Mom will know I'm not.

"So, the reason I invited you both to lunch..." The Creator starts. He takes a long sip of his old fashioned while Mom watches him, eager for him to finish the sentence in the way she wants it to be finished.

"Well, first," The Creator says, almost as if he's intentionally dragging out the tension as long as he possibly can, "let me ask you a question. How do you like being recognized? Being famous?"

"She loves it," Mom answers for me. "Absolutely loves it. And the fans adore her, too. They almost always say she's their favorite character."

I poke at my pasta.

"All right, good," The Creator says. "Because you're gonna have a lot more of it."

Mom's breath gets rapid with anticipation.

"... I want to give Jennette her own show."

Mom accidentally drops her fork with excitement. It clinks against the plate.

"I even have the name picked out. *Just Puckett*. Idn't that a fun name for your own show?" Dan asks with a smirk.

"Yes, yes it is! It's a very fun name," Mom chimes in.

"It can't happen for a while, because *iCarly*'s doing too well," The Creator says, trying to temper Mom's excitement. She nods along.

"We'll have to wait a couple years," The Creator reiterates. "But if you keep doing what you're doing and listen to me, take my advice, and let me guide you, I promise you I'll give you your own show."

"Oh, thank you," Mom says, tears welling in her eyes. "My baby deserves it. My baby deserves it."

Mom looks over at me and nods, urging me to smile with teeth. So I do. Even though I'm concerned. The Creator was very clear that his offer had a contingent—me listening to him, taking his advice, and letting him guide me. And even though a part of me appreciates The Creator, a part of me is scared of him, and the idea that I'll have to do everything he wants is intimidating to me.

"Why don't you seem happier? You're getting your own show," Mom says on our drive home.

"I am happy," I lie. "Very happy."

"Good," Mom says as she glances at me in the rearview mirror. "Because you should be. Everyone wants what you have."

34.

I've been on *iCarly* for almost three years now, and in some ways, things are easier. My friendship with Miranda has been a source of camaraderie and emotional support. I'm friends with the rest of the cast too, but my connection with Miranda is different and special. We Skype on the weekends and see movies at ArcLight after work. I now go there twice a week without batting an eye. Mom always joins. She'll lean over to me midway through the movie, her head bowing in resignation. "Their sound *is* very surrounded."

More important than my friendship with Miranda, Mom's not as stressed about the two things she's typically most stressed about: bills and my body.

Even though the consistency of my paychecks has helped bring Mom some financial comfort and stability, she makes her opinion of the size of those paychecks well-known.

"They should be ashamed of the salary they give you. Compared to network TV, it's jelly beans. JELLY BEANS," she tells me every day in my dressing room while she changes my clothes for me. "And no residuals either with Nickelodeon—or should I say Nickel-and-Dime-Alodeon."

Despite her complaints, I know deep down she's grateful, because this is a big step up from where we were before. The house payments are made on time and in full, and she no longer has to call bill collectors and beg for extensions.

She still monitors my lunches, but sometimes she lets me eat the food on set. My dinners are still mostly iceberg lettuce with dressing spray and ripped-up pieces of low-calorie bologna, but she'll give me two Smart Ones cookies for dessert. And my breakfasts have totally transformed. She *makes* me breakfast, which I never imagined would happen. She'll pour 2% milk on top of Honeycomb cereal—2%, not nonfat! And sure, Honeycomb cereal is still "one of the lowest-calorie breakfast cereals per gram," as Mom says (160 calories for 1 ¾ cups), but this is crazy. I've never seen her support eating like this.

A part of me wonders if Mom is supporting my meals a bit more because Miranda and Nathan eat breakfast and lunch in our joint schoolroom and it might look weird if I don't, or if I eat much less than them or something. But I don't ask her. I just let it happen.

My body is shifting a bit. My nipple buds have become very tiny breasts, and it's getting harder to hide them with my undershirt-pulled-through-underwear-legs technique. My skin is breaking out a bit too, which is new and weird and embarrassing. This past year, I've started wearing makeup on set, and even on my off days. I used to hate makeup, but now I want to wear it. To hide behind it.

I recently started shaving my legs, too—well, Mom does it for me, because she still showers me even though I'm sixteen. I didn't even know shaving legs was a thing until I heard a co-star's mom making fun of my "hairy legs" to my co-star, and then she laughed in a way that has haunted me every time I've shaved my legs since.

So now, even though Mom isn't as stressed about bills or my body, my legs are smooth and my nipples are past bud stage and my skin is red and bumpy in places and all of this feels awkward to me.

The show has progressively grown in popularity. Susan keeps throwing around terms like "cultural phenomenon" and "global sensation." The more the show's exploded, the more my fame has too. I've been on countless red carpets for fancy events and award shows and movie premieres. I've done talk shows like *Good Morning America* and *The Today Show* and Craig Ferguson and Bonnie Hunt's new one.

I can't go places anymore without being recognized. I no longer go to Disneyland, my favorite place, because last time I tried, I was walking down Main Street and so many people came up to me that they had to stop the Christmas Fantasy Parade midway through. Goofy looked pissed.

The kind of fame I have now is causing me a level of stress that I did not know was possible. I know everybody wants it, and everybody tells me how lucky I am to have it, but I hate it. I feel constantly on edge whenever I leave the house to go anywhere. I'm worried that strangers will come up to me and I get very anxious when interacting with strangers.

They'll shout things at me like, "SAM! Where's your fried chicken?!" or "Can you hit me with your buttersock?!" A buttersock is a prop my character frequently uses, and it's exactly what it sounds like: a sock filled with butter. My character carries it around to "beat people up" with.

Whenever someone shouts at me about chicken or socks, I'll laugh like it's a good one even though it's not a good one. I've heard this good one thousands of times, and it was a bad one from the get-go, but it only morphs into a worse one with each time I hear it. I'm shocked by how many people think they're original and say the same thing.

I'm so unimpressed by people. Even irritated by them. At times even disgusted by them. I don't know exactly when this happened, but I know it's a relatively recent switch and I know fame had something to do with it. I'm tired of people approaching me like they own me. Like I owe them something. I didn't choose this life. Mom did.

My anxiety causes me to be a people pleaser. My anxiety causes me to take the picture and sign my autograph and say it's a good one. But underneath that anxiety is a deep, unearthed combination of feelings that I fear to face. I fear that I'm bitter. I'm too young to be bitter. Especially as a result of a life that people supposedly envy. And I fear that I resent my mother. The person I have lived for. My idol. My role model. My one true love.

This complicated feeling crops up when I take a picture with a stranger and I see Mom standing off to the side, mirroring the smile she wants me to have.

It happens when she tells the person taking the picture to "Get one more! Or two more, just in case!" when she knows how much I dislike this whole thing.

It happens when she has me practice my autographs and tells me "It's getting sloppy. Little *C*, Big *C, U-R-D-Y*. They need to be able to read every letter."

It happens when she pitches me on what slogan to write to accompany my autographs. "See ya at the movies!" is the current winner, and Lord knows why. I'm not even in movies, I'm on TV. And kids' TV, at that—which, if anything, almost guarantees the fact that I will never be in any movies. The transition from child stardom to a legitimate career as an adult in the entertainment industry is a notoriously tough one—even for young actors blessed with roles in credible films with credible directors. But for kids who start out on kids' TV, it's a career death sentence. There's something about the one-dimensional, overly glossy image combined with the extent of the public recognition of that image that makes it nearly impossible to overcome. The second the child star tries to outgrow and break free from their image, they become bait for the media, highly publicized as rebellious, troubled, and tortured, when all they're trying to do is grow. Growing is wobbly and full of mistakes, especially as a teenager—mistakes that you certainly don't want to make in the public eye, let alone be known for for the rest of your life. But that's what happens when you're a child star. Child stardom is a trap. A dead end. And I can see that even if Mommy can't.

Fame has put a wedge between Mom and me that I didn't think was possible. She wanted this. And I wanted her to have it. I wanted her to be happy. But now that I have it, I realize that she's happy and I'm not. Her happiness came at the cost of mine. I feel robbed and exploited.

Sometimes I look at her and I just hate her. And then I hate myself for feeling that. I tell myself I'm ungrateful. I'm worthless without her. She's everything to me. Then I swallow the feeling I wish I hadn't had, tell her "I love you so much, Nonny Mommy," and I move on, pretending that it never happened. I've pretended for my job for so long, and for my mom for so long, and now I'm starting to think I'm pretending for myself too.

35.

IT'S A SUNDAY MORNING AND everyone else in the house is asleep. I reheat the mug of Mom's favorite raspberry royale tea that I first made an hour ago and wake her with it.

"Mommy," I say gently. "Here's your tea."

"Nnnnn," Mom half groans in her sleep while she twists onto her other side.

I eye the clock nervously, debating whether or not to keep trying to wake her. This is the third time I've tried, and technically the latest possible time I could wake her without us being late.

"Mommy," I say with a bit more urgency in my tone. "We have to leave for church in twenty minutes or we won't make it in time."

"NNNNN," Mom groans more aggressively.

"Do you not wanna go?" I ask.

"Mmm too tirrrrr," Mom mutters. Then she swallows and the words come out a little clearer. "I've worked too hard lately. I'm too tired."

She burrows her face deeper into the pillow and her breathing gets heavy. I study her.

I'm tired too. I've worked hard lately too. I actually think I've worked a lot harder than Mom has. And then I feel guilty for thinking this.

She does drive me to and from work, which has to be tiring, a part of me thinks. *Yeah, but I do homework on the drive, plus memorize lines, then spend ten hours on set rehearsing and performing and being "on" under bright lights and intense pressure, while she sits up in my dressing room perusing* Woman's World *and gossiping with my co-stars' moms,* the other part of me thinks.

I try and swallow these conflicting parts of me. They're unhelpful and distracting from the issue that needs to be resolved right now—whether or not we're going to church.

We haven't been to church in six months, our longest stretch ever. I'm concerned about this, but I've brought it up to Mom as much as I can without making things uncomfortable, and she just keeps reassuring me that we'll "definitely go back someday, when things settle down a bit."

I find it strange that we've stopped going to church since my career has taken off and Mom's health has normalized. I tried to broach the subject gently one night when we were driving home from work, but Mom started screaming and saying she was losing control of the steering wheel and that I was causing her tremendous stress that was putting both of us in danger, so I quickly learned to never bring up the subject again.

But now, in this moment, as I'm looking down at her sleeping, I'm starting to accept for the first time that our church days may very well be behind us. I guess Makaylah was right after all.

I used to think going inactive was a terrible thing, a sin to be ashamed of. But maybe it's not. Maybe it's a sign that things are going right.

Maybe people go to church because they want things from God. And they keep going while they're wishing and yearning and longing for those things. But then maybe once they get those things, they realize they don't need church anymore. Who needs God when you've got clear mammograms and a series regular role on Nickelodeon?

I let her sleep and start memorizing my lines for Monday.

36.

"I HAVE A STOMACHACHE," I tell mom as we walk back from ArcLight Café, where we met with my manager Susan for a quick lunch.

"Maybe the chicken on the salad was bad," Mom offers of the no blue cheese, no egg, no croutons, no dressing, no bacon Cobb salad—aka grilled chicken and lettuce—that we split for lunch.

"Maybe."

We're running down Sunset Boulevard to make it back to set on time. A half hour is hardly enough time for a lunch break, especially if you try to have it outside of set.

"Smile for the paparazzi," Mom orders me.

Without even spotting them, a vacant puppetlike smile crosses my face automatically. My eyes are dead, my soul is nowhere to be found, but a smile is on my face and that's all that counts.

FLASH, FLASH, FLASH. The light hurts my eyes.

"Hi, Glen!" Mom shouts to a paparazzo like he's her neighbor.

"Hi, Deb!" Glen says as he walks backward while snapping more photos. I'm shocked that Mom doesn't seem aware of how strange this whole interaction is.

We approach Nickelodeon Studios and cross into the parking lot. My smile immediately falls off my face. We race into my dressing room so I can change into my wardrobe for the next scene, and I go to the bathroom to take a quick pee beforehand. That's when I see it.

Blood. On my underwear. I'm immediately dizzy. I'm not exactly sure what this is, but I think it might be my period.

I first learned about a period—sort of—six years ago. I was ten, my neighbor Teresa was ten-and-eleven months. She never let me forget our eleven-month age gap, whether in attitude or explicit reminders.

"Do you know what a period is, or not? I feel like maybe you don't, since I'm older than you and know more things."

"Sure," I said, assuming she meant the period that comes at the end of a sentence.

"No, not *that* period. The *other* period."

"Yeah," I said again, thinking she must've meant a period in time.

"Again, not *that* period. The *other* period."

I racked my brain to think of what Teresa could possibly mean, then I had it.

"Oh. Yeah." I'm satisfied with myself, thinking, *Duh, a class period*, like for high school.

"You do?" Teresa was clearly suspicious.

"Yeah."

"Well I got mine. And I was scared at first to see the blood, but my mom taught me how to use pads and stuff. Then I went to HomeTown Buffet with all the women in my family to celebrate."

"Celebrate what?" I asked innocently, as I desperately tried to use context clues to figure out what kind of period Teresa was talking about. It definitely wasn't a class one. Nobody would celebrate that.

"To celebrate becoming one of them. Becoming a woman."

Teresa said it like it was something she'd been wanting her entire life, like it was some romantic, incredible, alluring thing. Becoming a woman. I was confused. I envied several things in Teresa's life—her pinball machine, her collection of Barbies (especially the ones with the short hair that Mom would never let me get because she thought it might make me want to cut mine), and yes, even her trip to HomeTown Buffet—a restaurant that my family deemed too expensive. But I did not envy her becoming a woman. Becoming a woman was the last thing I wanted.

Now, as I'm sitting here on the toilet with my blood-spotted underwear at my knees, I'm sure this is it. This is the thing Teresa was talking about.

"Um, Mommy," I call out.

Mom asks me what's up, and I swallow how mortified I am so that I can utter my next sentence.

"I'm bleeding."

The door bursts open before I even get to the "ing" in bleeding, and Mom wraps me in a big bear hug. While I'm on the toilet.

"Oh, Sweetie," she says with the gravity of someone consoling a friend who's just lost their beloved pet. "Oh, Sweetie, I'm so sorry."

Mom wraps a long strip of toilet paper around her hand and tells me to stuff it in my underwear while she goes to get Patti, my soft-spoken schoolteacher.

I watch the clock tick by ten minutes of slow-burning hell until Mom returns with Patti. Patti whips out of her back pocket a baby-pink wrapped square with a little strip of white tape across it. She wags it in front of my face like it's a hundred-dollar bill. She beams and pulls me into a warm embrace while Mom runs off to tell the AD why I'm running late.

"Congratulations, Jennette," Patti says softly into my ear. "Congratulations on becoming a woman."

I trudge onto our school hallway set, where our next scene is taking place. I can tell by the way the PAs and ADs are treating me that they've all heard the news. I'm humiliated. And ashamed. How did I let this happen? How did I become a woman? I don't know the answer, but I know the solution. I know what I'll do to fix this.

Tomorrow there won't be any 2% milk or Honeycomb or Smart Ones. I've been slacking and the slacking needs to stop. I need to get back to anorexia. I need to be a kid again.

37.

Mama I promise I'll be all right
I'll call to say I love you every night
I'm just trying to write the story of my liiiiiife

MOM AND I ARE SITTING in our room at the Hampton Inn & Suites in downtown Nashville, Tennessee, where we've been living for the past three months while I work on my country music career. We're splitting a Nutrisystem frozen lasagna dinner (we ordered the monthlong program to keep each other on track since Nashville has "so much more lard than LA," as Mom says) while listening to the final mix of my first single "Not That Far Away," a song written from "my" point of view (by a couple of songwriters I sat next to for a few hours) to my mother, about being on the road without her and how much I miss her, even though in reality I've never spent more than a few hours away from her in all my eighteen years.

I don't know much about music, but I know as I listen to this song that I find the rhythm un-rhythmic, the melody one-note, and the production outdated. I express none of these thoughts because of how much Mom loves it. Tears are streaming down her cheeks. Granted, I don't think they're just tears of joy. There's a weight to them too, a significance, and I think I know why. Life has imitated art, if you can call this song that. (You can't.)

My music career initially started as a result of the writers' strike of '07, when *iCarly* was put on indefinite hiatus until things got settled. During that hiatus, Susan suggested I start working with songwriters to put together demos to work toward a recording contract, because "that's what all the teen actors are doing nowadays." Susan represents Hilary Duff, who's had several albums go platinum.

"And I heard she doesn't even sing all the songs—that her sister sings half of 'em!" Mom chimed in excitedly. "No need to confirm or deny. My Nettie's gonna sing all her own songs."

Mom had me start posting covers on YouTube. Record labels saw those covers and two, Big Machine Records and Capitol Records Nashville, wanted to sign me. Mom decided on Capitol Records, because "Scott Borschetta's gonna be too busy with that Taylor chick; he won't have time for you."

So I signed with Capitol Records and lived here in Nashville for three months last summer to work on songwriting. Then *iCarly* started back, so I worked on the show Mondays through Fridays, flew out to Nashville on Friday night red-eyes, had songwriting sessions, laid down demos, took meetings, and did photo shoots for album cover artwork and various press releases, then flew back to California Sunday night to be ready for the show rehearsals on Monday. Currently the show is between seasons, so Mom and I are living here for a few months while I prep for my first tour.

I suspect this tour is going to be my first time away from Mom. And not because she's told me that outright, but because we share an email account and I saw an outgoing message from her to Marcus, where she told him the very thing I'd been dreading for my entire life.

"How come you're crying, Mommy?" I ask her as tears spill out of her eyes.

Mom arranges a bite of lasagna on her fork, then sets the lasagna'd fork back down in the frozen-dinner tray, as if taking a bite of it would just be too much for her right now in her emotional state.

"You just sound so beautiful," she says, but I know she's lying. Mom's I-think-you-did-well joy is not at all a tearful joy. It's more of an exhilarated, amped-up kind of joy. This here, whatever I'm witnessing right now, is something more, something deeper. I wish she'd tell me. I wish she'd just admit what I already know.

"Mommy..." I trail off, terrified for what I'm about to ask. Even though I already know what's happening, I want to believe it can't be true. I need to hear it from Mom. I need to confirm it.

"So much power in your voice. The chorus is really just... wow." Mom blots her eyes with a Kleenex.

"Mommy," I say again, slightly louder this time. I'm terrified of knowing, but I'm even more terrified of not knowing.

"... And then when you get back into the verse and you go to your lower register. I love your lower register," Mom says through tears. "It's got a kind of sultry thing."

"Mommy, do you have cancer again?"

I feel the color drain from my face right after I ask it. I've shocked myself that these words have come out of my mouth. I feel frozen. Mom looks just as shocked as I do. Her tears stop.

"What? No." She tries to laugh it off. "Why would you think that?"

I take a deep breath because I know she's lying right to my face, and I know she's doing that to try and make me less scared, but it's making me more scared. Why is she lying to me about something so significant?

"I saw your email to Marcus. Where you said your cancer came back."

Mom looks down and the tears return, no different from the ones a half minute ago. My heart feels heavy as I watch her little body shake and heave with sadness. I get up from my seat at the desk and sit next to her on the edge of the bed. I hug her. She feels so small in my arms.

"I don't want to miss your tour," she sobs, sounding like she really means it. I'm baffled. How can she care about that stupid tour right now?

"I'm not gonna go on the tour," I say, like it's as obvious of a decision as it feels to me.

Mom breaks away from our hug and lifts her head as her sadness switches to anger.

"Net, you have to go on this tour. Don't talk crazy like that, okay? You scare me when you talk like that. You have to go on this tour, no matter what, all right? You're gonna be a country music star."

"Okay."

Mom goes back to crying. I go back to hugging her.

38.

THE GENERATION LOVE TOUR IS a mission to get my new single, "Generation Love," on the radio. The reps at Capitol have arranged for me to perform for a bunch of radio stations across the country, in what they consider an "unconventional radio tour." Most artists go perform radio tours in the soundproof boxes that are radio stations, in the hopes of impressing a few radio execs enough for the execs to add the artist's song to their lineup, but my label suggested that we leverage my fanbase from *iCarly* to show radio heads the "value" I carry. So instead of performing in soundproof boxes to two or three radio reps, I'll be performing in each radio station region's local mall to thousands of screaming tweens.

Our first stop is in Hartford, Connecticut, or maybe it's Philly, Pennsylvania. It's hard to keep the schedule straight. Regardless, I get used to it quickly enough.

I wake up at eight, groggy. We usually have a few hours left to drive on the bus, then Stewy, our bus driver, pulls into the motel that the label's rented for a half day, just enough time so that each of us on the bus can shower. I go first, and then Paul, the sweet guitarist with the thick twang, goes next. I have a crush on him. Josh, the other guitarist, who looks like a shorter, beefier Conan O'Brien, goes after that. Then goes Dave, the earring-wearing videographer documenting the tour. Next is whoever this week's regional representative from the record label is, then the press representative from the label.

While the rest of the group is showering, I do press on the bus. We find a place to eat lunch, then have a sound check, then we have two or so hours to kill before the show. After the show, I sign autographs for three hours, get back on the bus, and then Stewy drives us to the next place.

The experience itself is overwhelming, performing in malls for thousands of kids. I get so nervous that I practice the songs twenty to thirty times before our set begins, and sometimes blow out my voice before I even get onstage. Press and the autograph signings afterward are emotionally exhausting. There are a few interactions that feel worthwhile, that seem like this experience actually means something to the kids and their families, but the rest of the crowd just feels like sheep to me.

"Hey, Samantha Puckett! How'd you get outta juvie?!"

"Ha ha, good one."

"Where's your fried chicken?"

"Ha ha, good one."

"Do you really beat up people in real life?"

"Ha ha, good one."

My dead-soul smile spreads across my face and I look in their cameras while their mom apologizes fifteen times for not knowing how to operate it.

But other than the work itself, there are two things I'm noticing about this tour.

The first thing I'm noticing is that a part of me is enjoying myself. The part of me that doesn't feel guilty for enjoying myself in the midst of such unfortunate circumstances—Mom's cancer and being away from her while she faces it with frequent rounds of chemotherapy and radiation treatments. This enjoying-myself part of me feels fresh and new and exhilarating. I feel free. I'm even able to shower myself.

I'm realizing for the first time how exhausting it is to constantly curate my natural tendencies, responses, thoughts, and actions into whatever version Mom would like most. Without her around, I don't have to. I miss her deeply, and my heart aches over what she's going through, and I certainly feel a lot of guilt about the ease I feel these days, but that ease is undeniable. Without her monitoring and weighing in on my every move, my life feels much easier.

The second thing I'm noticing is that I'm eating. A lot. I'll eat cinnamon Pop-Tarts in the mornings, then I'll eat lunch and dinner with the band, both meals out. And I'll order from the adult menu. And rarely salads. And rarely substitutes. Burgers and fries.

Without being monitored by Mom, each bite I take feels rebellious. I hear her voice at every meal, telling me, "Dressing on the side. No more bites. That's junky. You don't want a watermelon butt. Mind over matter." But her voice can't stop me from eating. I'm horrified by this reality, but simultaneously drawn to what's on my plate with an attraction that can only be described as lust.

The fullness I feel after my meals is nice. And new to me. But it's immediately usurped by a deep sense of guilt. Guilt that this is not what Mom would want. That Mom would be disappointed in me. The guilt drives me to eat more—boxes of Cheez-Its and store-bought cookies and pieces of candy or Fruit Roll-Ups or whatever goodies are on the bus—sometimes until my stomach aches and feels like it's about to burst. I go to bed unable to sleep on my stomach because I'm so overstuffed. I weigh myself in the hotel rooms that have scales in them, and the number keeps climbing, climbing, climbing. I'm horrified with every pound gained but also feel unable to stop. I have been starving myself for years, and now my body is begging for me to stuff myself.

This new relationship to food deeply confuses me. For years I have been in control of my diet, my body, myself. I have kept myself rail-thin and my body childlike and I have found the perfect combination of power and solace in that. But now I feel out of control. Reckless. Hopeless. The old combination of power and solace is replaced by a new combination of shame and chaos. I do not understand what is happening to me. I am terrified of what will happen when Mom sees me.

39.

I DID NOT EXPECT A hampton Inn & Suites to be the place where I have my first real kiss, and yet here we are. Room 223. I'm standing in front of the kitchenette and my lips are touching Lucas's. He's holding my chin softly. I can't tell whether I like that or not, but I do like the kiss. It's more natural when you like the person than when you're doing it on-camera.

He pulls away.

"I really like you. Have a good night," he says, or I think he says. I don't really know what he's saying. And I don't entirely care. I'm too busy in my head, thinking about the fact that I'm eighteen years old and I finally just had my first kiss. Finally.

I watch him walk down the hallway. I don't like the cut of his jeans or his long hair, but I like his Queen shirt and the shape of his sneakers. I don't like how much he talks about music, but I like how much he likes me. I don't like how awkward he is, but I like how nice he is. I shut the door behind him. My vagina feels funny but I figure I'll worry about that later.

I shut the door and sit down on the couch. I don't know why in movies women always shut the door and then lean against it after the guy leaves. Couch sitting is much more natural.

I'm sitting here going over it all in my mind. Lucas and I first met a few months back when I had a show here in Nashville. He was hired to be the bandleader and play electric guitar for the show. The other band members said he was really good. The best in town.

We spent a lot of time together that first week while we were all rehearsing. He was very nice to me, and at first I didn't think much of it, since he's twenty-seven and I'm eighteen, but then I noticed him looking at me a lot and I started to wonder if maybe he liked me.

By the third rehearsal day, he started offering me rides home, which I took because I was starting to like him. I felt queasy around him in an uncomfortable but good way. On the last rehearsal day, he invited me to come into his house and listen to a Queen album with him. I was so excited.

We listened to *News of the World* front to back while sitting on his wooden floor. He kept scooting closer to me and brushing his hair behind his ear, which was mildly repulsive to me coming from a man. That repulsion confused me because at the same time I deeply wanted him to kiss me. Or maybe it's not that I wanted *him* to kiss me, maybe it's just that I wanted to be kissed in real life. Either way, he didn't. He drove me home to the Hampton Inn and dropped me off. And then the next day I left for the radio tour.

I didn't see him much during tour because he wasn't on the road with us the entire time, but he was flown out for a few of the shows, the ones not in malls but rather on bigger festival stages when we did full-band sets instead of acoustic ones. In between seeing him, we'd text every day and have phone calls whenever I got some privacy, which is hard to come by on a tour bus. He'd say things like "I miss you so much" and "I really really really like you," both of which made me uncomfortable but I didn't know why. On one hand, I liked that he was saying these things to me. On the other hand, I felt physically unable to say them back, like I couldn't get the words out of my mouth.

I'd get excited to talk to him but then the excitement waned whenever we'd actually talk. He'd talk about music and reference all these different songs that I didn't know, which was fine, if there were other things we talked about too. But there really weren't. It was either music or he'd be showering me with generic compliments like "the sun rises and sets in your eyes" or "you're my favorite person I've ever met."

The few times that he joined us for festival dates were okay but a bit awkward since the rest of the band was around too. There was no space for private conversations, and yet I was all right with that. When Lucas tried to pull me aside to have one, I'd come up with excuses for why I couldn't. I was tired, needed to prepare for press, practice my songs, respond to emails from my managers or Mom or Miranda. I've been so unsure about him for the past month.

But now the tour's over and I'm back in Nashville for a week to record some new songs. And I'm staying at the Hampton Inn, room 223. And I'm sitting on the couch in 223, processing the fact that I just had my first kiss with him. And as much as I'm relieved to have my first kiss over with, I'm even more relieved to know that now I am sure about him. I'm sure I need to end this, whatever this is.

I pull out my phone to text him, but just as I'm about to, there's an odd pulse in my vagina. It feels warm. I reach my hand into my pants and pull it out. My fingers are wet. This is gross. I need to shower. I'll text him after.

40.

I'M WALKING OFF THE PLANE and tugging my shirt down so it lies flat. I'm sucking in and trying to look as thin as possible. "Maybe Mom won't notice. Maybe if I tug my shirt again she won't notice; maybe if I hold my breath for ten seconds she won't notice," says my OCD voice, formerly known as my Still Small Voice, but which I've since accepted as the pounding voice of mental illness. It's more sporadic than it used to be, and almost exclusively related to food and my body, but it's still here.

I take a deep breath and step on the escalator heading toward baggage claim. A young dad with a nervous laugh asks for a picture for his daughters.

"Sure, as soon as we get off the—" He starts arranging the girls in front of me before I can finish my sentence. He snaps a picture just as he nearly trips off the escalator. He nervous laughs again.

As I step off the escalator, I look out to the lineup of people waiting and there I see her. The sight of her shocks me, and for a moment I'm more focused on her appearance than I am on mine.

She's lost a dozen or so pounds, which is hugely noticeable on someone with as small a frame as she has. Her face is gaunt and sickly. Her bones protrude from under her skin. She doesn't have any eyebrows or eyelashes. She's wearing the turquoise Ugg hat I got her for Christmas to cover up her bald head. I'm shocked at the sight of her. I don't know what to say.

Dad is standing next to her but he might as well not be. I can't focus on anything but her. I can't believe she didn't warn me of this in any of our five daily calls.

By the time we exchange hugs and "I love yous," I've settled slightly. I've adjusted just enough to be able to take in Mom's reaction, which is the same reaction as mine toward her: a combination of shock and horror with a vacant smile on top.

I feel sick to my stomach while I wait for her to tell me how ugly I am. How fat I've gotten. How I've made horrible mistakes. How I'm incapable of handling life on my own. Of keeping myself in order. I brace myself while we pile into the car (a Kia Sorento replaced our old Ford Windstar).

"Net, what happened?" She doesn't face me when she asks it. She stays looking out the window at the bumper-to-bumper traffic on the 5. "You're getting chunky."

"I know. I'm sorry."

"We've gotta get you on a diet. This is getting out of hand."

"I know."

I'm full of remorse, for sure. But there's also a piece of me that picks up a little bit of enthusiasm, a little bit of a lift in spirit, because this is the mom I know. She's not weak, or frail, or soft, or beaten down by cancer like whoever the person was that I saw as soon as I got to baggage claim. Whoever that wilted excuse of a person was, I refuse to believe that person is my mother. The mom I know is the person sitting in front of me, the person who is strong-willed and forceful and sometimes vicious. This is the mom I know.

41.

"Come on, take a sip."

"No thanks."

"Come on."

"I've never had alcohol before. And I'm only eighteen. Couldn't I get in trouble?"

"No one's looking, Jennetter. You're fine."

"I dunno."

"The *Victorious* kids get drunk together all the time. The *iCarly* kids are so wholesome. We need to give you guys a little edge."

The Creator always compares us *iCarly* kids to the kids on his other hit show, *Victorious*. I think he thinks it'll make us try harder.

"I don't know if drinking is what gives a person edge."

I look at The Creator's drink. He picks it up and sloshes it around. It's some sort of whiskey mixed with coffee and cream. I do like coffee.

"One sip."

"Okay."

The Creator hands me his glass and I take a sip. I hate it.

"It's great."

"Don't lie to me. I don't like when you lie to me."

"I hate it."

"That's better, Jennetter."

The Creator laughs. I've done well. I've pleased him. Mission accomplished. It's the same mission I have every time I get dinner with him, which has gotten more and more frequent lately as my new contract for the spin-off he promised me is being worked out. The Creator is doing the thing that I've heard from my co-stars he does with every new star of a show that he's making—he takes you under his wing. You're his favorite. For now. I like being his favorite for now. I feel like I'm doing something right.

"So are you excited to have your own show?" The Creator asks.

"Sure."

"Sure? That's it?"

"No, of course I'm excited. I'm so excited."

"Good. 'Cuz I could give a new show to anyone, you know. But I didn't choose anyone. I chose you."

"Thank you."

"Don't thank me, I chose you because you're talented."

I'm confused. He just said he could choose anyone, which made me feel not special and now he's saying he chose me because I'm talented, which makes me feel special again. This kind of confusion is normal around him. I take a sip of water while I try and figure out what to say next. Luckily, I don't have to.

"How'd you like the steak?"

"It was good."

It was terrible, actually. Well, great and terrible. Great in terms of flavor, terrible in terms of how much I'm gonna be fixating on it for the rest of the night. I ate too much of it, and too many roasted potatoes, and too many brussels sprouts, and a roll, and glazed carrots. I couldn't stop myself. I ate everything. I feel so full. I'm disgusted with myself.

Mom's got me on a Nutrisystem diet again like we did back when we were in Nashville. We do it together, when we're together. But that's the thing—we're not together as often these days. She's consumed with her cancer stuff and I'm consumed with my TV stuff.

When Mom's not around to motivate and coach me, I can't seem to force myself to eat a cardboard cinnamon roll that tastes more like a protein bar wrapped around itself. I can't seem to order the dressing-less salad. I can't keep up my diet without Mom. I'm a failure without her.

"Are you okay?" The Creator asks.

"Of course."

"Good, 'cuz you should be okay," he says gently. "You're about to star in your own TV show, for crying out loud. You know how many kids would kill for that opportunity? Every last one of them."

I nod along. He reaches out and places his hand on my knee. I get goose bumps.

"You're cold," he says, concerned.

I don't think that's why I got the goose bumps, but I agree. It's always best to agree with The Creator.

"Here, take my jacket."

He takes his coat off and drapes it around me. He pats my shoulders and then the pat turns into a massage.

"Oof, you're so tense!"

"Yeah…"

"Anyway, what was I saying?" he asks while he keeps massaging me. My shoulders do have a lot of knots in them, but I don't want The Creator to be the one rubbing them out. I want to say something, to tell him to stop, but I'm so scared of offending him.

"Oh, right," he says, remembering his train of thought without my help. "Every kid out there would kill for an opportunity like the one you've got. You're very lucky, Jennetter."

"I know," I say while he keeps rubbing me.

And I do. I do know. I'm so lucky.

42.

"I CAN'T BELIEVE MY baby girl is moving away," Mom says, in a way that's different from how Grandma would say it. Grandma would be weeping and saying it loud enough for the neighbors to hear. Mom says it quietly and can hardly make eye contact. Unlike her bill extension calls with Sprint PCS, this is not for show. I appreciate the ways in which Mom is different from her mother.

"It's just for work days. I'll come home on the weekends if I don't have to go to Nashville."

Mom sighs.

"That's a big 'if.' I'm hardly gonna see my baby. Who's gonna keep your eating on track? How are you gonna shampoo your hair?"

"Well, I did it on tour."

"Yeah, but I saw pictures. It looked greasy." She sniffles.

"It's just the best option, since I don't drive and you can't anymore."

Even though it's just a fact, Mom looks down. I can tell I've hurt her feelings.

"I might be able to drive again someday," she says timidly, like a child would to seek reassurance from an adult.

"I know you might," I say with loaded positivity, the way an adult would to reassure a child.

We both look at her wheelchair, the wheelchair she's recently been given to utilize "when she needs," an allotment that has gotten more and more frequent by the day. In the moment her doctor told her he thought she could use one, we both pretended it would be fun. She said I could push her around at Disneyland and I said yay. Then I went into the hospital bathroom and sobbed but there was no toilet paper left in the stall so I used a toilet seat cover to dry my eyes. And then I went back out and said yay again.

This goddamned wheelchair is the furthest thing from a fucking yay. It's a death sentence. Neither of us can admit it, but that's what it is. Once you're a cancer patient with a wheelchair, you're never gonna be one without it. You're gonna die a wheelchairing cancer patient. Fuck this.

"All right, sorry about that," Grandpa says as he comes out of the house to meet us in the driveway. "I'm ready to go now. Clean pants." He gestures to the pants he just changed into after spilling his entire tumbler of coffee on the first pair.

I take a seat in the back, surrounded by the moving boxes I already piled into the Kia. I watch as Grandpa lifts Mom into the shotgun seat, folds her wheelchair up, and piles it into the trunk. And with that, we're off to my apartment. My first-ever solo apartment.

We pull up to the Burbank complex a little over an hour later. The complex is okay. It wouldn't have been my first choice, but it makes sense logistically. My new managers (I switched during season three of *iCarly*) arranged for Nickelodeon to pay for my lodging here and for a production assistant to take me to and from work. (I don't drive since Mom says it's probably too difficult for me and that my energy in cars could better be spent elsewhere, like "learning lines or planning tweets.")

I would never admit this to Mom, I've only told her I'm devastated about being away from her, but I'm excited too. I feel guilty about that excitement, considering the fragility of her health, but the feeling is undeniable. I get to be on my own. I get space to myself. Life to myself.

Grandpa carries Mom into the apartment while I carry the first few boxes.

"I got you a present, Net," Mom says as Grandpa sets her down on the couch. Since Nickelodeon's paying, Mom insisted on the pre-furnished place. She pulls a wrapped gift from under her arm.

"You didn't have to do that."

"I even curled the ribbon," she says as she hands the DVD-sized present to me. She's gotten more desperate these past few months. She's gotten more desperate and I've gotten more angry. I don't know if my anger is a direct result of her desperation, but it's at least a partial result of it. I can't fucking handle how desperate she is. The sicker she gets, the cuter she becomes in her intonation, the more innocent she becomes, the more she pleads with me. It's like she's begging me to not slip away, and I want to scream, YOU'RE THE

ONE SLIPPING AWAY! I could swear she can tell that I want to scream because she doubles down on the cuteness. Which makes me want to double down on the scream. But I don't. I keep it in. And then she looks at me with her big eyes and I know she doesn't, she couldn't, but I almost feel like she's enjoying this. I almost feel like she's enjoying the pain. Like it's a representation to her of how much I care.

"Aren't you gonna open it?" Mom asks.

"Oh. Right."

I unwrap the present. It's a DVD of *The Sting*. Mom loves Robert Redford. I do too, but she loves him more.

"I figured we could watch it tonight after you unpack."

"Oh, okay. That'll be great."

"Yeah, yeah," Mom says, removing her hat to scratch her bald head. "And then, um, I was thinking... I don't have chemo tomorrow, so I could spend the night. You know, if you want."

She looks at me, doe-eyed, wringing her hands nervously. I immediately know what this is. This is not Mom spending the night. This is Mom spending every night for the foreseeable future. This is Mom moving in. I don't want her to spend the night.

"Sure, you can spend the night," I say.

And I continue to say it every single night for the next three months, until eventually, she doesn't even ask it anymore. She just expects it. This is not my first-ever solo apartment. This is *our* apartment. We are roommates.

43.

I'M SITTING ON THE LOG ride at Six Flags, stuffed into the front seat of the log with five *iCarly* crew members tucked into the seats behind me. My co-worker Joe, the one seated directly behind me, keeps touching me. At first I couldn't tell if it was an accident since I know he's in his thirties and has a girlfriend, but now it's happened so many times that I'm sure it's on purpose. I say nothing because the truth is it feels nice. The truth is I want him to touch me like this.

Our friendship has been flirty for the past few months, ever since we were the first two in the room before a table read. Joe and I got to talking and he mentioned his favorite movie, *Dazed and Confused*, which I went home and watched that night so that we'd have something to talk about the next day. I wanted so badly to impress him since he was older and wiser than me. We swapped Words with Friends usernames and Joe started offering me rides home from work, where he'd play Daft Punk albums front to back and explain to me what made their music so genius. I didn't really like the electronic sound but I loved that Joe wanted to teach me why I should.

Now he's touching me. The way he's touching me. This is another level. Or so I assume. I've never been touched like this before, so I don't know exactly. Sure, there was the kiss with Lucas at the Hampton Inn, but since then, romance has been nonexistent in my life. All I know is that this feels like more than just a friendly touch. My whole body tingles when his hand lands on my back. The sensation is exhilarating and overwhelming and scary. In this moment, I know that one way or another, we're going to be together.

44.

"MIRANDA AND I WERE GONNA have a sleepover," I lie as I fix Mom and me a plate of steamed vegetables for "dinner." I already ate dinner earlier on set and felt awful about it. I'm too ashamed to tell Mom.

"What am I gonna do alone without you?" Mom asks genuinely, fighting back tears. "I'll miss you more than anything. I just love you so much, Net."

"I'll miss you too, Mommy. This is just something Miranda and I have been planning for a while." I lie twice with this one.

The first lie is that I'll miss her. I won't miss her. I will be happy to have space from her. She's been sleeping in my bed every night since we moved into my not-solo apartment and it's hard to sleep because she clings to me all night long.

The second lie is that Miranda and I are having a sleepover. We have sleepovers every couple of weeks, but not tonight. Tonight, Joe is going to stay with me. But Mom can't know about Joe because Mom would never approve. Mom only approves of me hanging out with two types of boys—Mormons and gays. And even then she wants to supervise the hangout. "Just because a boy reads Third Nephi..."

I set the plate of steamed vegetables in front of Mom. She pokes at a cube of squash before forking it into her mouth.

"Yeah, but *I* need you right now, Net," Mom says, looking down.

"I'll be back tomorrow," I say gently, hoping this will comfort her enough for us to be able to move on from the topic. There's a long pause where I wait for Mom to say something. She looks off and her eyes glaze with an intensity that seems dissociative. It scares me. Just as I'm about to ask her what's going on, she snaps her head toward me, picks the TV remote up off the coffee table, and chucks it at my head. I duck aside to avoid it.

"You're LYING to me, you LIAR," Mom says, spitting as her face contorts. "I'm gonna find out what's going on. Mark my words, you FILTHY LITTLE

LYING WHORE."

Mom's been harsh with me before, but she's never spoken to me like this.

"And you better bet your ass I'll be able to sniff the lies on you tomorrow when you come back," she says dramatically. It's obvious to me how much Mom wanted to be an actress. "Right, Mark?"

Mom whips her head around to my dad, who has been here the whole time not saying a word, as usual. He nods quickly, scared of her wrath. Fed up, I grab my backpack and start to head out.

"I'm gonna figure out what you're up to, you LIAR!" Mom screams. My nervous system jolts, but I pretend to ignore her. I head out the front door, letting it slam shut behind me.

* * *

Joe picks me up on the corner of Sunset and Vine. The passenger door on his Ford Taurus is slammed in and jammed shut from a years-old accident, so I crawl over him in the driver's seat to sit down in the passenger seat. I'm still shaking from the interaction with Mom. I look at Joe.

His eyes are glassy. There's a sweet/rotten smell radiating off him. I'm disappointed. Tonight was supposed to be our first night together as an official couple. I wanted it to be romantic and magical and momentous. Instead, Joe's sad and drunk and I'm trying hard to resist the disillusionment.

"Did you do it?" I ask anxiously.

"Yes, I broke up with her. I wouldn't be here if I didn't," he says, his words slurring.

"Right... how are you?"

He snort-laughs. "How do you think I am?"

Joe looks down, like he feels bad for snapping. This side of him comes out when he's drunk. He starts driving to the Sheraton Universal where I booked us a room. I'm concerned that he's driving while drunk, but I fear bringing this up because I know it will make him more erratic.

By the time Joe gets us there and we get to our room, it's past midnight. Joe tries to get the key into the key slot but he's too wobbly, so I take the key and shove it in.

"I could've done it," he says.

Joe stumbles in after me and immediately collapses onto the bed. At first I think he must be really tired, until he rolls over onto his back and I can see that there are tears streaming down his cheeks. His chest heaves. He makes that gross hiccup-y cry sound.

"What's the matter? What's the matter?"

"What have I done? What have I dooooone!" he sobs. "We were together for five years. *Five years*. We just moved in together, we were gonna get married."

I lie down next to him and hug him. I'm the big spoon. He rattles on about his regret and remorse. If I were good enough, he wouldn't be feeling this way. He wouldn't be sad.

"I thought you wanted this," I say, looking for reassurance.

"You won't even have sex with me!" he wails.

It's true. I won't have sex with him. Even though my family stopped going to church, there are still a few rules of the religion that for whatever reason I can't bring myself to break. One of them being no sex before marriage.

We've been seeing each other for the past three months. We keep things secretive at work, which really causes the tension to build up. Then after work most nights we get together for a few hours, at his place if his girlfriend's not around, at his friend's place if she is. We've made out and rubbed on each other, but we've never had sex and I've never even touched his penis.

"I'm sorry, I'm just not ready," I tell him with a finality that makes me proud.

"Well can you give me a blow job at least?" Joe lifts his head off the bed like a hopeful, needy puppy.

"Um. I don't want to do that."

Joe throws his head back onto the pillow and the tears are replaced with a sharp anger. "This is ridiculous. My needs aren't being met."

"We can make out," I offer.

"I don't want to *make out*. I'm thirty-two years old."

I feel stupid for suggesting the idea, and embarrassed for not being sexually advanced enough to meet Joe's needs. Even though I'm eighteen, I feel like a child.

"You're too young for me. This is never gonna work." Joe starts to get up off the bed.

"Okay okay, I'll do it," I say, immediately disappointed in myself.

Joe lies back down and sprawls out lazily like he's already over the idea but might as well go forward with it since we're both here. He unzips his pants and pulls out his penis. I look at it for a long time.

"What am I supposed to do? I've never done this before."

"Yeah, it's not a turn-on when you say shit like that."

I've seen a certain shortness to Joe at times, but this feels different. I could justify his behavior as him being drunker than normal—since I've never had alcohol myself (other than that splash of The Creator's spiked coffee), this is hard for me to gauge, so I usually just guess how much he's had by how crooked he's walking or how slurred his words are. I could also justify his behavior as him being overwhelmed with grief from his breakup, but honestly, I don't even need to justify it as anything, because I'm so desperate to be with him. He's so much older than me and cooler than me, and I've never felt this way about anyone before, so I know we must have something special.

I dive forward. And then I start doing it. Licking it and sucking it and hoping that's what I'm supposed to be doing and hoping I'm doing it in a way that's pleasurable to him. But I have no idea. I've been an actor for a dozen years. I'm nothing without direction.

"I'm about to finish," Joe says with a gasp. It sounds like it's a good thing. I don't know what's about to happen. "Speed it up a little."

"Thank you," I say. Direction!

And then suddenly, something that tastes like warm liquid plastic shoots into my mouth. I spit it out onto the bedspread.

"Something came out! OhmyGod, something just came out!"

"Yeah. It's cum." Joe looks at me with dull annoyance.

"What's cum?"

Joe turns on his side, facing away from me, and clutches a pillow tight to his chest. He takes a long breath.

"What have I done?" he asks.

45.

"ALOHA." THE PRETTY FOUR SEASONS Resort Maui employee greets us as she drapes a floral lei around my neck and a nut lei around Joe's. Joe's eyes linger on the employee for .2 seconds too long. I hate the bitch. I make a mental note to work on jealousy someday, whenever I get around to it.

We check into the hotel, reiterating multiple times that the reservation is under my name and not Joe's. Whether it's the age difference between Joe and me, or just sexism, nobody seems to believe that a trip to the Four Seasons might be my doing and not his.

Granted, it's not exactly my doing. It's Nickelodeon's doing. This was each cast member's fifth season wrap gift—four nights and five days at the Four Seasons Resort Maui at Wailea for the cast member and one guest.

Of course Joe's my guest. We've been together for a year at this point, and our relationship has settled into a nice groove. Sure, 50 percent of the time things are chaotic and tumultuous—Joe's drunk and I'm hysterical; Joe's upset that I'm too possessive and I'm upset that Joe's gotten back into debt three weeks after I paid it off for him—but the other 50 percent of the time, things are great.

We watch reruns of *Survivor*. We have stupid-but-fun inside jokes. We laugh a lot. We still haven't had sex, but I've gotten better at giving blow jobs.

This relationship looks and feels to me like a huge step up from my parents' relationship—they had the screaming, tumultuous, fighting part, but none of the fun. The only problem is that Mom still doesn't know about our relationship.

Mom had to move out of my apartment a few months back to be closer to her oncologist in Orange County now that her appointments are near daily. Now that we're not physically in the same space together, Mom calls me ten or so times a day to keep up-to-date on my life—how big of a role my character has in any given episode of the show, if I've been auditioning for anything else lately, pitches for why I should get back into country music (I quit my recording contract after Mom's cancer took a turn for the worse). I'm worried about how I'm gonna get through a four-night and five-day stay at the Four Seasons without Mom knowing who I'm with.

We decide I'll tell Mom I'm with Colton, my gay friend she approves of because there's no way his penis is entering me, who will then join in three-way calls to help me out so Mom won't know I'm lying.

Lying to Mom is difficult for me. Whenever I lie to her to protect my relationship with Joe, I hang up the phone and weep into Joe's arms from the guilt I feel. I tell him I wish I could be honest with her, I wish she could meet him, I wish I wasn't scared of her. And Joe runs his hands through my hair and comforts me.

I feel the wedge between Mom and I growing by the day. With every lie I tell, I feel myself slipping further away from her. With every pound I gain, every binge I partake in, I feel myself getting more disconnected from her.

I'm so confused and troubled by this wedge. I'm desperate to feel close with her, but also desperate for that closeness to be on my terms, not hers. I want her to know me for who I'm becoming. I want her to allow my growth. I want her to want me to be me.

But that feels more like a fantasy than a possibility, for now at least. So for now, I lie.

We're three days into the vacation and the plan is going smoothly. Each day, Colton and I three-way-call Mom to tell her about our snorkeling adventures and off-roading Jeep drives and white-sand beach walks. She laughs along as Colton gives follow-up details that scream I'm-definitely-not-walking-through-a-Burbank-Target-right-now.

But in the late afternoon on day three, Joe and I are paddleboarding on the beach in front of the hotel when he spots it and tells me to duck. I look to see what he's talking about and there in the distance near one of the banana-yellow cabanas, I see a squat, little paparazzo snapping photos of me and Joe.

Shit. Shit shit shit. This is a disaster. We swim to the sand, dump the paddleboards, wrap some fancy towels around ourselves, and hurry into the hotel's back entrance. The paparazzo snaps photos of us the whole time.

By the time we're in our room, I'm panicking, rattling off the list of ways Mom might punish me, disown me, or threaten me. Joe unsuccessfully tries to keep me calm.

Eventually, I've been hysterical enough for long enough that I'm completely emotionally depleted. I fall asleep on the bed by six p.m.

The sight I wake up to the next morning is not the beautiful palm trees out the window; or the shimmering, turquoise water; or a young, happy newlywed couple canoodling in a hammock in the distance. It's my cold, hard iPhone screen with a glaring notification that terrifies me.

Thirty-seven missed calls from Mommy, sixteen voicemails, and four missed emails (we no longer share an account—I recently created my own, thanks to Joe's encouragement). I open the top email:

Dear Net,

I am so disappointed in you. You used to be my perfect little angel, but now you are nothing more than a little SLUT, a FLOOZY, ALL USED UP. And to think—you wasted it on that hideous OGRE of a man. I saw the pictures on a website called TMZ—I saw you in Hawaii with him. I saw you rubbing his disgusting hairy stomach. I KNEW you were lying about Colton. Add that to the list of things you are—LIAR, CONNIVING, EVIL. You look pudgier, too. It's clear you're EATING YOUR GUILT.

Thinking of you with his ding dong inside of you makes me sick. SICK. I raised you better than this. What happened to my good little girl? Where did she go? And who is this MONSTER that has replaced her? You're an UGLY MONSTER now. I told your brothers about you and they all said they disown you just like I do. We want nothing to do with you.

Love,
Mom (or should I say DEB since I am no longer your mother)

P.S. Send money for a new fridge. Ours broke.

I hunch over and bury my head in my hands, breaking into a sob. Joe rubs my back and assures me that my mother is not okay, but I assure him it's the opposite. I'm not okay. Maybe she's right. Maybe I've lost my way. Maybe I'm an evil monster.

"You can't let her get to you like this," he says.

I pick up my phone and urgently start typing TMZ into my search bar. Joe reminds me we agreed not to look at the pictures—he knows my body image isn't good—but I don't care. I need to see them. I need to see if Mom's right.

She is. I look awful. My body and face repulse me. I do look pudgy. I no longer wear one-pieces but I still wear board shorts to hide my ass, which is curvy and womanly and disgusts me for being those things. Joe tells me my tits look great in my bikini top but I don't see it. I think boobs are hideous. I hate them. I wish I was flat-chested and curve-less. I wish there was nothing sexual or suggestive about my body.

My tears are replaced by my venomous self-loathing. Joe, sensing a shift in me, nabs the phone out of my hands and tells me it's going in the hotel safe. I don't object.

Over the next two days, my phone stays in the safe and my bathing suit stays flung over the bathroom door handle, where I last left it. Joe and I try to make the most of our remaining time in Hawaii by going on hikes and drives and other activities that don't involve me removing any clothes in public. By the last morning of the trip, I've been distracted enough and my phone's been far away enough that I've almost forgotten the paparazzo incident and the vicious email from Mom.

But then Joe and I are packing up our bags and out of the corner of my eye, I see him discreetly entering the code on the safe. He pulls my phone out and goes to tuck it into his pocket. I ask to see it first. He reminds me this is a bad idea and that it won't be anything but harmful for me if I look at it, but I can't not. I want to see it. I need to see it.

As soon as the phone's in my hands, I know I've made a mistake, but it's too late now. Forty-five missed calls from Mom. Twenty-two unread emails from her. I start reading through the messages frenetically, and each one gets more aggressive than the last—she calls me a dimwit, loser, scumbag, devil child. Joe says we're running late for the airport. I don't care.

I read another email. This one's titled "Letter To Your Fans." I open it up and find a scathing note attached, a note that Mom tells me she's posted to an online Jennette McCurdy fan club in an attempt to get my fans to flee from me. She says that she's gonna steal all my fans, that she deserves them more than I do, that she swears to God she's gonna sign up for Vine and they're all gonna love her comedy videos.

I wonder if Mom's bluffing, so I check the fan club she referenced. No bluff. There's Mom's message right on the front page of the fan club. I almost can't believe it.

I go back to my email and another new message from Mom has popped up. I open it:

YOU caused my cancer to come back. I hope you're happy knowing this. YOU have to live with this fact. YOU gave me cancer.

I draft a response to her, asking if we can just sit down and talk this out face-to-face. I'm sure that if she'll just grant me that, I can explain myself enough to earn her approval. I'm desperate, pleading.

My dear Nonny Mommy—

Please can we at least just meet up in person to talk about this? Please. Just me and you. We can sit down and talk this out. I can answer any questions you have. Please Mommy. I hate letting you down. I would do anything to not disappoint you. I feel confident that if you knew the whole situation you wouldn't think these things about me. I love you so much. I want to be close to you again. I miss you.

Love, Nettie

I click my phone off and tuck it into Joe's pocket. He asks what she said. I tell him nothing. I'm numb. Catatonic. The entire plane ride home, I don't say a word.

Over the past few years, Mom and I have grown apart in a way that I never thought was possible. Between fame and Joe, the strain between me and Mom has gotten nearly intolerable. Plus there's the strain of her cancer. Maybe all of this is actually just about the strain of her cancer.

Why can't she admit that she's dying? Why can't I admit that she's dying? I hate her for caring so much about fame and she hates me for caring so much about Joe. There seems to be more hate than love for each other right now but maybe we're both just scared. Maybe we're just letting this wedge between us grow because deep down we both know that soon enough this wedge will be out of our control.

The plane lands. While we're circling the tarmac, I open my email draft to Mom. I hit send. Moments later, my phone pings with a response from Mom:

Sure, we can meet up. P.S. Reminder to send fridge money. Our yogurt has soured.

46.

"Jennette? Will you sing 'Wind Beneath My Wings' at my funeral?"

Mom and I are sitting at the Panda Express on Cahuenga Boulevard for Mom's birthday dinner. Mom's chewing steamed broccoli and I'm chewing steamed cabbage and we're both going through the motions of our relationship because that's what we do nowadays.

This started the first time we got together after the Hawaii trip. Dad drove her to my place and lifted her up out of her wheelchair and set her down on the couch. While we waited for our tea to steep, I waited for her to bring up the Joe situation since I thought that's why we were meeting up in the first place—to talk about it. But she never brought it up. She just asked me trivial questions about work, and I asked her trivial questions about the last episode of *NCIS*. Mom's big into Mark Harmon.

When's she gonna bring it up? I wondered. And I kept wondering until, before I knew it, our two hours together were over and Dad came back to pick her up and take her home.

By the time we're here at the Panda Express on Cahuenga Boulevard, this way of communicating—polite small talk with an undercurrent of pain and resentment—has been our new reality for several months, enough time that it's not new anymore. That's why it shocks me that Mom has asked me to sing "Wind Beneath My Wings" at her funeral.

Mom's cancer falls under the category of things that we pretend don't exist because they're uncomfortable to talk about. Mom asking this question is a breach of our unspoken rule. I don't know how to process this, or how to proceed.

"Um..."

"You've gotta do it with emotion, though. You've gotta believe your words. It won't work if you're only giving fifty percent."

I haven't even agreed to sing it yet and Mom's already giving me performance notes. "Uhhh..."

"Lemme hear you try it."

"Mom, we're in Panda Express, I'm not gonna—"

"Just try it."

"'*It must have been cold there in my shadooooow...*'" Involuntarily, my singing voice starts pouring out of my mouth. My body is programmed to Mom-on-Demand. A nearby employee watches me out of the corner of her eye as she mops.

"'*To never have—*'"

"More emotion, more sadness. Feel it, Angel."

"'*To never have sunlight on your faaace...*'" A little heavy on the vibrato, but Mom's into that sort of thing.

"Good, stop. I don't wanna burn you out. Your performance peaks early. So are you gonna do it?"

I feel obligated. It's Mom's dying wish. The only problem is I don't think I have the range to sing it. I'm okay in the verses where I can use my lower register. But once the song hits that soaring chorus, it's way out of my range.

Back at my place, Mom asks me to pull the song up on YouTube so I can practice along and give her a taste of what the final performance will be.

"I thought you didn't want to burn me out."

"Well, we're practicing so far ahead—hopefully—that it won't matter."

Mom's pointed choice of words—or word, rather—hits me hard. *Hopefully*. I feel furious with her, then immediately guilty for feeling furious. I must be a terrible person to be able to feel fury at my mother while she's slowly dying.

I throw the energy of my guilt into meeting Mom's wish. Maybe that'll clear my conscience. I pull up the song on YouTube, and another tab with the lyrics. And then I begin. The verse is, as expected, fine. But once I get to the "'*Did you ever*'" part... it's confirmed. Out of my range.

"Well, it's because you didn't do any vocal warm-ups," Mom assures me. "Do some vocal warm-ups and try again."

I do ten minutes of mee-may-moos before trying again. But then I try again and it's the same issue. I try one more time, just to make sure.

"It's out of my range," I finally admit.

"Don't say that," Mom says sharply.

"I'm sorry."

"You'll get there. I know you'll get there. You've got plenty of time to practice—hopefully."

I don't want to practice the song my dying mother has instructed me to sing at her funeral. I don't want to think about my mother's funeral. I want to go back to ignoring the things that make us uncomfortable to talk about. As much as I thought I hated it, I want to go back to pretending.

"Why don't you just try it a couple more times tonight, sweetheart?" Mom urges as she removes her Ugg hat to scratch her bald head. On the surface, it seems like such a sad gesture, but I could swear she's doing this manipulatively.

I click back to the beginning of the song. The twinkly 1980s intro starts. I try again.

47.

"You're going the wrong way," I tell Grandpa over speakerphone as I watch him from my window.

"Woops."

He pulls a 180 with Mom's wheelchair and starts heading in the opposite direction. I'm looking down at them from the courtyard-facing window of my apartment. I chose this apartment for its view, or rather, for what's not its view. The most desired units in the complex are the ones facing Sunset Boulevard, looking right out onto the bustling city. But there was no way I would've gone for one of those, because those complexes face Nickelodeon Studios, and plastered on the side of Nickelodeon Studios is a bright purple-and-yellow billboard for *iCarly*, complete with my fake smile and cheesy airbrushed hairdo. There was no way I was waking up every morning to face myself.

After a few wrong turns and elevator button pushes, Grandpa and Mom finally make it up to my unit. We chitchat for a few minutes over tea before heading back down to the parking structure so Grandpa can drive us to lunch.

"Where do you wanna go?" I ask. *Please don't say it, please don't say it, please don't—*

"Wendy's?" Mom suggests innocently.

"Sure," I say through a tight smile. There's nothing inherently wrong with Wendy's. In fact, I'd go so far as to say there are several things inherently right with it. We've all tried the Frosty.

My tenseness isn't coming from Wendy's, it's coming from Mom's reasoning for suggesting Wendy's. She knows I have money and could take her anywhere she'd like, and yet she chooses Wendy's not because she likes it, but because she can go and tell her friends or fellow churchgoers how humble she is, how down-to-earth, that even on a day as special as her birthday, all she did was eat a side salad from a fast food restaurant.

This thing in Mom drives me nuts. This thing where she yearns to be pitied. She's got stage four cancer, she's already plenty pitied. She doesn't need to throw Wendy's on top of it.

Grandpa pulls out of the structure and gets to the first stoplight. The stoplight that sits directly in front of the giant, terrifying *iCarly* poster. I start organizing his messy back seat pockets out of anxiety. I pull out papers, crumpled-up receipts, dirtied napkins, and a copy of Sean Hannity's *Conservative Victory*. Grandpa looks over his shoulder to see what I'm doing.

"You wanna borrow that? I'm done with it. Excellent read. Very excellent read." He raps on his dashboard as punctuation.

"Maybe." (No.)

"There she is!" Mom says as she snaps a photo of the giant poster with her disposable Kodak camera. She has at least a hundred photos of that same billboard.

As she takes the picture, the camera drops out of her hand and to the floor. I stretch down to pick it up, and by the time I sit upright with it, Mom's convulsing. Her hands are clenched into tight little balls and her face is contorted so that one eye is squinted shut and her mouth is scrunched up entirely to one side. Her convulsing looks like the rocking of somebody in a mental hospital. I'm horrified.

I tell Grandpa something's wrong. He takes the Lord's name in vain. Mom says nothing because she can't. Grandpa looks both ways to make sure the coast is clear, then cuts across the street, going through the red light and into the Nickelodeon Studios parking lot. Carl, the friendly security guard, recognizes him since Grandpa visits me on set often. Grandpa tells Carl to call 9-1-1.

By this point, Mom is frothing at the mouth. I'm sure she's dying. Grandpa tells me to get her to lie down. I unbuckle her seat belt and pull her onto my lap. This is the most terrifying moment of my life.

The ambulance arrives impressively fast. They yank Mom onto a stretcher and buckle her in. She's still convulsing. They wheel her into the ambulance. One of the EMTs recognizes me, so he lets me ride with Mom. It's one of the rare times I'm grateful to be recognized.

I grip Mom's hand and squeeze it. I tell her everything's gonna be okay even though I'm sure it's not. The siren starts blaring from the ambulance. It sounds warped when you hear it from inside the vehicle that's making it. The driver pulls a right out of the parking lot. As I'm squeezing my dying mother's hand and watching froth spill out of her mouth, we pass the poster again. I see my dead-eyed grin and my stupid fucking outdated hairstyle. My life is mocking me.

48.

It's the day before Christmas Eve. Mom's been in the ICU for a week, unresponsive. She had a seizure as a result of her brain tumor, which is apparently a "pretty regular occurrence," the doctor tells us, as if the regularity makes it any less horrific.

Marcus, Dustin, Scottie, and I sit in a row in the waiting room while Grandma and Grandpa visit with her in the ICU. We're all quiet.

Finally, I offer to go pick up some Burger King for all of us because I'm desperate for a distraction. And food is the perfect distraction. None of the boys want anything. They "can't eat" right now, they tell me. I envy them. I envy that their sadness and stress translate to a lack of hunger.

I go to the Burger King across the street. I order a Whopper and fries and a Coke Icee, and some tacos and chicken sticks to go with it. The ordering and the eating happen in rapid succession and both feel out of my control. Afterward, my stomach feels distended.

I consider making myself throw up. I've heard about this before, but never actually tried it. Now seems like as good a moment as ever to try. I shove my Burger King bag into an overstuffed trash can and head back to the hospital. I rush through the entrance doors, cut through the lobby, and hop on the elevator, excited about my new plan. I get off the elevator at the ICU. My brothers are no longer in the waiting room. They must be visiting Mom. I head to the two-stall bathroom and make sure no one else is in there, then I kneel on the cold, hard, tiled hospital floor and shove my fingers down my throat. Ow. I poke the back of my throat. It hurts, but nothing comes out. I try again. Nothing. One more time. Still nothing.

Fuck this. I give up. I wash my hands. I'm a failure at not eating and I'm a failure at getting rid of the food I do eat.

I hurry down the hallway and push open the heavy door that leads to Mom's ICU room. Marcus, Dustin, and Scottie are standing around her. You can barely make out the shape of her little body underneath the hospital sheets and blankets.

"She's awake," Dustin tells me.

I rush over to her bedside and take her hand in mine. I love the way her hands feel. They're small and her fingers are short. Her skin is shiny and warm.

"Net," she says as she turns her head feebly to look at me. My eyes well with tears. Maybe she's gonna be okay after all. I can't believe it. I'm elated.

"The boys said you stopped at Burger King. You don't need to be eating that stuff. Lotta grams of fat in a Whopper."

I beam. A tear trickles down my cheek. Mom's gonna live. For now, she's gonna live.

"I know, Mama. I know. I did get it without mayo…"

She sighs. "Still."

49.

MIRANDA'S CRYING. I'M CRYING. WE'RE both crying. We can't stop crying. For me, it's not that *iCarly*'s ending. It's not that today is our last day ever taping *iCarly*. That I'm fine with, even excited about, definitely ready for. Even though I'm wary of starting my spin-off, I'm glad to at least be saying goodbye to this project that makes me feel like I'm living every day in the *Groundhog Day* movie, doing the same thing over and over again.

The reason I'm crying is that I don't know what will become of my friendship with Miranda. We've gotten so close. Like sisters, but without the passive-aggression and weird tensions. I have my judgments around female friendships being catty and petty and backstabby, but that couldn't be further from the truth with Miranda.

With Miranda, it's always been so easy. Our friendship is pure.

An AD hands me and Miranda a tissue. We blow our noses hideously and get back on our marks to do one last take of the final scene we're shooting together. The sadness takes both of us over. We hold each other and cry.

This feeling of sadness and ending is really common on sets. You get to know the people around you so intimately because you're around them more than you're around your family. For a period of time. And then you aren't anymore. And little by little, you realize you start talking less and less to the people you thought you were so intimate with. Until you don't talk to them at all anymore. And it makes you wonder if you were ever really intimate with them in the first place or if it was all just a facade. If the connections were as temporary as the sets they were made on.

I don't like knowing people in the context of things. *Oh, that's the person I work out with. That's the person I'm in a book club with. That's the person I did that show with.* Because once the context ends, so does the friendship.

I yearn to know the people I love deeply and intimately—without context, without boxes—and I yearn for them to know me that way, too. And as much as I think I know Miranda deeply and intimately, I don't like that I know her through the context of *iCarly*, because *iCarly* is ending, and I don't want our friendship to end with it.

50.

"Are you sure?"

"I'm positive."

"Now's not the time to throw us away. Now's when you need us most."

"I don't think so. I think... if I go through these next few months with you, I'll get too attached."

"Why don't you want to be attached? Isn't being attached to someone a good thing? Isn't that what love is?"

"I'm just worried about being attached while my mom's, you know..." I can't say it out loud. The realer it becomes, the more I can't say it out loud. Doctors have been saying that Mom's health is rapidly declining for a while, long enough for me to question their use of the word "rapidly." Regardless, it's declining. She's wheelchair bound. She's weaker than I've ever seen her. The cancer has spread to just about everywhere. The end is near. I bite my nail.

"Like, since I'm more attached to her than anyone, I worry all that attachment toward her will just pile onto whoever I'm with," I say.

"Well, that's fine with me. I want the pile. Pile it on."

Not the response I was hoping for. I backpedal.

"Maybe I misspoke. I just think it's a distraction from what I need to be focusing on. Family."

"I'm a distraction?"

"No. Yes. I don't know."

I scratch my head. I want out of this moment, this moment in Tony's Darts Away—Joe's favorite vegan joint in Burbank.

"Look, if you don't love me anymore, you can just say it. I can take it," he says, his voice cracking on the last part, betraying his words.

Just then his vegan sausage and beer come. The timing of food at restaurants is always impeccably in line with the phrase you'd least like someone to overhear.

You almost have to appreciate it, it's like the waiters work on this.

"I do love you."

"Then why are you breaking up with me?" Joe takes a big bite of his sausage. An obnoxiously big bite. He's got vegan mayonnaise smeared all over his lip. It's disgusting.

Maybe this is why. Maybe it's not about the Mom stuff at all. Maybe I'm just over it. His chewing bothers me most of the time. The baby voice he overuses makes me cringe. His jokes aren't funny. He lacks ambition. He drinks too much. He has anger issues. Our age gap no longer feels cool to me and instead feels a little embarrassing for both of us.

I wonder what laundry list of flaws he's racked up about me at this point. What could he say? I'm selfish. I'm possessive. I'm not social enough. I don't like his friends. I'm too judgmental. I don't give him enough attention.

Joe's still chewing the same bite. He's been chewing this same bite for a goddamned minute. Why not just take smaller bites? There's an easy solve to this, Joe.

"Did you hear me?" he asks. "If you still love me, why are you breaking up with me?"

Something switches in me in this vegan mayonnaise–filled moment. All my patience is gone. I'm in a vegan dive bar, smelling beer I don't care to drink with basketball and football games I don't care to watch blaring from the excessive amount of TVs around me. I'm sitting on a bar stool with uneven legs opposite a man I no longer love. I am numb. I am done.

"Look, I just am."

51.

MIRANDA'S DRIVING AND I'M SITTING shotgun in her Porsche Cayenne, where we spend 50 percent of our time together these days. And we spend a lot of time together these days. There was no need to worry about context; our friendship has gotten stronger since *iCarly* ended.

We hang out three or four times a week. Usually one of the nights is a sleepover, like last night. Typically the sleepover is at Miranda's place, but last night we stayed at the St. Regis Laguna Beach because our series wrap gift was a night there.

The sleepover might as well have been at Miranda's place because we didn't do anything that made our sleepover any more St. Regis-y than our other ones. We sat in the room and watched some movie about the porn industry starring Amanda Seyfried, and decided that, even though the movie was mediocre and we don't know how to pronounce her last name, Amanda Seyfried is a walking angel of beauty. We talked about how sad and miserable we are and how we feel guilty about it because we have so much to be grateful for. We watched *Dance Moms* until we fell asleep—between Abby Lee Miller's abusive tactics and the intensity of the parents, we relate deeply.

We left the hotel not long ago. Miranda makes her way toward the nearest freeway on-ramp. We're complain-laughing about something while Katy Perry's "Roar" plays in the background (we once saw the Rolling Stones together, but who are we kidding, we're twenty-one-year-old females and Katy Perry does much more for us than Mick Jagger). My phone rings. Mommy.

"Hello?"

"Net! Net! Help me!"

"Whoa whoa, slow down, what's the matter?"

"Help! I'm scared."

"What are you scared of?"

"They're taking me back for my surgery."

Mom's been set to have this surgery for a while. The breast implant from her mastectomy recently started leaking, so the doctor needs to go in there, clean up the leakage, and repair the implant—supposedly a fairly easy procedure.

"It's gonna be fine. It's just a minor surgery."

"Something's not right, Net. Something's not right."

I hear a nurse in the background. "Ma'am, no phones are allowed here."

"Please, Net! Do something!"

"What do you want me to do?"

"I don't know! I need you!"

She sounds panic-stricken. There's a trembling to her voice that I've never heard before. It terrifies me. Dad takes the phone.

"Hey, Jennette?"

"Yeah?"

"She's just emotional right now. She's on the hospital bed, they're rolling her to the room for her surgery now. I'm with her. Everything's fine."

"Should I come?"

Mom shouts "Yes!" Dad says "No."

I ask again. "Should I come?"

"No, it's fine," Dad says. "They'd be done by the time you got here. It's gonna be quick—totally harmless. The doctors are great. I'll call you afterward."

Cool. I turn up "Roar." Miranda keeps driving.

"Everything okay?"

"Yeah. It's nothing."

She doesn't press. We drive in silence for a few minutes and then we start talking again, about whatever. Something's off, I can feel it in my gut. We stop for gas, then keep driving. My phone rings again. Dad.

"How'd it go?"

"Hey. Mom's not okay."

"What?"

"Apparently her body couldn't withstand the surgery."

"Wait, what? I thought it was gonna be harmless—"

"She's in a coma."

"But you said the doctors were great—"

"She's not doing well. You need to get to the hospital right away."

I hang up the phone, numb. I tell Miranda what's happened. She offers to drive me to the hospital. I say okay. I stare out the window. Miranda stops at a red light.

"It's Sigh-Fred," Miranda says plainly. "I looked it up."

52.

"Mommy. Did you hear me? I said I'm so skinny right now. I'm finally down to eighty-nine pounds."

I uncross my legs. I lean forward, desperate.

"Eighty-nine!"

I'm grateful that since Mom's been in a coma I've stopped binging. In fact, I've eaten almost nothing. I've been losing weight rapidly.

Beep. Beep. Beep.

As the hospital machines keep beeping, I slowly settle into the fact that my big news isn't gonna wake Mom up. I wipe the tears from my eyes just as the boys come back up from the cafeteria. We don't say anything to one another. We don't need to. They sit around Mom's body and we all just stare at her.

I glance at the clock. It's two thirty, two hours since we were told Mom has less than forty-eight to live. I wonder how much time she has left. Where her lifetime falls within those forty-eight hours. Does she have forty-four hours left? Ten? Two? Every moment feels so slow and so heavy. I'm trying to hold on to each moment but they just keep ticking on. I've never felt worse.

"Cam ooda dieeeee."

All of us whip our heads to Mom. What the fuck. She spoke. She feebly, barely, inaudibly spoke, but still, she spoke.

"Cam oooooda dieeeeeee," she says again.

Marcus leans forward. "No, Mom, don't say that. You're not gonna die."

"CAM OODA DIE," she says with a hint of anger. There she is.

Dustin snaps his fingers. "Canada Dry!"

Mom's eyes widen with confirmation. We all crack up around her, harder than we would have if she wasn't dying. There's something about these life-or-death moments that just beg for some levity. They're too difficult otherwise. Too excruciating.

Marcus runs to the hallway to get a Canada Dry from a vending machine. He comes back, pops it open, and tilts it to Mom's mouth. We all share a smile. This is good, right? This is a good sign. Mom's speaking some version of words and slurping down Canada Dry. This means she's gonna be okay. This means she's gonna make it. Right?

I'm desperate, I know. I'm clinging, I know. But I'll cling if I have to. I can't let her go.

* * *

Mom was moved out of the ICU wing a week and a half ago and has been in a regular wing since. So much for forty-eight hours. Take that, Dr. Wiessman. That's what I think sometimes. Until he assures me and the boys—which he does often—that this does not mean she will have some sort of a miraculous recovery. He doesn't want us to get our hopes up. As much as I wish I could argue with him, I know I can't. I see it. She shits in a bag and breathes from a machine. This isn't gonna turn around.

For the first week of her hospitalization, the boys and I stayed at a hotel nearby while we waited for her to die. But then she didn't. So after a week, we checked out of the hotel. Life resumed back to normal, or as normal as it could be. Dustin stopped taking sick days and went back to work. Marcus flew home to Jersey. Grandpa and Dad alternated work shifts so someone could be with Mom most nights, while Scott stayed with her during the days. I visited each day after I got off work on my spin-off, which had started taping. I'd go from slinging a buttersock and shouting my cheesy lines on the brightly colored, overlit *Sam & Cat* soundstage to sitting in a hospital bedside chair with outdated upholstery, surrounded by the smell of sanitization and the feel of death.

Today is no different. I just finished shooting a scene where I confront some mean school bullies and slap somebody with a ham sandwich. And now I'm here. Watching a nurse change my mother's shit bag while she side-eyes me. I know what's coming, and it is pure hell.

"Are you...?" the nurse asks. If this hadn't already happened twenty-five times in this hospital, I'd be shocked someone had the audacity to ask me if I'm Sam

Puckett while I'm sitting across from my dying mother.

I don't respond. I narrow my eyes and hope the nurse recognizes how inappropriate it is that she's asking this right now. She doesn't.

"You look like Samantha Puckett. Sam. Are you her?"

I sit in this feeling of utter hopelessness toward the state of humanity while the nurse disposes of my mother's feces.

"No," I say. Rudely.

"You look *just* like her. Spitting image. Do you mind if I take a picture so I can show my niece? She's not gonna believe how much you look like her."

I lean back in the chair. It squeaks. "No. I'm not taking a picture."

I look at Mom. It's wild how much cancer has changed her shape. She used to have curves, all four foot eleven of her. She had thighs, a bit of an ass, and boobs too (well, boob, if you're only counting real ones, the other one was the implant post-mastectomy). She had a small waist and narrow shoulders. She had shapeliness. Now her stomach is distended, her boobs have shriveled, her legs are twigs. Her arms look longer in an almost monkey-like way—they just dangle at her sides. She looks less human to me.

"Iluyooo!" Mom lobs into the abyss. This is one of the only phrases she has left in her. She has so many brain tumors that are so big in size that she's all but brain-dead. And yet she still remembers how to sort-of say "I love you." It makes my heart physically hurt.

"Iluyoo!" she says again, her head bobbing around and no connection behind her eyes. I bite my lip 'til it bleeds.

I try looking at Mom while I'm here at the hospital with her—to savor her, to remember her. But at the same time, I don't want to remember her like this. So every time I look at her, within moments, I look away again. Sometimes I'll force myself to grab her hands and tell her I love her and that I'm here for her, but most of the time I'm not strong enough to do that. So instead, I sit in the chair in the corner, and I look at her occasionally, but otherwise I look out the window and try not to break down.

My phone pings with a text from Colton. He's asking if I want to get away for a few days, take a road trip to San Francisco. He knows I'm struggling and thinks this will help take my mind off things. I check in with Grandpa that Mom's at a "stable" place for at least the next few days, and Grandpa says she is.

I take one quick look at Mom while she spews some gibberish. I can't get out of this hospital fast enough. I get up, kiss her on the forehead, and leave.

53.

I'M SITTING SHOTGUN IN COLTON'S Dodge Charger. He's driving. We're reminiscing about the first time we met, on a movie shoot in Utah nearly ten years ago. We're fifteen miles from San Francisco when he suggests we pick up a little alcohol to drink back at the hotel. I've never had alcohol before, more so because I was scared of it after seeing Joe's relationship with it than because I'm holding on to any Mormon values or anything.

But if there's anyone I'd try drinking with, it's Colton. He's warm and energetic and has a way of making everyone around him feel accepted. Plus he's gay, so I don't have to worry about any sexual tension.

We crack open the bottle the second we get to our hotel room and pour a shot's worth each into the two plastic courtesy cups from the bathroom. We open a packet of Sour Patch Kids so we can suck on them as soon as we take our shots.

"You ready?" Colton asks excitedly. I nod. He counts us in. "One, two, three."

We plug our noses, swallow our drinks, and suck on the Sour Patch Kids.

"I don't feel anything," I say, confused.

Colton agrees, so we take another shot.

"Okay, still not much, but now I feel, like, a slight dizziness."

Colton agrees, so we take another shot.

"Ooh, I think I'm starting to feel it."

Colton agrees, so we take one more, just in case.

Before we can determine how the fourth shot feels, we've jumped on the beds, played hide-and-seek in the hotel hallway, and snuck into the pool even though it's closed. We've planned a short film we're gonna make together where we're handcuffed to each other for a week. We've tried to find handcuffs. Luckily, we haven't.

The next morning, I wake up energized, mascara smudged all under my eyes like a raccoon, still wearing yesterday's outfit.

"That was one of the best nights of my life," I declare.

Colton agrees, and we debate taking another shot. Ultimately, we decide we'll wait until nighttime so we have something to look forward to.

And my God am I looking forward to it. I can't believe I've waited so long to get drunk. It's an incredible, one-of-a-kind feeling. When I'm drunk, all of my worries disappear—hating my body, the shame I feel about my eating habits, coping with my dying mother, starring in a show I'm humiliated to be a part of—it all just goes away. When I'm drunk, I'm less anxious, less inhibited, less worried about what Mom would want or think of me—in fact, when I'm drunk, the voice of Mom judging me evaporates completely. I can't wait for tonight.

54.

KNOCK-KNOCK-KNOCK.

I jolt awake, startled by the noise. Ow. My head's throbbing. I rub my temples. This must be what it feels like to be hungover. I've only heard about what it feels like to be hungover, but I've never actually felt it for myself, despite the fact that I've gotten drunk almost every night for the past three weeks since having my first sip of Tennessee Honey Jack with Colton in San Francisco. Up until this point, every time I've gotten drunk, I've been able to wake up the next morning unscathed, regardless of what and how much I drank. But today's different, for whatever reason. Was it the tequila? The whiskey? The rum? The wine? Mixing all four? Who knows.

KNOCK-KNOCK-KNOCK.

Shit. What time is it? I check my phone: 8:05 a.m. Fuck. I forgot to set my alarm. I was supposed to leave for a flight five minutes ago. This must be the driver that Nickelodeon sent.

"I'm coming!" I shout, trying but failing to put on my best I-definitely-did-not-just-wake-up voice.

I yank open the front door. The suit-and-tie-clad driver is nowhere to be found. Instead it's Billy—my jovial contractor sucking on a cough drop—and his three crew members.

"He-hey!" Billy says cheerily as he bounds in, not waiting for an invitation. His guys trail behind.

I totally forgot Billy was coming today. I shouldn't have forgotten, being that he comes almost every day.

I bought a house three months ago. Everyone was telling me it would be a good investment. Plus the idea was exciting to me. My first home. It would be free of must and mold and hoarding. It would represent how far I've come.

I got a beautiful three-story hillside house that was turnkey so I could move in immediately and not worry about having to do any remodeling. I even bought the display furniture so that I wouldn't have to think about decorating the place. My vision for this house was to not have any—to let someone else have the vision and let myself enjoy it.

Within weeks of moving in, I learned the entire infrastructure needed to be dug out and replaced. A pipe broke and the shower leaked onto the living room display furniture, ruining all of it. The kitchen sink and one of the toilets clogged. The deck chipped and a stair broke. This thing was not turnkey. This thing looked good on the surface, but underneath it was falling apart.

As Billy and his guys barrel up the stairs, I step onto my porch and crane my neck over the ledge to see if the driver's down below. He is. Of course he fucking is. And not only is he, but he is with his arms crossed and his gloves on and his car running and his trunk popped. Drivers' level of preparation and timeliness has always been irritating to me.

"I'll just be a few minutes!" I shout down to him.

"All right, ma'am! But we really should leave any min—!"

I slam the door in the middle of his sentence. I'm becoming an angry person with no tolerance for anyone. I'm aware of this shift and yet have no desire to change it. If anything, I want it. It's armor. It's easier to be angry than to feel the pain underneath it.

I rush upstairs, drag a suitcase out of my closet, and open it up on my hardwood floor. The guys start banging and hammering in the bathroom to work on the shower while I crouch down and haphazardly stuff socks, underwear, pajamas, jeans, and shirts into my suitcase.

I hold up a jacket, debating whether or not I'll need it for this trip. Is it cold right now in New York? I toss the jacket aside and opt for a hoodie instead. I shove it in my bag, shut the lid, and sit on it to try and get the zipper up. Shit. I forgot toiletries.

I'm frantically jumping up to grab each respective item as it pops into my mind. It's chaos. I rummage through my bathroom cupboard and grab some makeup items, a travel toothbrush, a mini floss, and mouthwash. I toss them in the front flap of my suitcase when my phone starts buzzing. I swipe it open.

"Yeah, Dad?"
Hammer-hammer-hammer. Drill-drill-drill.
"You should get down here."
"Really?"
Hammer-hammer-hammer. Drill-drill-drill.
"Yeah..."

I throw my body onto my suitcase again. Why won't this thing shut? I yank the zipper harder. The part of it I yanked on breaks off in my hand. I chuck it.

"Are you sure? Because I'm supposed to leave for a flight right now, the car's downstairs waiting for me."

I hear Dad take a breath on the other end of the phone. He sounds stressed.

"Where you going?"

"New York, remember?"

"For what?"

Drill-drill- LOUDEST DRILL I'VE EVER FUCKING HEARD-*drill*.

"The Nickelodeon Worldwide Day of—" I stop, realizing how ridiculous this sentence sounds. "I don't know; some thing I'm supposed to be hosting. So I really shouldn't go?"

"They say it'll happen today."

I freeze, shocked for a beat, but not for long. I've experienced this moment many times before. Somebody says Mom's gonna die, and then she doesn't. I go back to tugging on the zipper.

"Yeah, but..." I start, knowing Dad will know what I mean.

"But what?"

Never mind. I always forget Dad never knows what I mean.

"But people have said this so many times before. If this is just another false alarm, I really shouldn't head down. Nickelodeon's gonna be pissed if I bail on this thing."

A beat. Knocking starts up again at my front door. The driver's probably checking in on me. Dad swallows.

"You really need to come down."

"Fine."

I hang up just as I finally get the zipper shut. I'm sweating by this point. I stand up, cross over to my bed and sit at the foot of it for just a moment to try and collect myself before heading down to see my mom for possibly the last time I ever will. I'm trying to process this intense reality, but I'm really struggling to because *hammer-hammer-hammer. Drill-drill-drill. Knock-knock-knock.*

55.

I'M SITTING ON THE COUCH looking at Mom as she lies in the hospital bed that's been set up for her here in the living room of the ole Garbage Grove hoarder house. The couch was removed to make enough space for it. Mom's been in hospice care for the past three weeks, so this is not an unusual sight, though she's typically sitting up instead of lying down like she is now, and her breath is shallower than I've ever heard it.

Scottie and Dustin sit nearby. All of us are silent, the effect of years of emotional exhaustion. I'm surprised none of us are crying, but it's like we have no tears left. We've been through at least a dozen dress rehearsals of our mother's death. We remember the VHS tape.

My phone pings with a text. Nickelodeon is reaching out to say no worries at all on me missing the Worldwide Day of Whatever. I send a thank-you text back.

Another text comes through, this one from the guy I'm currently stringing along. Current Guy and I "met" via Twitter. We arranged to meet up in person. I invited some friends so I wouldn't get murdered. Once I knew he was safe to be around, we went to fancy dinners and laser tag and minigolf. We even went to Disneyland together to watch the fireworks. (I splurged on a VIP guide so we wouldn't stop any parades and piss off Goofy.)

Current Guy is wonderfully sweet and thoughtful and romantic. But I don't love him. Maybe it's because I don't have space in my heart to love anyone right now while Mom's dying, or maybe that's me trying to blame a genuine lack of connection on grief. Grief is a great scapegoat. Regardless, I'm discovering just how powerful of a tool it is to not love someone.

Loving someone is vulnerable. It's sensitive. It's tender. And I get lost in them. If I love someone, I start to disappear. It's so much easier to just do googly eyes and fond memories and inside jokes for a few months, run the second things start to get real, then repeat the cycle with someone new.

That's where I'm at right now with Current Guy. The distraction has been nice, but I'm ready for a replacement.

I whip out my phone to check the text from him.

What are you up too?

I'm no stickler on spelling but Jesus Christ get your "tos" right. That's it. I'm ready to end things. I draft a text.

Hey—I'm really sorry but I just can't do this right now. My mom's gonna die and I really need some time to just be alone. I hope you can understand.

Send. Done. Simple as that. I look back up at my dying mother. A text pings.

Don't say that, boo. Your mom's not gonna die.

He ignores the rest of my message. I roll my eyes. I've told him twelve times that Mom's dying of cancer but he acts like she has a sprained ankle. He has no concept of loss. I feel like the world is divided into two types of people: people who know loss and people who don't. And whenever I encounter someone who doesn't, I disregard them.

I'm in a constant state of irritation these days. I just don't want to deal with people anymore. I set my phone facedown on the arm of the couch. I look at Dustin, then Scott, then Mom. Her breathing looks so strenuous. She's struggling to hang on. I hate this.

Mom takes a sharp breath in, then out. The hospice nurse locks eyes with Dad, gives a slight nod. Dad looks at us. Mom's gone.

We're all numb. We don't cry. We just sit. In silence. Finally, I pick up my phone. A hundred messages have poured in. Everyone's heard. *E! News* broke the story. How the fuck they already know, I have no idea.

I go to my text tab, then click on the chain with Current Guy. I stare at his last text: *Don't say that, boo. Your mom's not gonna die.*

I text him back: *She just did.*

after

56.

WE EACH SAY OUR GOODBYES, WHICH just involve us staring numbly at Mom's dead body. The nurse wheels Mom's hospital bed out and into the hospice van.

Dad asks us what we should do and suggests we get out of the house, go somewhere. None of us respond. He pitches the South Coast Plaza, a luxury shopping mall about twenty minutes away. We pile into the car.

I need an iPhone case, so we head into the Apple store. A small, upbeat employee with white teeth and a receding hairline approaches us.

"Well hey there, how's your day goin'?" He flashes a smile. We meet him with blank stares. Reading the room, Apple guy drops the smile and redirects. I appreciate this about him.

"Anything I can help you guys with today?"

I get my phone case and we're out of there in five minutes. We head to a small café on the same level for lunch. I order a salad, dressing on the side to make Mom proud. I don't eat a single bite of it. I feel lucky, grateful even, that trauma has finally resulted in my lack of hunger. Sure, Mom died, but at least I'm not eating. At least I feel thin and valuable and good about my body, my smallness. I look like a kid again. I'm determined to keep this up. I'm honoring Mom.

That night, I get home to my big lonely house. Billy and his guys left all their tools out since they're returning tomorrow. Tarps cover the living room furniture. I sit on one of the tarps and look around. I think I might hate this house.

I fidget. The tarp crinkles and makes an annoyingly loud sound. I don't know what to do with myself. I open a bottle of whiskey and drink a few gulps straight from the bottle, then text Colton and a few other friends to see if they'll keep me company.

We all head to Little Tokyo and sit down at a sushi place for dinner. I down a bottle of sake. The menus are passed around. I want everything. I want to eat all of it.

I'm so confused. This past month, I haven't been able to even think about food. Every day, I've been living off whiskey, Coke Zeros, and two individual bags of barbeque Baked Lay's. What the fuck is happening? I'm starving. Ravenous.

I haven't been engaged in a single second of the ten-minute conversation. I'm sure everyone has mistaken my silence for grief. But this isn't grief. This is my secret food obsession.

By the time the waitress comes around, I can't decide what to order, but I'm drunk enough that I just choose the first thing I see—the teriyaki bowl. I tell myself I'll just eat the steamed cabbage on the side, maybe a few bites of steamed rice, but by the time the piping-hot bowl is placed in front of me, I can't hold back. I devour every bite as quickly as I can. I order another bottle of sake, another side of steamed rice, some egg rolls, and a bowl of ice cream for dessert. I drink the full bottle and eat every bite of the food.

We get back to my place and my head is spinning from the alcohol. We play a board game and listen to music, but I'm just going through the motions. My mind is only on one thing—the amount of food I ate and what I'm going to do about it.

I try and rush everyone out of my house as quickly as possible, which is a hard thing to do when you're the one who invited them on the day of your mother's death to keep you company. As each person leaves, they double-check that I don't need anyone to stay overnight with me.

As soon as they're all gone, I race up my stairs and into my master bathroom. Billy's equipment is all sprawled out, so I tiptoe around the piles to get to the toilet. I lift the lid, crouch down onto my knees, and shove my fingers down my throat.

Nothing. Fuck. I try again, harder. Ow. I poke my throat and taste a little blood. I must've scratched it raw. Oh well. I'm making this happen. I take a steady breath, shove my fingers back as far as I can, as hard as I can, and finally vomit spews up and out of my mouth, landing in the toilet. I look down at it, at the little chunks of rice and chicken and the frothy melted ice cream. I feel victorious.

So what if I fucked up and ate? So what if I failed? So fucking what? All I have to do is shove my fingers down my throat and watch my mistake be undone. This is the start of something good.

57.

I'M LOOKING AT MYSELF IN the mirror while I do my hair and makeup for Mom's service. I'm doing everything she liked best, which also happen to be the things that I like least—hot curling my hair, overlining a bold red lip, and scraping eyeliner along my sensitive tear ducts. The end result is a bit more severe than I would've hoped, but I don't have time to redo it so this will have to do.

I pull on my black dress robotically, zip it up, and throw on a pair of heels. Marcus, who's been staying with me this week, drives. His wife Elizabeth sits shotgun. I'm in the back. I use the hour-and-a-half ride down to make up my mind. It's a big decision, and it deserves a chunk of dedicated thought.

The ride down is hell. Bumper-to-bumper traffic, and Sara Bareilles's "Brave" is the biggest song on the radio right now, so it blares from the speakers every third song. On a regular day, Sara's fine, but the last thing I want to hear on the day of my mother's funeral is how much Sara Bareilles wants to see me be brave. I try to ignore it. I shut my eyes to focus, trying hard to find an answer.

Am I or am I not going to sing "Wind Beneath My Wings" at Mom's funeral?

During these last few months of Mom's life, her request has tormented me. I've been thinking about it constantly. I even practiced the song every night last month until my neighbor taped a piece of paper to my door that read: NO MORE BETTE MIDLER.

Due to some lingering Mormon beliefs, I think this means Mom will be looking down at me today, disappointed, from her throne in the Celestial Kingdom—the highest kingdom of heaven in the Mormon faith. No way Mom wound up in the Terrestrial or Telestial trash kingdoms. Gross.

I'm whipped out of my train of thought when Sara starts pulling out all the stops on that final chorus. You know what? Maybe she's right. Maybe I should be brave. Maybe I should sing "Wind Beneath My Wings" at Mom's funeral. For Christ's sake, literally. My afterlife depends on it.

Marcus turns into the parking lot of the Garden Grove 6th Ward of the Church of Jesus Christ of Latter-day Saints, the church we grew up in. We walk up the front steps and in through the back door. I haven't been here in years, but it looks and smells exactly how I remember it. Carpet cleaner and burlap, baby. White tiles in the entryway, blue carpet in the hallways, pictures of Christ in various settings with disciples plastered everywhere. (Long hair on a guy does nothing for me, but the man does have a great jawline.)

Marcus and Elizabeth peel off to greet people so I'm left alone. I head to the family waiting room and take a seat next to bleary-eyed Dustin, Scottie, and Grandma. I reach in my purse and pull out the "Wind Beneath My Wings" sheet music that I printed out last night, just in case. I thumb it and go over the words to make sure I have them memorized. I'm mentally singing it to myself, cringing when I get to the chorus. Shit. I know in my heart that I'm incapable of singing this song, but I feel like I have to. I can't break the last promise I made to my dying mother.

I see the pianist walk by and I'm about to hand her the sheet music, but just then, the pallbearers show up to bring Mom's casket into the room. They are milking their moment. Pallbearers love the spotlight. My brothers are crying. Grandma's wailing. "There aren't enough cold cuts! We underestimated the turnout!"

I'm the headliner of the eulogy lineup, so I have all the eulogies to sit through while I go back and forth on whether there's any way I can attempt the song. I would say I could bring the whole song down a step or two, but then the verses will be too low. I would say I could tweak the chorus melody, but let's be real, you don't "tweak" a Bette Midler melody. Bette knew what she was doing.

It's my turn.

I walk up to the podium. I'm shaking. Since I didn't give the sheet music to the pianist, my only option left to sing "Wind Beneath My Wings" at Mom's funeral is to just blurt it out a capella. I clear my throat, take a deep breath, and then I just... start crying. It's a guttural cry that puts my *Hollywood Homicide* audition to shame. I keep crying. And keep crying. Until the Bishop taps me on the shoulder.

"We only have the chapel for another fifteen minutes. We have to prep for John Trader's baptism."

I walk offstage. No Bette Midler.

58.

"Thanks for being such a good sport," our assistant director tells me with a pitying, appreciative glance.

"Uh-huh," I say monotonously while two children bounce on me as we get ready to rehearse this scene for the seventh time so the kids can get their marks right. I've seen The Creator fire children for little reasons, like if they lose a line or don't hit their mark, so on rehearsal days like today, our directors like to be extra sure the kids know what they're doing so that they don't lose their jobs.

I hear that phrase a lot these days. "Thanks for being such a good sport." I hear it on a daily basis: not only from our assistant director but from my managers every time I'm on the phone with them, from a writer or producer at least once a week, even from a network executive who sent me a five-hundred-dollar gift card to Barneys with that very phrase inscribed on the attached note.

I know why I'm hearing this phrase so often. It's because my co-star Ariana Grande is a burgeoning pop star who misses work regularly to go sing at award shows, record new songs, and do press for her upcoming album while I stay back and angrily hold down the fort. I understand on a surface level why she has to miss work. But at the same time, I don't understand why she's allowed to. I booked two features during *iCarly* that I had to turn down because the *iCarly* team wouldn't write me out of episodes to go shoot them.

I've tried to calm myself down by thinking the whole situation through. Okay, fine. Maybe they couldn't let me shoot the movies because they would've had to write me out of episodes completely, whereas for my co-star, they let her do her music obligations because she's just missing rehearsal days and parts of shoot days but not entire weeks.

Then this week happened. The week where I was told Ariana would not be here at all, and that they would write around her absence this episode by having her character be locked in a box.

Are you. Kidding me.

So I have to turn down movies while Ariana's off whistle-toning at the Billboard Music Awards?

Fuck. This.

There was a time when I took the "Thanks for being such a good sport" comment as a true compliment. I took pride in it. Mom always taught me to be one growing up, always wanted me to be one so I'd book more roles and build a good reputation to help my acting career grow. So when I was called one, I knew I was doing something right. *Yep. I'm a good sport. I'm a good egg. I'm the good one, the one who's not difficult, the teacher's pet.*

But now, I'm over it. I've become a bitter person and I'm resigned to that fact. I can't change my circumstances, so why try to change who I've become as a result of them? I'm done being a good sport. I resent being a good sport. If I wasn't such a good sport to begin with, I wouldn't be in this predicament in the first place. I wouldn't be on this shitty show saying these shitty lines on this shitty set with this shitty hairstyle. Maybe my life would be entirely different right now. I fantasize about it being different.

But it's not different. It's this. This is what it is. Ariana misses work in pursuit of her music career while I act with a box. I'm pissed about it. And I'm pissed at her. Jealous of her. For a few reasons.

The first is that she had a much easier upbringing than I did. I grew up in Garbage Grove in a goddamned hoarder house with a cancerous mom who constantly wept about not being able to afford rent and utility bills. Ariana grew up in Boca Raton, Florida, an incredibly wealthy, idyllic town, with a healthy mom who could buy her whatever she wanted, whenever she wanted—Gucci bags, fancy vacations, Chanel outfits. I don't even want Chanel outfits—I don't like the way the fabric looks—and yet I'm jealous that she had them.

The second is that when I initially got a development deal with Nickelodeon for my own show a few years ago, I thought it was gonna be just that... my own show. This was supposed to be *Just Puckett*, the harrowing tale of a brassy juvenile delinquent-turned-school counselor. Now it's some half-baked two-hander—*Sam & Cat*—about a brassy juvenile delinquent who, with her "ditzy best friend," starts a babysitting company called "Sam & Cat's Super Rockin' Fun-Time Babysitting Service." This is not harrowing.

The third is that Ariana is at the stage in her career where she's popping up on every 30 Under 30 list that exists. And I'm at the stage in my career where my team is excited that I'm the new face of Rebecca Bonbon, a tween clothing line featuring a cat with her tongue sticking out. Sold exclusively at Walmart. And I frequently make the mistake of comparing my career to Ariana's. I can't help it. I'm constantly in the same environment as her, and she doesn't exactly try to hide her successes.

At first, I managed my jealousy well. When she came skipping onto set saying she'd be performing at the Billboard Awards, I didn't care. So what? She's pursuing a music career—a thing I quit doing because I hated it. And in her pursuit of that career, she's going to go sing some cheesy pop song on a stage, a task that sounds truly awful to me. I was unfazed.

Then she came trotting onto set saying she'd be on the cover of *Elle* magazine. That one got to me, but only out of my own insecurity. Am I not pretty enough to be on covers of magazines? Would I be the one on covers if this show wasn't a two-hander? Is she robbing me of opportunities that would have been mine? I stuffed down my jealousy and carried on.

But what finally undid me was when Ariana came whistle-toning in with excitement because she had spent the previous evening playing charades at Tom Hanks's house. That was the moment I broke. I couldn't take it anymore. Music performances and magazine covers... whatever, I'll get over it. But playing a family game at National Treasure, two-time Academy Award–winner and six-time nominee Tom Hanks's house? I'm done.

From that moment on, I didn't like her. I couldn't like her. Pop star success I could handle, but hanging out with Sheriff Woody, with Forrest Fucking Gump? This has gone too far.

So now, every time she misses work it feels like a personal attack. Every time something exciting happens to her, I feel like she robbed me of having that experience myself. And every time someone calls me a good sport, all I feel is how much I don't want to be one. Fuck being a good sport, I'd rather be playing charades with Tom Hanks.

59.

COLTON AND I ARE CHUGGING tequila Pocket Shots in the back seat of Liam's 2009 Toyota Corolla while he drives. The Pocket Shots are disgusting. We almost gag with each one down, but we keep on chugging. We want to be nice and obliterated by the time we arrive.

"How you guys doing?" Liam coyly asks, wheeling around while he's at a stop sign. This is the fifth or sixth time he's asked it, and every time, he looks right at me like I'm the only one whose answer he cares about.

Liam and I met at Colton's friend's Cinco de Mayo party a couple months back. He was making himself some fajitas from the buffet table. Six foot two with a shaggy haircut and wide-set eyes, I beelined for him. We bonded over margaritas and our mutual attraction to each other. The stuff of substance.

"Couldn't be doing better," I slur as I split another Pocket Shot with Colton. *God, I'm so fun.*

"Good. Good," Liam says with a wink. I've always been impressed by a man who can make a wink not creepy. He keeps driving.

I haven't had sex yet, but it's starting to feel like an appropriate time. I'm not scared of it anymore. I'm not scared of anything anymore, because I don't really care about anything anymore since Mom died.

Liam seems like a solid person to lose my virginity to. I like him just fine but I don't care about him in a deep way, so I don't have to fear growing attached to him the second after we have sex—which is a genuine fear of mine since I've heard about this feminine weakness a hundred times. I want to do anything to avoid it. I don't want to be some weak, smitten woman who falls for a man just because he was inside her. I want to be stronger than that.

Liam and I are gonna do it soon. I just know. Maybe tonight we'll kiss for the first time and then maybe in a week or two we'll finally have sex, once enough tension has built up that we just have to break it. I'm excited as I fantasize about it. I chug another Pocket Shot.

Twenty minutes later and we've arrived at the dance club where our friend Emmy is having her twenty-first birthday party.

Colton and Liam help me hobble in since I'm so wasted and wearing such high heels that I'm not walking straight. We get inside and head to the bar. We order three drinks and guzzle them.

The party itself is fine, a little boring even while inebriated. I see Emmy watching Liam out of the corner of her eye. I hate when females are so obvious with their crushes. If you're obvious, some other little bitch can come along and exploit that crush, use it against you, betray you with it. I learned this from Mom's long-winded speeches about trusting women even less than men. "Men, they'll hurt you without ever really knowing you," she often told me. "But women... women will know you deeply, intimately, and then hurt you. You tell me which is worse."

And so I don't trust women. I just observe them. I watch them act desperate and weak and pathetic. It's so embarrassing to be a woman. I study women like Emmy so that I can be different from them. Better than them.

I nurse another drink as I watch Emmy chat up Liam overanimatedly. And for too long. And with too many flirty blinks and hair tucks and "inadvertent" touchings of his arm. She's doing it all wrong. Poor thing. I do the opposite of Emmy and ignore Liam completely for the rest of the party. It's almost too easy.

Two hours later we're back at my place. Liam dropped Colton off on the way home, so it's just the two of us. Liam throws me onto the bed and takes off my copper dress. I'm dizzy. The room is spinning. I'm wasted. I'm confused. Where the fuck am I?

"What's happening?" I finally ask.

"I'm having sex with you," Liam says in a tone that nauseates me. It's halfway to a baby voice, the same inflection as what a baby voice would do, but without jumping up an octave.

I kind of want to stop. This is not at all how I intended to lose my virginity. I never expected it would happen tonight. I thought tonight would be all about the magical first kiss, and the virginity thing could be done in a week or two. I thought I'd have time to mentally and emotionally prepare.

But I also kind of want to keep going. Who cares about the rituals and preparation? If anything, I'm relieved to be getting my virginity over with.

Fuck it. I say nothing. I squint my eyes to try and ground myself in some way so I can see straight. Finally I do. Liam's holding my hips as he pumps into me repeatedly. A bead of sweat is trickling down his forehead. Gross.

Liam eventually pulls out. He cums. I don't.

The next morning, I wake up in a puddle of sweat. I feel suffocated. Trapped. Like I'm in a straightjacket. My eyes fly open. Liam is spooning me. He must've been spooning me all night with the amount I'm sweating. I try and break free, but I can't. A fucking giant is draped over me. That's the thing about being a small woman. Every man feels like a giant. I squirm. That doesn't work either. Finally, I start poking him until he wakes up, then I pretend that I wasn't poking him and that he must've just felt something.

He looks me deep in the eyes and smiles at me. Says that last night was amazing. I lie to him by agreeing. Figure I'll come up with a plan to ditch him later on when I'm alone.

He tries to hug me more but I tell him I really have to pee. I jump up to go to the bathroom and suddenly realize how incredibly sore I am. Walking hurts, so I waddle instead. I get to the bathroom and pull down my underwear to pee. There's some blood on them. I know it's not my period—I haven't gotten it for years because of my various eating disorders. It must just be from having sex for the first time.

Peeing stings and burns, so I do it in little spurts, as if prolonging the pain will make it hurt any less. It doesn't. Finally, I'm done.

I spend ten minutes washing my hands, lathering them up, then washing them, then lathering them up and washing them again. I'm stalling. I don't want to go back in there with Liam. Something about his presence makes me uncomfortable.

Knock-knock-knock.

"You all right in there?"

I tell him I'm not feeling well. He leaves.

I Postmates myself some breakfast. Eggs and bacon and toast and potatoes and a latte with whipped cream. I eat rapidly, desperately, until I'm halfway through. *I can stop here. I'm full, I don't have to keep going. I can interrupt the cycle.* I chuck the takeout box in the trash. Overwhelm floods my whole body. I rush to the bathroom, lift the toilet lid, and purge my breakfast. I wash up.

Usually I'm depleted by this point but this time I'm not. I'm still filled with pent-up anxieties. I need to rid myself of these fucking feelings.

I run back to the trash can and pull out the takeout box. I stuff my mouth with eggs and chew rapidly. *Fuck what am I doing I need to stop I need to stop.* I spit out the half-chewed eggs into the trash can. I grab a perfume bottle from the bathroom and squirt some on the remaining food to guarantee that I won't eat any more of it. But then I eat more of it. The perfume makes me gag. I throw up.

60.

"YOU'RE LOOKING GREAT."

"You're really starting to blossom."

"You've never looked better, but I'd stop where you are. Any more and you'll start to look bad-thin."

"Your body looks outstanding."

These are all comments spoken to me over the past few weeks by producers, agents, and crew members that I work with. I have gotten more positive—and creepy—comments on my body over these past few weeks than I ever have before.

I have over a decade's worth of eating disorder experience at this point. There were the anorexic years, the binge-eating ones, and the current bulimic ones. The more experience I've got, the more I recognize that the body is hardly a reliable reflection of what's going on inside it. My body has fluctuated frequently and drastically throughout this decade, and no matter how it's fluctuated, no matter whether my body is a kids' size 10 slim or an adult size 6, I've had an issue underneath it.

People don't seem to get that unless they have a history with eating disorders. People seem to assign thin with "good," heavy with "bad," and too thin also with "bad." There's such a small window of "good." It's a window that I currently fall into, even though my habits are so far from good. I'm abusing my body every day. I'm miserable. I'm depleted. And yet the compliments keep pouring in.

"I've gotta say, when you're doing run-throughs and you walk out the door for a scene, it's really hard for me to not focus on your ass. I hope it's not creepy that I said that. I meant it as a compliment."

61.

It's Monday, my favorite day of the work week for two reasons. The first is that this is our shortest rehearsal day. The second is that every Monday, when we come in for the table read, we get an updated schedule dropped on the table in front of us so we can see episode titles, directors, and shoot dates for upcoming episodes. And each time that schedule is dropped in front of me, I get to see my name there on one of the episode titles as director.

I signed on to do the spin-off mostly to placate Mom. But I also did it because The Creator promised me this very thing—a position as director on one of the episodes. Sure, directing one of The Creator's shows is not exactly the best way to flex your creative muscles, since The Creator is ever-present during the shoot, adamant about his own ideas, and not very receptive to anyone else's. But getting to direct an episode of television is a chance to make the industry finally see me as something more than just a kids' TV actor. It's a way of showing that I have value outside the box I've been put in. I really want this.

The dates of my directing job have been pushed a few times, but I've repeatedly been assured that this is just because of scheduling conflicts with other slated directors. I've also been assured that the newest dates that I've been given—dates for one of our final episodes—are locked. I'm set to direct.

I grab my coffee, sit down in my chair, and watch as our production assistant drops the updated schedules in front of each person at the table. Come on, Bradley, let's pick up the pace here.

"Here you go," he says as he drops the salmon-colored sheet in front of me.

I pick it up and look down toward the bottom of the page to the place where the final episodes are listed. The place where I should be seeing my name in one of those little "directed by" boxes.

But instead, I see two letters: N/A. It must be a typo. I look around to meet anybody else's eyes, but there are only a few crew members in here so far, and our ever-sewing wardrobe person isn't gonna know a thing about this.

My breathing gets weird and rapid. I look around for any of our producers who might know something about this, but none of them are in the room yet. I can't believe it. I feel like I just got the wind knocked out of me.

Executives and producers start filing in. I lock eyes with one of them, the one I trust most out of these people I don't trust.

We'll talk about it later, he mouths.

No. I don't want to talk about it later. I want to sort through this now. What the fuck is happening? They can't possibly expect me to sit here and be a professional and do a table read when they've just taken away the one thing that I wanted out of this whole process.

I fight back tears as I realize that I've been foolish. I believed that these people would do what they said they would. Give me what they'd promised. Now that I've shown up to work every day, been a professional, swallowed my anger, and carried a show for almost forty episodes, now that they've gotten what they wanted out of me—they're taking away the very reason why I was doing all of those things in the first place. I feel betrayed.

After the table read I call my agents and managers and they advise me to play ball, to be the "good sport" I've always been. But I'm so fucking tired of being a good sport. I don't know how much longer I can be one.

* * *

It's Friday of the same week. A shoot day. It took an hour and a half for Patti—my makeup artist but also one of my dear friends in this crew—to do my makeup because I couldn't stop crying. I'm a mess. I'm distraught. I feel deceived and hurt and angry. I've told Patti what's going on, so she's even accompanied me a few times to various producers' offices as I try and garner a conversation with them, but each time I'm rejected. No one will speak with me. Everyone is tight-lipped. They're clearly all in this together, and not in a fun *High School Musical* clap-it-high kind of way.

I pull on my costume sluggishly and head down to set. I haven't memorized my lines because I don't care anymore. I wish they would just fire me. This place is toxic and bad for my already poor mental health. I want out.

I arrive to set for a scene in a boxing ring. (One of my castmates plays a boxer who is managed by a ten-year-old.) I thumb through my lines, silent.

We start rolling. First take, I get through—barely. Second take, I get through—barely. Third take—I don't get through at all. In the middle of my second line, my breathing gets away from me and speeds up, like it does whenever a panic attack is coming on. Shit. I see stars. I'm afraid I'm gonna pass out. Then I collapse on the floor. My chest heaves. Drool spills out of my mouth as the most hideous, intense cry of my life pours out of me. In front of everyone: the cast, the crew, the extras.

Finally, one of my co-stars, the one who plays the boxer, picks me up and carries me off set. He takes me to my dressing room and sits with me. Patti joins. They comfort me and tell me they understand. They're here for me.

Then someone knocks on the door. I'm immediately frozen with fear. Patti shouts that we'll be out in a minute. A booming voice from the other side demands to come in. I can tell it's one of our producers.

"Yeah, not now," Patti says rudely to the producer on the other side of the door. I love her. I appreciate her. She has the balls to stand up to these people.

"Can I just talk to Jennette for a minute? I feel for her," the producer says.

A part of me believes them. Or at least wants to believe them. Another part of me is suspicious. I choose to believe them. I allow them in. They ask if we can speak privately. The others leave.

They sit down on the couch opposite me.

"I like how you've decorated the place," they joke, since I've added absolutely nothing to this cold box of a dressing room.

I don't laugh. They clear their throat.

"I'm assuming this is about your being removed from the directors' slate."

"It's about a lot of things."

A beat. They proceed.

"I want you to know that I vouched for you. I wanted you to direct. And there's somebody else here who doesn't want you to direct. Very badly, they don't want you to direct. So badly that they said they would quit the show if you did. And we can't afford that. So we had to remove you from the slate. I just want you to know that it's not your fault."

I'm stunned. I have no words. The producer gets up and exits, shutting the door quietly behind them.

Somebody didn't want me to direct? So much so that they said they'd quit the show if I did? I don't even understand how something like this is possible. I make myself throw up again and again and again. I don't know how else to deal with everything happening around me. I don't know how else to cope with so much of my life being so out of my control. I look around at the white walls. Maybe I should decorate the place. The prop master knocks on my door to deliver the buttersock for my next scene.

62.

I'M WALKING AROUND WHOLE FOODS buying groceries for the week. I'm coughing up the big bucks for my produce and frozen meals because I'm hopeful that if I spend an obscene amount for a bag's worth of food, I will be less likely to throw it up.

By this point, I'm starting to realize that bulimia is not sustainable for me. My throat bleeds daily, my teeth feel softer, my cheeks look puffier, my stomach struggles to digest food, and I've gotten a handful of cavities since this started. I think I want to change, but so far, willpower has gotten me nowhere. Every morning I tell myself I'm not gonna throw up today, and every morning by ten a.m. I already have. Since willpower clearly hasn't worked, this Whole Foods thing is me trying a different strategy.

I pull a frozen meatloaf meal from the shelf and inspect the nutrition label for calories and fat: 440 calories, 15 grams of fat. No way. I put that shit back.

Another one of my brand-new strategies is lowering my calorie intake like I did when I was a kid. I figure that if I keep my calories low, maybe the urge to throw up will go away and I'll be able to keep my food down. At least this is what I tell myself on the surface. But deep down, I know the truth.

The truth is that I wish I had anorexia, not bulimia. I'm pining for anorexia. I've grown humiliated by bulimia, which I used to think of as the best of both worlds—eat what you want, throw it all up, stay thin. But now it doesn't feel like the best of both worlds. It feels terrible.

I'm filled with so much shame and anxiety every time after I eat, I literally don't know what to do to make myself feel better except throw up. And after I'm done, I half do. Half of me feels depleted, exhausted, like there's nothing left, which is helpful. The other half of me now has a splitting headache, a sore throat, vomit sliding down my arm and tangled in my hair, and even more shame on top of the initial shame since now I've not only eaten but thrown up, too. Bulimia is not the answer.

Anorexia is.

Anorexia is regal, in control, all-powerful. Bulimia is out of control, chaotic, pathetic. Poor man's anorexia. I have friends with anorexia, and I can tell they pity me. I know they know because anyone with an eating disorder can tell when anyone else has an eating disorder. It's like a secret code you can't help but pick up on.

Now that I've got my Whole Foods plan and my anorexia mission, I'm feeling motivation that I haven't felt since Mom died. Sure, most things are out of my control. Losing people I love, being on a show I'm ashamed of, directing jobs being pulled from me—but this? This I can control.

I push my cart a bit farther down the aisle and pick up some black bean hamburger patties: 180 calories a patty, and 5 grams of fat. I place this delicate angel of a food into my cart with great reverence since it is on my side. Helping my mission.

I push my cart forward. My phone starts ringing. Grandma.

I've never much liked my grandma. As a toddler, I hated the way she stroked my back and ran her hands through my hair. It was like she didn't know how to touch from a nurturing, comforting place, she only knew how to touch from a seductive place. It disgusted me.

When I was growing up, Grandma's favorite hobbies were gossiping on the phone and getting perms and complaining. Her feet hurt, her shirt's too tight, her perm's not the right color, Louise never called back, Grandpa's not home from work early enough, gas is too expensive, Souplantation took cornbread off the menu.

It's not just that she's a bitter old woman dryly airing her grievances with a cigarette hanging out of her mouth, which would be funny at least. She's always teary-eyed, always wailing, always making her problems everybody else's.

For all these reasons, I don't like or respect her. And I don't think she likes me much either, but she would never admit that because she's too busy crying about me not liking her.

Since Mom died, I've tried to work on our relationship a bit. I'll try to text her back when I can, I'll call her every few days, and I'll send her an email once a week. There is way more maintenance to this relationship than I would like, and even so, it's not nearly enough for her, which I'm told every time we do talk.

I'm emotionally spent, but I keep giving to this relationship because I don't want to be a dick and cut off my daughterless grandmother.

I tuck my phone back in my pocket. I head down the aisle and find some frozen vegetables. Pull out a bag and set it in my cart. My phone starts ringing again.

Grandma.

I text her: *I'll call you in a minute.*

I tuck my phone back in my pocket, this time with some irritation, and head to the produce section. I grab a bag of pink lady apples, some carrot sticks, and a coconut that I'm not sure what to do with but it looks nice so why not.

She calls again. I want to throw my phone. Instead I answer it, leaving a hint of irritation in my delivery so Grandma can tell I'm annoyed.

"Grandma, can I call you when I'm home? I'm getting groceries."

She's wailing. She says something, but it's indiscernible through the wails. I'm concerned. I ask if everything's all right. She keeps wailing. I ask again.

"You... you... You never call meeeeeeee!" she finally gets out.

Every time she calls wailing, I assume it's because Grandpa died. His health is rapidly declining. I know she knows I jump to this conclusion because I've told her before. I've asked her if she can try to taper her screaming and crying. Every time I tell her this, she assures me she'll never do it again. She does it every time.

I tell her sternly that I'll call her back when I get home, then hang up my phone. It starts ringing again. By now it's not only me that's stressed, but the makeup-less yogi with the hemp tunic who's shopping in front of me. I envy her glass skin. She eyes me. I'm embarrassed.

Grandma calls again. I give up. I leave my grocery cart where it is and head out of the store. Glass Skin looks pleased. I wonder if I should try microneedling.

I cross the parking lot, and in the time since I've been in the store, a thunderstorm has started. One of the rare annual LA thunderstorms. Typically, I avoid driving in the rain because I don't like driving to begin with, let alone when there's rain involved. I get in my Mini Cooper and just as I turn on the engine and my windshield wipers, she starts calling again. It's hooked up to Bluetooth, so her voice blares through the speakers. She's still wailing.

"Grandma," I say evenly, trying to calm her down. She's hysterical. She blubbers through some speech about me hanging up on her. I pull out of the parking lot and take a right, heading down the main street that leads to my home.

"Grandma," I say again, as evenly as I can even though my face is growing hot with anger. "I was getting groceries. We're on the phone now. Why'd you call?"

Her tears turn to venom immediately.

"No need to get nasty with me, *bitch*."

My grandma frequently refers to me as "bitch." She always throws a little extra salt on the word too, for effect.

"Grandma, like I've said before, if you keep calling me names and guilting me every time we get on the phone, I'm gonna block you."

"Don't threaten me, *little girl*."

"I'm not threatening you. I'm telling you a fact."

"*I'm telling a fact*," Grandma repeats, mocking my voice. "All my other grandkids call me way more than you do," Grandma complains.

"How are you?"

"How do you think I am, huh? Did you hear anything I've just said? You don't treat me well. Your mother must be rolling in her grave."

I wish I could just roll my eyes at this last thing she says, just write her off as an old batshit woman. But I can't. Mom stuff is my soft spot, the spot that can't be breached. I won't allow Mom to be used against me. And if she is, I take desperate measures.

"Okay, Grandma, I'm hanging up and I'm gonna block you."

"Don't you dare! Your mother will weep tears up in heaven."

She always fucking does that. If she knows something hits me in a deep way, if she knows it hurts, she shoves the knife in deeper and twists it around. How can a grandmother *want* to cause her grandchild pain? I know she's had a hard life, I know she's sad and desperate for attention, and I know she's hurt by my coldness toward her, but still. I do not think there are any excuses for her behavior.

"Bye!" I hang up the phone. She calls repeatedly. I pull over, swipe my phone open, and push block. It feels good. It feels right. A surge of built-up stress leaves my body. I can breathe normally again.

I get home and I walk up my front steps, slowly because of the rain. I get inside, my arms empty since I left Whole Foods in a huff. I was planning on starting my low-calorie anorexia meal plan tonight, but I'm too spent by now. The plan will have to wait. I order Postmates—bacon, brussels sprouts, and french fries and beef skewers from a place up the street that I like. I pour myself a filled-to-the-brim glass of tequila to go with.

I chug down the tequila before the Postmates even arrives. By the time it does, I'm famished. I devour it as quickly as possible. As soon as I'm done, I throw it all up.

Fuck it. This works for me. Bulimia helps me. My grandma is blocked and my body is empty and these are things that I need.

63.

I'VE BEEN GOING THROUGH THE motions at work for weeks. I glance at my lines in the mornings, making no effort to memorize them for rehearsals. I completely tune out between takes and for press—the back half of lunch break is typically crammed with interview after interview for all the teenybopper magazines. Ever since the directing situation, I'm counting down the days until the show is over.

Twenty days left after today. Just four more episodes. And even still, I'm not entirely sure I'll be able to push through until then.

I'm starting to expect I'll have a bulimia-induced heart attack. It's hard to admit it, but a part of me actually wishes I would. Then I wouldn't have to be here anymore. My thoughts have gotten dark and dramatic like this in recent weeks. And while at first I was aware of the shift, and concerned, it no longer feels like a shift. It just feels like me.

The disappointments in my life are piling up, and with each added disappointment, so grows my misery. Mom's death alone would've taken everything out of me, but since then, the pile has gotten bigger and bigger.

I can't get a hold on my bulimia. It's taken me over and I've stopped fighting. What's the point? It's stronger than I'll ever be. It's easier not to fight it. It's easier to accept it, embrace it even.

I've come to terms with the fact that I don't like acting. While I was able to push through the season for the promise of directing, now that that opportunity has been taken away from me, I feel that all I've ever been and all I ever will be is an actor. A has-been actor, because who's gonna wanna hire me when I've spent almost ten years on Nickelodeon? How will I ever get a "real" acting job, anything out of this phony, bizarre sphere? I never went to college and have no real-life skills, so even if I wanted to get a profession outside of the entertainment industry, I'm years away from that being a realistic option.

Men are not doing it for me either. They all just feel like distractions. And even so, I'd rather distract myself with a bottle of wine a night, or a full glass of straight whiskey, whatever's on hand. I'll even drink vodka, even though my body's started rejecting it by breaking out in puffy welts every time I have some. Doesn't matter to me, the buzz is worth the welts.

I'm hopeless. And I can't help but carry that hopelessness with me. I walk slowly, my shoulders hunched. My eyelids are in a perpetual droop. I can't recall the last time I smiled unless it was for a scene.

If I didn't know any better, I'd say my bad energy is what's rubbing off on everyone around me and bringing the on-set vibe down to the miserable slump it's been in lately. But I do know better. I know the real reason.

The Creator has gotten in trouble from the network for accusations of his emotional abuse. I feel like it's been a long time coming, and should have happened a lot sooner.

I appreciate the amount of trouble he's gotten in. It wasn't just a slap-on-the-wrist sort of thing. It's to the point where he's no longer allowed to be on set with any actors, which makes communication in between takes complicated.

The Creator sits in a small cave-like room off to the side of the soundstage, surrounded by piles of cold cuts, his favorite snack, and Kids' Choice Awards blimps, his most cherished life accomplishment. He watches our takes on four separate monitors, one for each camera, that are set up in his lair. Whenever he wants to give us a note, he tells it to an assistant director, who then has to run across the entire soundstage to give it to us. So our shoot days went from about thirteen hours to about seventeen. The general on-set vibe these days can best be described as malaise meets "dear God please let's get this over with."

We're on the last scene of the day, one that takes place in one of our main sets —a robot-themed restaurant where all the waiters are, you guessed it, robots. My character is supposed to jump up on a table and tackle someone... or something. I don't know or care. The scenes, the actions, the lines—they all blur together at this point.

I've done the stunt a few times. Between the stunt and the long hours and the bulimia, I'm spent. All I want to do is get home to some whiskey.

Finally, just past one in the morning, we wrap. I get home, pour myself a full glass, and down half of it before showering off my false eyelashes, my caked-on foundation, and my hair spray–stiff hair. By the time I'm out, the whiskey's kicked in. I'm bleary-eyed when I check my email. Messages pile in—half of which I won't even look at because I apply the same haphazard approach to my inbox folder as I do to everything else in my life these days. I'm about to X out of the window when I spot an ominous subject line hovering near the bottom of the unread email string. It's from my management company, saying we need to talk first thing in the morning.

I click out of my email, top off my glass, and try to fall asleep.

64.

THE NEXT MORNING I'M ON the phone with Agents 1–3, Managers 1 and 2, and Attorneys 1 and 2. I don't remember when exactly the team got so big, and I'm still not sure why—I can't remember the last exciting idea anyone on this team had and half the time they just echo what someone else on the conference call said then laugh for too long—but apparently this is what you do when you get successful in showbiz.

"Wait, they're cancelling the show?" I say, unable to hide my glee.

"Yep, we knew you'd be excited," Agent #1 says.

"Best part is..." Agent #2 starts in, pausing for dramatic effect (I swear agents are the best performers.) "... they're offering you three hundred thousand dollars."

I pause. This doesn't sound right to me. "Why?"

Manager #2 chimes in. I can tell he feels intimidated by the rest of the men, so by the time he finally chimes in, whatever he says spills out rapidly as if he's been prepping himself to say it, working up the confidence while the others have been talking.

"Well-think-of-it-like-a-thank-you-gift," he blurts out in one mushed-together phrase. He lets out a sigh of relief after he spits it out, like he's done his part and now he doesn't have to speak again for the rest of the call.

A thank-you gift? I'm suspicious.

"Yeah, a thank-you gift," Manager #1 repeats. "They're giving you three hundred thousand dollars and the only thing they want you to do is never talk publicly about your experience at Nickelodeon." Specifically related to The Creator.

"No," I say immediately and instinctively.

A long pause.

"N-no?" Agent #3 finally asks.

"Hell no."

"It's free money," Manager #1 offers.

"No it's not. This isn't free money. This feels to me like hush money."

A strained silence. One of them clears their throat.

Through the years, I've slowly learned that the entertainment business is one where what's being said is rarely what's being talked about. This way of operating not only disagrees with me but seems genuinely impossible for me to adapt to. Everyone else seems so able to position things discreetly and choreograph their phrasing so that the heartbeat of what's being said is delicately danced around, but what winds up happening is that I usually just don't understand what's being talked about and have to ask outright.

There are occasional times, however, where I do get exactly what's happening, like this time right now. And in these instances, instead of asking outright what's going on, I'll just say it. The results vary. Sometimes it's laughter. Sometimes it's discomfort. This time it's discomfort.

"Well, I-I wouldn't think of it that way if I were you," Manager #1 says with a nervous laugh.

"That's what it is, though. I'm not taking hush money."

"Well, um, okay. If you're sure..." Agent #1 or #2 says (their voices are indiscernible).

And with that, they all hang up. *Click. Click. Click.* Until I'm the only one left on the conference call line. I hang up too and sit on the edge of my bed.

What the fuck? Nickelodeon is offering me three hundred thousand dollars in hush money to not talk publicly about my experience on the show? My personal experience of The Creator's abuse? This is a network with shows made for children. Shouldn't they have some sort of moral compass? Shouldn't they at least try to report to some sort of ethical standard?

I lean back against the headboard of my bed and cross my legs out in front of me. I extend my arms behind my head and rest them there in a gesture of pride. Who else would have the moral strength? I just turned down three hundred thousand dollars.

Wait...

I just turned down three hundred thousand dollars. That's a lot of money. I've made a decent amount on this *Sam & Cat* spin-off, but definitely not enough that three hundred thousand dollars doesn't make a difference. Shit. Maybe I should've taken it.

65.

THE SHOW HAS BEEN OVER for three and a half weeks and the story the press has run with is that it ended because I was upset that my co-star was getting paid more than me, which is upsetting to me because it's untrue. My manager told me it was cancelled because of a sexual harassment claim against one of our producers.

Whatever. They've got to blame someone, so they've chosen me, and there's nothing I can do about it.

Except to tell the truth. Which I consider doing on multiple occasions but never bring myself to do because speaking out about the show and my time at Nickelodeon will just keep my connection to the show and Nickelodeon at the front of people's minds. If anything, it will cement my position as "girl on Nickelodeon." As "Sam."

I hate being known as Sam. I absolutely hate it. I've tried to find some peace with it, but I haven't. When people say, "You look like that girl from *iCarly*," I just say, "Nope, not me." Every single day, many times a day, people shout at me things like, "Sam!" "Fried chicken!" or "*iCarly* girl!" and then ask for a picture. I say no and walk away. Sometimes they'll call after me and say that I'm rude. I keep walking.

I will, however, take a picture with anyone who knows my actual name because I genuinely appreciate the courtesy. But anyone else—nope.

I know I've grown bitter. I know I've grown resentful. But I don't fucking care. I feel like that show robbed me of my youth, of a normal adolescence where I could experience life without every little thing I did being critiqued, discussed, or ridiculed.

I started to thoroughly dislike fame by the time I turned sixteen, but now at twenty-one, I despise it.

It doesn't help that I'm famous for a thing I started when I was a kid. I think of what it would be like if everyone was famous for a thing they did when they were thirteen: their middle school band, their seventh-grade science project, their eighth-grade play. The middle school years are the years to stumble, fall, and tuck under the rug as soon as you're done with them because you've already outgrown them by the time you're fifteen.

But not for me. I'm cemented in people's minds as the person I was when I was a kid. A person I feel like I've far outgrown. But the world won't let me outgrow it. The world won't let me be anyone else. The world only wants me to be Sam Puckett.

I'm aware enough to know how fucking annoying and whiney this all sounds. Millions of people dream of being famous, and here I am with fame and hating it. I somehow feel entitled to my hatred since I was not the one who dreamed of being famous. Mom was. Mom pushed this on me. I'm allowed to hate someone else's dream, even if it's my reality.

66.

I'M IN THE BACK SEAT of an Uber with Colton. I'm wearing a very little black dress and some too-high heels. I figure the higher the heel, the better the chance of it taking away some of my insecurity. So far, no such luck.

Bulimia kept weight off me for the first few months. But since those first few months, bulimia has betrayed me. My body seems like it's retaining whatever food it possibly can. Refusing to get any smaller and, in fact, getting bigger.

I've put on ten pounds since those first few months of bulimia, when I was Mom's goal weight for me. These ten pounds are the first thing I notice when I wake up in the morning, the last thing I notice when my head hits the pillow at night, and the thing that I most often notice throughout the course of any given day. I'm obsessed with these ten pounds. Tortured by them.

I don't understand. Why won't my body do what I want it to do? Why won't bulimia help me out anymore? I thought we were friends. I thought bulimia had my back. Clearly it doesn't. Clearly I had this whole relationship wrong. Yet I can't seem to get out of it. I feel stuck to, enslaved by, codependent with my bulimia.

The driver pulls up to the bar and lets us out. Colton and I spill onto the street and rush into the bar, where some friends are already there nursing their drinks.

"Happy birthday!" they all shout at me simultaneously. One of them passes me a shot of tequila. I throw it back, then another. And another.

Within an hour, I'm wasted. Fifty or so friends have shown up by then, and we're all having a decent enough time, when I'm frozen by the image of my friend Bethany walking toward me. She's carrying a cake with candles.

Shit. Not cake with candles. Anything but cake with candles.

Bethany extends her free arm out and squeezes me into a tight one-armed hug. Even with just one arm, it kind of hurts. Bethany is a strong woman.

"You're, like, not a good hugger," she says in her trademark upswing, Valley girl lilt.

"Yeah, well…"

"I brought a cake. It's vanilla, your favorite. And it has this, like, really cool vanilla buttercream topping that's supposed to be, like, amazing."

"Great," I lie.

"I know, right? Wanna do cake now? Let's do cake now." "Hey!" she shouts to the crowd of people, snapping her fingers. Everyone starts singing.

I'm too drunk to be able to fully make out the blur of figures standing in front of me singing in a range of keys. Why is "Happy Birthday" the hardest song ON EARTH to sing, when it's also the most popular song on earth? What kind of sick joke is this?

At least cha-cha-cha's aren't in style anymore. I'll take what I can get. The singing ends and everyone stares at me, waiting for me to blow out the little flames on the little wax sticks.

This is it. This is why I didn't want a cake and candles in the first place. I didn't want to have to deal with my birthday wish. At twenty-two, this is the first birthday wish I'll be making where I won't know what to wish for because the thing I've been wishing for all my life is done. Over. Case closed. The thing that I secretly hoped through all these years I had some control over, I now know that I don't, and never did.

My entire life's purpose, keeping Mom alive and happy, was for nothing. All those years I spent focusing on her, all the time I spent orienting my every thought and action toward what I thought would please her most, were pointless. Because now she's gone.

I tried desperately to understand and know my mother—what made her sad, what made her happy, and on and on and on—at the expense of ever really knowing myself. Without Mom around, I don't know what I want. I don't know what I need. I don't know who I am. And I certainly don't know what to wish for.

I lean forward and blow out the candles, wishless.

"You've gotta try the cake! The buttercream frosting!" Bethany shouts, already cutting the cake and divvying it up. She hands me the first slice.

I take a bite and make big "ooh, that's good" eyes, hoping this satisfies Bethany. It seems to. She claps her hands repeatedly and jumps up and down. I head to the bathroom to throw it up.

67.

I HAVE HOPE. FOR THE first time in years, I have hope. I've been offered the lead role in a new Netflix series—NETFLIX <cue confetti>—and this is no two-hander, baby. This is all about me. Well, actually it's an ensemble, but I'm the lead and, considering the network upgrade, I'll take it.

Granted, "taking it" wasn't the easiest of choices. I had expressed early concerns about the pilot script. The polite term for this in acting is to say, "I don't respond to the material," even if the exact language might be something more like, "I'm terrified this might be trash." But my agents had urged me to do the project because the paycheck was pretty good, the only other projects I was being offered were cheesy sitcom roles and reality shows, and they said it's worth it to make the connection with a respectable up-and-coming company like Netflix. This seemed like good logic to me, so I signed the contract.

It's October 1st when I touch down in Toronto, the cleaner, friendlier New York City I'll call home for the next three months of my life. I arrive at my hotel apartment excited, inspired even. I'm convinced that my life is turning around, that this new job is exactly the motivation I need to jump-start getting my life on track.

I'm starring in a real show. No more kids' shows. Kid show stars can be messes with all their alcohol abuse and bulimia. But real deals—Netflix stars—aren't messes. Real deals have their shit together.

So the day I get into Yorkville, the neighborhood in Toronto where I'm staying, I begin my real-deal endeavor with a trip to the bookstore to pick up a stack of self-help books. I plow through them in a week and come up with a solid affirmation-type mission statement of a plan, a mission statement that I think sums up the gist of all the self-help knowledge I've accumulated over the past week.

I will focus on myself. I write the phrase in my diary and touch it five times. (This is one of my OCD tics that lingers. I also twirl every time I enter my bathroom, but at least that one's kinda fun.)

I know focusing on myself won't be easy. It will take continuous effort, time, and attention. It will mean working on my issues, facing them head-on instead of letting them serve as distractions or trying to pretend they're less than they are. It will mean doing THE WORK. The soul-scraping introspection it takes to understand where bad habits and insecurities and self-sabotaging patterns come from and why, plus the motivation to challenge and change those bad habits and insecurities and self-sabotaging patterns even as they continue to get triggered over and over again by various life events.

I am ready to clear everything and everyone out of my life if necessary. I am ready to focus solely on myself.

Until I meet Steven.

* * *

It's the first day of shooting. I'm sitting in my trailer, thumbing through the scripts for episodes two through six when a terrible realization hits me.

I may be a part of Netflix's first-ever dud. I don't respond to these scripts even more than I didn't respond to the pilot. The budget is lower than expected—not that there's anything wrong with a low-budget project, it's just that that's not exactly the type of budget you want for a sprawling postapocalyptic drama about a small town where a virus breaks out and everyone over twenty-one starts dying. There hasn't been a single Netflix rep present for any of the welcome-to-the-show cast and crew pre-parties, which makes no sense to me. There's always a network rep present at those things.

I pick up the phone and dial my agents. One of them takes the call, and after I express my concerns, he explains to me that the reason no Netflix rep has been on set is because this show is a partnership between Netflix and a Canadian network called CityTV. CityTV is the production company, and Netflix is just the distributor.

Oooohhhhh. Oh oh oooohhhhh.

So this isn't a Netflix (cue confetti) show. This is a CityTV (cue... something else) show.

A part of me wishes I hadn't asked, that I could still be sitting here naively thinking I'm on a Netflix show. And the other part of me wishes I'd asked sooner so that I could've gotten out of this not-Netflix show.

I hang up the phone and sit here in my trailer, looking at my reflection in the mirror. I'm so ashamed of myself. Of my career. I'm aware there are worse things than starring on television shows you're not proud of yet the awareness doesn't change a thing. This is the truth for me. I am ashamed.

I want to do good work. I want to do work I'm proud of. This matters to me on a deep, inherent level. I want to make a difference, or at least feel like I'm making a difference through my work. Without that feeling, that connection, the work feels pointless and vapid. *I* feel pointless and vapid.

I know that if I make myself throw up right now, my cheeks will swell and my eyes will get watery and that's gonna be noticeable on-camera. But I can't help it. I need to. The shame that I feel is intolerable. I need my coping mechanism. I need the depleted feeling I get after a good purge. I jump up from the couch, but just then, there's a knock at my door. It's our production assistant ready to take me to set. Shit, there's no time for a purge. I descend the trailer steps and follow after the PA as we walk toward our first shot of the day, which takes place outside in the middle of a snowstorm.

There, through the flurry of snowflakes and harsh winds, I see him: auburn hair, soulful green eyes, and charmingly bad posture, wearing chinos and a puffer and a beanie with a pompom at the top of it. He's leaning against a Star Wagon trailer, with one foot resting on the tire while he smokes a cigarette—*so* edgy. He's speaking on his iPhone in a combination of broken Italian and English.

"Aayyyy. Aaayyy. All right. Ti amo. Ciao, Ma."

He calls his mother on breaks? This boy is too good to be true. He hangs up his phone and tucks it into his coat pocket. He pulls out a fresh cigarette and lights it.

"Steven! We're setting up," the production assistant calls out to my new love. So Steven is an assistant director on our shoot. My heart skips a beat. This means

I'll get to see him every weekday for the next three months.

"'Kay," Steven says plainly, then he heads to set.

I'm already fantasizing about how I'm going to wind up with Steven. The self-help books said to be flexible when goal setting, to be willing to adjust and tweak accordingly, and my God am I willing to adjust and tweak. I am ready to abandon my goal of focusing on myself. I don't want to work on my shame and humiliation and grief and bulimia and alcohol issues.

Maybe it's not so bad that I'm on this CityTV show. Maybe it deserves some confetti after all.

68.

AFTER TWO AND A HALF painstakingly long weeks of "coincidental" crafty run-ins, Steven invites me on a date.

We grab drinks at a bar called Sassafraz, right up the street from the hotel I'm staying at. Steven orders a rye and ginger. I order a gin and tonic.

There's a sweetness to Steven that's so far from typical nice-guy sweetness, which is—let's face it—dull. His sweetness is somehow cool. Maybe it's his voice that makes it that way. Oh my *God*, his voice. It's my favorite thing about him—quiet and gravelly, probably from his two packs a day, but that's fine, we can deal with the lung cancer later.

Steven has an edge to him that's somehow balanced out perfectly by how unassuming he is. I've never seen someone so edgy seem so humble, and vice versa. He's a walking anomaly. I am taken with him.

For our second date, we go to Jack Astor's—a chain restaurant in Canada; think TGI Fridays—and split some nachos and soup. I throw them both up in the bathroom, refresh with a Listerine strip, and head back into the dining area, with Steven waving me over. I can't believe that just weeks ago I was ready to work on ridding myself of bulimia. It feels like such a part of me, such a staple habit. I'm relieved to still have it to lean on.

We have a couple of drinks, then go back to my place for a couple more while we watch stand-up specials on my laptop. There's an ease and a comfort to our dynamic. We talk about what we want out of life and what we don't. What's weird about being in our early twenties. Past relationships. Past hurts. Hopes. Dreams. The good stuff! We talk until one in the morning, make out on my couch for an hour, then keep talking 'til four.

Our third date, we go out dancing (Steven's idea). I get wasted enough to completely lose my inhibition. Steven and I dance together. What should feel impossibly lame feels impossibly magical and it's all because of Steven. I've never felt this way about a guy before. Even my feelings for Joe—who, up to this point, I would have considered my first love—seem so immature, so childish compared to whatever this is. This is real. This is pure. This is deep. I feel completely understood and seen by Steven, and he seems to feel the same way.

Our fourth date, we watch *The Voice* at Steven's place. His taste in television shows is... questionable, but I'm happy to watch Christina Aguilera lob canned compliments at the show's contestants if it means spending time with Steven. We finish a bottle of tequila between the two of us and, as we get to the last few drops, start making out on his couch. He takes off my shirt, then his pants. He puts on a condom. He's responsible, too?!

We have sex for the first time and it's incredible. The typical commentary that rattles through my brain during sex is nowhere to be found.

The times I've had sex have always felt like a thing that's happening in the background of what's going on in my head. I throw in some moans for good measure so they can't tell. But not this time. This time, I'm lost in the moment. Steven makes me forget myself. I love that.

I start to cry. Steven asks if I'm all right. I tell him the truth. I'm crying because I'm realizing that this is how sex is supposed to feel. He kisses me harder. We have sex a few more times. He asks me to sleep over. He says he wants to never not fall asleep next to me. Christina compliments a young woman wailing a Whitney Houston number. All is well.

69.

I'M IN MY LIVING ROOM sitting on my overstuffed couch. Billy's jackhammering away upstairs. I've been back home in California for three long weeks and the magical fairy dust of Toronto has settled.

My fixation on Steven had curbed my anxieties about the quality of the non-Netflix show and the overall state of myself, but now, without Steven in close proximity, the anxieties are back.

Will this show end my career? Or worse, will it explode into another embarrassing phenomonen that eclipses my identity?

What is my identity, even? What the fuck is that? How would I know? I've pretended to be other people my whole life, my whole childhood and adolescence and young adulthood. The years that you're supposed to spend finding yourself, I was spending pretending to be other people. The years that you're supposed to spend building character, I was spending building characters.

I'm more convinced than ever that I need to quit acting. That it doesn't serve my mental or emotional health. That it's been destructive to both. I think about what else has been destructive to my mental and emotional health... the eating disorders, of course, and the alcohol issues.

And then I realize that, as much as I'm convinced that I need to quit these things—acting, bulimia, alcohol—I don't think that I can. As much as I resent them, in a strange way they define me. They are my identity. Maybe that's why I resent them.

The stress of the realization draws me to the toilet, just like any stress does. I purge. By the time I get back to my couch spot, I see a missed call from Steven.

Steven and I became official the day I left Toronto and my God was I relieved. I was terrified of our relationship being nothing more than a blip. A fling. Something to pass the time that would have otherwise been spent bored in a workplace. That would mean I misread, misinterpreted. Was foolish. I was convinced there was something real between us, but I needed the label to back me up, support my reality.

The morning my flight was set to take off, Steven woke me up with a love letter asking me to be his "woman." Leaving him was true agony. The moment of getting into my cab and saying goodbye was one of the most intense feelings I've ever felt in my life—shaky, terrified, passionate, and powerless. I had no idea where the future would take us, especially with us being long distance. It's possible that the past few months have just been a fantasy, a delusion. Maybe Steven will go back to his life, and I'll go back to mine, and we'll just fall into our usual old patterns and slowly forget about each other, even with a label.

That's why now, when Steven's calling me, I'm relieved. I know what this call means. Last night while we were on our nightly three-hour FaceTime, he mentioned he was going to look at flights to LA and call me in the morning if he was able to get on one last-minute because we couldn't stand being apart from each other any longer. This call means he was able to get on one. This call means Steven is coming out to visit me... today. This call means our relationship wasn't a fling.

* * *

Steven's plane lands. He only packed a carry-on since he's only staying for a couple days, so he's in his Uber quickly and we text back and forth his whole ride over. I cannot wait. I kick Billy out. He leaves his tools everywhere. (WHEN will this guy be done with his refurbishments? It's been over a year.)

There's a knock at my door. I let Steven in. It's wild to see him in person after only seeing him through a phone screen for three weeks. We're timid at first. The conversation is slow. I'm terrified. Is this LA us? Was magical us Toronto Us and LA Us is whatever this is?

Finally, after the longest three minutes of my life, Steven grabs me into a hug and we start making out. He takes off my clothes and I take off his and he takes a condom out of his pocket (of course he does) and pulls it on and wields his condom-clad penis toward me and I am enthralled. We fuck three times on the couch and afterward we start talking and everything feels back to normal. Easy. Comfortable. The awkwardness was just the sexual tension. Yay.

After an hour of cuddling and chatting, Steven goes to the bathroom to pee. He walks back into the room slowly and with a concerned look on his face. He stops in the archway of the living room, keeping his distance from me. He seems guarded. He doesn't say anything.

"What?" I finally ask.

"Jenny..." Steven says worriedly.

"What?" I ask again, more concerned than before. "You're freaking me out. What's going on?"

"It's just..." Steven looks down and scuffs his socks against the hard cherry wood floors. I have no idea what Steven is about to say, and his hesitance is nerve-wracking to me. I just want him to get it out.

"Do you have a problem?" he finally asks.

"A problem?" I ask.

"Yes. A problem."

"I'm not sure what you mean..."

"There's vomit residue on the toilet seat."

"Ooooh, that's it?" I ask, trying to play it off casually. "Well, I wouldn't really consider it a problem, it's more of just a... thing I do."

He's not buying it.

"You know, like how you smoke." I try to level with him. "You smoke cigarettes, and I make myself throw up. They're just things we do."

"No, they're different," Steven assures me. "Bulimia can kill you."

"So can cigarettes."

"Yeah, but I'm gonna stop."

"Right. So am I."

Steven sighs.

"I really just want you to be okay and healthy, Jenny."

"Well I mostly am."

"But you're not."

"But I mostly am."

He gives me a long, hard look. He's never looked at me like this before. It's pitying and parental. I don't like it, but there's something to the depth of it that makes me realize he's not going to budge. I'm not going to be able to convince him.

"Look, Jenny, you need to get help for this or I... I can't be with you. I can't watch you do this to yourself."

I'm taken aback. *Really?*

His eyes answer back. *Really.*

Well, shit.

70.

I'M SITTING IN LAURA'S CENTURY City office. It's my first time in a therapist's waiting room and not at all what I expected. Aren't these places supposed to be clinical? This room is anything but. It's cozy and inviting. Granted, Laura is a therapist–slash–life coach, so maybe therapists that are multi-hyphenates do more decorating. I'm skeptical.

There's a turquoise crocheted pouf in one corner next to a bookcase filled with rows of self-help books. I'm sitting in an orange chair with a cream knit blanket folded over the back of it. "Boho chic." Maybe I would've known this if I'd read the Yelp reviews, but as soon as I saw those five stars, I booked an appointment and never looked back. Plus, who wants to read a review from someone who takes the time to write a review? Can't trust 'em, too much time on their hands.

I'm in the middle of stroking the soft blanket draped over me and planning my opener. I wanna start this thing on a light note. I don't want to be another sad sack who plops down in a therapist's chair and whines about their troubles while the poor therapist regrets their degree. Laura comes out to greet me.

"Jennette?" she asks, even though I'm the only one sitting in this waiting room and the only one with an appointment scheduled for this time.

I humor her. "Laura?"

She smiles big, revealing one of the more beautiful smiles I've ever seen. Laura must be using Whitestrips too.

"Hi!" She moves toward me in a way that can best be described as a float. I'm not sure whether she floats because of her floral prairie skirt that flows across the ground with every step she takes toward me, or whether she floats because that's just who she is. I'm intrigued by her.

She pulls me into a hug. I'm typically not a hugger, but there's something about Laura's warmth and immediate trustworthiness that causes me to surrender to her embrace. She smells like fresh laundry. I take a whiff, hoping it's discreet. Gimme that Snuggle sheet scent, Laura.

Laura pulls away and holds on to both of my forearms while looking me in the eye, intimately. Everything about my interaction with Laura so far would typically put me on the defensive, if Laura were anyone else. But Laura is Laura. The regular rules don't apply here.

"Let's get started, shall we?" she asks with, I swear to God, a twinkle in her eye. Yes, we shall, Laura. We. Shall.

I sit down opposite Laura in her little office, which aesthetically resembles her waiting room. My opener's gone after being so disarmed by her.

She asks me what brings me in, and I tell her about the Steven ultimatum, and how I love him and want things to work out between us, so I agreed to come here.

"All right, well that's fine. But therapy is a thing *we* have to decide to do. *We* have to want to change, not for someone else, but for ourselves." Laura takes a long sip of tea. "So Jennette, do you want to change?"

"Yeah," I say, knowing that even though there's more nuance to it than this, this is what I should say. It's almost like Laura is the casting director and I'm the child actor, trying to say exactly the thing that will earn me a callback. Yes, I can swim. Yes, I can pogo stick. Yes, I want to change.

"Okay, good," Laura says.

Laura asks me what I'm currently struggling with in life, why exactly Steven suggested I come here, and I dive right in—Mom's death, bulimia, alcohol issues, the works. I try to give her the succinct elevator-pitch version. I figure we've got more sessions to unpack the specifics.

In her buttery voice, Laura gives me a rundown of how we're going to work.

"I take a holistic approach to recovery, so our sessions will incorporate a lot of variety. Today we'll focus on a life wheel so that we can gauge where you're starting out and use this as a benchmark to track your progress over time."

I nod along. No idea what a life wheel is, Laura, but let's get it spinnin'.

"Over the next four months, we'll go grocery shopping, cook together, discover your hobbies and passions through experimentation, read a stack of eating-disorder-specific books and take notes on what does and doesn't resonate with you, and explore balanced and non-obsessive physical activity options together." (My eating disorder translates into exercise as well. I run a half-marathon twice a week and five to ten miles every other day.)

All of this sounds well and good to me, especially since Laura will be by my side through it all, and I'll lose Steven if I don't. Where's the dotted line, baby? Sign me up. I'm ready to change.

71.

I CATCH A WHIFF OF BURNING toast and dog piss—the unmistakable smell of my spray tan. I wonder if Dwayne "The Rock" Johnson caught a whiff of it too. Even if he can smell it, he doesn't let on. Bless him.

I'm standing backstage at some Teen Choice People's Choice Fan Favorite award show—they all blur together—waiting for the commercial break to end and my segment to begin. I'm wearing overpriced heels with straps that dig into my ankles and a two-piece turquoise floral set, even though I don't like floral patterns. This is the outfit that was approved by the network, so this is what I'm wearing.

The Netflix show hasn't yet been released, so I'm still only known for Nickelodeon stuff. They're still airing new episodes of *Sam & Cat*, so I'm still on the cover of all the tween magazines with a sassy hand on my hip and a bright smile on my face, portraying the image of a carefree starlet with the world on a string. Tee-hee.

Even though I've been seeing Laura for a month, I feel worse off than I did when I initially sat in her tufted chair. Firstly, because Steven, who is the reason I sat down in Laura's tufted chair in the first place, is out of town working on a show that shoots in Atlanta, so I'm unable to lean on him for support. And secondly, because now I'm aware of just how bleak things are. I'm no longer able to remain in denial about how much of a problem my alcohol consumption is (a big one) and my bulimia is (a bigger one). I'm no longer in denial about the extent of my grief over Mom's passing (insurmountable).

The first three weeks of my program with Laura were all about gauging exactly where I'm at by collecting info. And so far, I don't like the info we've collected.

I'm binging and purging five to ten times a day and drinking at least eight or nine shots of hard liquor a night. The first three weeks with Laura have shown me just how dark my situation is, just how much of a failure I've become.

But now we're on week four of our five-sessions-a-week schedule. And week four is the first week where, instead of just assessing how pathetic my day-to-day life really is, Laura starts to help me toward change. We've already identified my main binge, purge, and alcohol triggers, and RED CARPET EVENTS came in near the top of the list in all caps—not only because of the stress and nature of the events themselves, but because red carpet events inevitably come with lots... and lots... of food. And lots and lots of food means lots and lots of opportunities to binge and/or purge. Because of this, Laura and I decided that, for the next few months, Laura will be my plus-one to all these events so she can monitor my behavior and serve as emotional/mental support.

The lights are low. I can see the crowd. Laura's sitting in the front row. I make eye contact with her. Laura smiles and starts to mouth, *You've got this*, but just as she gets to the *th* in "this," a mother trying to corral her fleet of young children scuttles past her. Laura makes an "excuse you" face until she realizes that the mother is Angelina Jolie. "Excuse you" face turns into "oh, you go right on ahead you glorious angel" face.

I try to meet Laura's eyes again, even for a quick second, before the lights come back on. I'm desperate for her support. I'm sure that I'm penetrating her soul with my desperation, but it doesn't matter. I've lost her to Angelina. Not that I can blame Laura. I get it.

The camera operator, Chip—I don't actually know his name, but there's a 90 percent chance that any given camera operator's name is Chip—starts giving me the five-finger countdown. I swallow my nerves.

The lights shock me when they come on. It doesn't matter how many random tween/teen/kid awards shows I participate in, I never get used to the lights. They are blinding, and I'm amazed how more people onstage giving or accepting awards for things that don't matter don't squint while they're up here.

I start talking, saying whatever's on the prompter, with a big smile and my "fun" voice. I notice my hands are doing a lot of big gestures, but I can't seem to control them. The whole thing is an out-of-body experience.

Nick Jonas waltzes out and accepts an award, and the lights are off again. I gasp for air like somebody coming up from holding their breath underwater for too long. I look down at my hands. I can't see them because my eyes haven't yet adjusted to the lights being off, but I don't need to see them to know that they're shaking.

I'm approached by a security guard who carries himself like a man who takes his wings extra spicy just to prove a point. As I'm escorted to the backstage area, I feel little heat streams running down my cheeks. Shit. Tears.

Finally, when we get to the dingy backstage tunnel with fluorescent lighting, I can get a good look at my hands. They're shaking and clenched in little stiff balls. I don't need any more evidence than this. I'm having a panic attack. And I know exactly why I'm having one.

I haven't thrown up all day. Laura only agreed to be my plus-one if I would agree to meet up with her ahead of the event so that we could eat lunch together. Laura knew that my instinct would be to starve myself before the award show, which could then lead to a binge and purge later.

She ordered a healthy lunch for us and sat there patiently while I picked at my food like a tantrum-y three-year-old.

"I know you don't want to, but you need to eat. You can't go do something like this without having some food in your stomach."

We sat there for nearly an hour, my food untouched, when the car pulled up to take us to the event. I pushed my seat back and stood up until Laura gave me "no way" eyes. I knew she wasn't getting in that Cadillac Escalade until I followed through on my end of the bargain. I forced a few bites into my mouth, Laura encouraged me to take a few more, and we were off.

The ride over to the pavilion was hell. I couldn't focus on anything except for the shame I felt about how much food I had consumed, the calories in that food, and the fact that I couldn't rid myself of it. All I wanted was a toilet, and all I got was forty-five minutes in LA traffic with some adult contemporary slow jams on the radio. (Laura's taste in music is questionable.)

"Um, you okay, ma'am?"

Not now, Spicy Wings. I'm in the middle of a discreet breakdown. I mutter some half-word response, wipe my eyes, and push open the door to the backstage area. The first thing I see is, of course, the buffet table. The inevitable backstage buffet table, piled with crudite, olives, mini sausages, shrimp cocktails, mini grilled-cheese sandwiches, popcorn chicken, and cheeseburger sliders.

FUUUUCK. Cheeseburger fucking sliders. I'm dying to cram some meaty, cheesy sliders into my mouth and then throw them up in the bathroom. The act of purging gives me a rush of adrenaline and it's so physically exhausting that I hardly have space for anxiety after I'm finished. I need the fix.

But I know I shouldn't. That's why Laura's here. Laura! That's what I need. I need Laura. Where is Laura?

I frantically scan the room. Manny from *Modern Family* chats with Sheldon from *The Big Bang Theory*. Fergie talks to Kristen Stewart, who stands in the corner biting her nails. At the other end of the room I spot Laura, beaming as she compliments Adam Sandler. It's clear she has a crush on him. Who doesn't? Shirtless Adam Sandler in the "shampoo is better" scene from *Billy Madison* was true porn for me as a child.

I'm torn. Do I interrupt Laura's engaging discussion with America's Favorite Goofball–slash–Occasional Indie Darling to tell her I'm in the middle of a panic attack? Or do I rush over to the buffet table and stuff my face with a slew of snacks, then go throw them up in the bathroom? Do I get my fix?

I beeline for the buffet table and don't even grab a plate. I double-fist some cheeseburger sliders and start shoving them into my mouth. I turn my back so no one can see what I'm doing. I take bite after bite. I'm done with the first slider and halfway through the second one when I hear...

"I think it's great that you're eating. I would love it if you could slow down a little bit, though. And I want to make sure we step away to a private area afterward so that you can process your emotions without purging. How does that sound?"

My heart sinks. My cheeseburger slider does too. I feel it like a rock in my stomach. I know Laura means well, but in this moment I hate her. I hate that she's disrupting my ability to purge.

"You know what? Why don't we just head out now?" Laura suggests. She must have spotted the dried tear tracks on my cheeks, or my clenched hands, or she might just have such a good read on me that she knows how devastated I'll be at having to keep down the sliders.

We pile into the car and immediately, I start to sob. The panic attack is in full force. It feels like death.

"NOOOOO! NOT THE SLIDERS!! WHY DID I EAT THE FUCKING SLIIIIIDERS!!!" I wail.

"I know, baby," Laura says affectionately. She strokes my hair. "You're doing great. You're doing great."

Really? It doesn't feel like I'm doing "great." It feels like I'm in the middle of a full-fledged breakdown after white-knuckling my way through three teleprompter lines and not being able to cope with eating two Rich People's White Castles. Laura assures me it's normal to have these types of reactions after not purging, since my body's been so used to the habit for so long and the habit has been a source of emotional suppression for me. But it doesn't feel normal. My reaction feels humiliating but impossible to curtail.

I continue wailing. The driver looks ahead blankly. If this guy's not reacting to a hysterical bulimic who's getting orange spray tan on his freshly polished leather seats, I hate to think what else he's witnessed in the back of his Cadillac.

"Can you flip the radio to KOST 103.5?" Laura asks politely.

The driver switches the radio. Gloria Estefan starts singing "Rhythm is Gonna Get You."

"Mom used to loooove Gloria Estefannnnnn!" I sob, collapsing into Laura's lap. I notice her toe tapping. The rhythm did in fact get her.

"Jennette..." Laura says, pausing to rub her lips together, which she does every time she feels like she's about to say something important. "This is what recovery looks like."

One of the more excruciating emotional disconnects for me is when someone says something they think is poignant and I receive it as complete bullshit. This is one of those disconnects. To make the disconnect even worse, Laura SHUTS HER EYES and repeats herself.

"This..."

NO Laura, please don't give me that dramatic pause for emphasis. DO NOT give me that dramati—

"... is what recovery looks like."

72.

I SIT DOWN IN THE tufted chair opposite Laura and let out a sigh. But not like a heavy sigh, more one of those sighs that come out when you've just accomplished a task that you're both glad to be done with and also desperately want to brag about having done.

I finally made it happen. I've gone a full twenty-four hours without making myself throw up. Maybe it doesn't sound that impressive, but it is for me. It's been three years that I've been binging and purging every day, many times a day. I have felt controlled by this eating disorder. Even since beginning my work with Laura, I haven't gone a full day without making myself throw up. I'll struggle through our sessions, and then as soon as I'm back home, I'll purge until I've fully relieved myself of the pent-up emotional turmoil that's accumulated since my last one. I'll visit Laura the next day and regretfully inform her of my failings. Then we start over and we try again. The pattern has proven grueling, and the disappointment in myself has proven overwhelming. But now, I finally made it happen.

Since our session yesterday morning, I have not purged once. My sigh is the sigh of a fucking winner, and Laura can tell. With the hint of a smile, she asks if I have something to share. I tell her the good news. She claps, then asks how I was able to do it, how I managed.

That's when my pride starts to fade. It was really hard, and I'm not convinced I'll be able to do it again. To not throw up for twenty-four hours, I've been journaling near constantly to get my feelings on paper, which is a challenging task since I struggle to identify my emotions. Is "all of the uncomfortable ones" an option? I've had a few bouts of sobbing and I called Laura three times last night, since she opened up that line of communication in an effort to help me make some tangible progress.

The task of FEELING this confusing, overwhelming blob of emotions instead of distracting myself with bulimia is daunting. Bulimia helps me to rid myself of these emotions even if it is a temporary, unsustainable fix. Facing these emotions feels impossible. If I can't even clearly identify them, how will I possibly be able to tolerate them?

I express my fears to Laura, and she assures me it will be a step-by-step process. It will take time. But we will get there, together. I feel comforted. Then she explains to me that now that I've experienced what it's like to not make myself throw up for a day, now that I know I can do it, we need to delve deeper. While this experience was meant to serve as motivation for me, we can't just treat the problem and not the cause. In order to get to what's underneath the bulimia, what's driving it, we need to unpack my life in a more comprehensive way.

"Okay..." I'm hesitant. What will this entail? I hate the uncertainty.

"I want to understand more about Little Jennette," Laura says tenderly. "I understand you felt a lot of pressure, that you had a lot of responsibility at an early age. But I want to get into some specifics."

Always with the childhood, these therapists. I've seen enough movies and TV shows to know that this is the classic therapeutic scapegoat. Some shit happened in your childhood, it messed you up, that's why you are the way you are.

But not me. I didn't have an alcoholic dad, my brothers didn't torture me when my parents weren't home. We were poor, sure, and lived in a hoarder house, yes, and Mom had cancer when I was very little, which was very scary. But otherwise things were fine. I relay this to Laura, gently suggesting in my tone that I refuse to play the game of boohoo-my-childhood-was-wuff.

"Okay," Laura says with a glint of a knowing smile that irritates me deeply for some reason. This irritation confuses me. I'm typically so fond of Laura.

"Tell me about your mom. Tell me about your relationship with her when you were a kid."

Immediately I'm defensive. Why does she want me to talk about Mom? What's wrong with Mom? Nothing's wrong with Mom. Mom was perfect. I know in my gut that I don't believe this, that it's a lot more complicated than this, but why on earth would I tell Laura the specifics? I've never told anyone the specifics and I never will. I don't even fully understand them. And I don't want to. I don't need to.

"Mom was wonderful. She was honestly, like, the perfect mom."

"Oh yeah? What was so perfect?"

I throw on my best fake smile. Laura's sharp. I'm sure she can see right through most of her clients. But not me. I didn't star on shitty sitcoms for a decade and not learn how to sell a line I don't believe in.

"Just everything, to be honest. She took care of me and my brothers, I'm sure that was really hard for her."

"That was her job."

I feel interrogated, like I can't say the right thing. I speed up, trying to explain myself.

"Well, but I mean this was different from most parents." Shit. I hated how that came out.

"How so?"

I pause to compose myself. Laura won't rattle me. I speak in an even, measured tone.

"She sacrificed everything for me. She constantly went without so she could take care of me. She put me first, ahead of herself."

"Hmm. And do you think that's healthy?"

What kind of fresh hell is this? What is this impossible-to-ace quiz? I have no idea how I'm supposed to be answering to make Mom look good.

"Well, I mean, I put her first too, so that kind of balanced it out. We balanced each other... putting each other... first... out."

Laura holds a look at me. An unreadable look. She says nothing. The silence is deafening.

"We were best friends," I clarify.

"Oh? Did your mom have any friends her own age as well, or was her main friendship the one she had with you?"

What do you want from me, Laura?! I squirm in my seat.

"Are you comfortab—"

"I'm extremely comfortable."

"Did your mom have any friends her own—"

"Yeah, no I heard the question," I say in bitch-voice.

Laura looks slightly startled. I feel sorry. Her tone this entire time has been a gently curious one, even though I've been treating it like a personal attack. Maybe she doesn't mean anything by her questions. Maybe this is all harmless.

"Sorry."

"It's absolutely fine."

Couldn't it have just been fine, Laura? Did it have to be "absolutely" fine? *Why is she bugging me like this*, I wonder. I smile at her, tenser than I'd like. She smiles back, softer than I'd like.

"So..." she starts.

"She had acquaintances, yes. She always said she didn't really have time for friends." Before Laura can sidle in with another question, I get ahead of it. "Which makes sense to me because she was really busy taking me to auditions and to set and everything."

"Ah, yes." Laura nods a wistful nod. "So when did you first want to start acting?"

I know a trick question when I hear one.

"Actually, Mom wanted me to start acting because she wanted me to have a better life than she had."

"Oh, so you didn't want to start acting? Your mom wanted you to start?"

"*Yes*," I say with a little more heat on it than I would've liked. "Because she wanted me to have a better life than she had. It was very kind and generous of her."

"Okay."

"It was."

"I understand."

Beat.

"Can you tell me the first time you were aware of your weight or your body in a..." Laura pauses to find the right words. "... significant way?"

This one I don't want to answer but I feel like if I wiggle around it Laura will just come right back for the jugular with her follow up. I tread with caution.

"Well... when I was eleven I was concerned about getting boobs, so Mom taught me about calorie restriction to help me out."

"To help you out?"

"Yes."

"What do you mean, to help you out?"

"Well, I was concerned about getting boobs."

"Right. But how does your mom teaching you about calorie restriction help you out?"

"Because watching my calories meant I could delay adulthood."

Laura holds another of her trademark unreadable stares at me. Even though I can't gauge the specifics, I can tell there's a lot of speculation going on. I feel the need to add more.

"Plus for acting. I always played characters younger than me, so if I wanted to keep booking, looking younger was important. By teaching me calorie restriction, she was helping to ensure my success."

I give a little nod to punctuate my statement. I'm hoping that moved the dial on Laura's judgment, but after a few seconds I can tell it didn't.

"Jennette, what you're describing is... really unhealthy. Your mother essentially condoned your anorexia, encouraged it. She... taught it to you. That's abuse."

My mind flashes back to the first time I heard the word "anorexia," when I was sitting on the paper-covered table in room 5 at Dr. Tran's office. Suddenly I feel just like that little eleven-year-old girl who was confused and scared and uncertain. That eleven-year-old girl who was doubtful that I knew the whole truth of my situation, who was unsure that my mother was the hero she pretended to be, but who shoved that doubt down.

I feel tears welling in my eyes. I'm embarrassed. I'm well-trained in crying and not crying on cue, so I resort to my usual tricks—gritting my teeth to distract from the tears and blinking a few times rapidly to try to churn them away.

"It's okay to let it out." Laura leans forward.

SHUT THE FUCK UP, LAURA. I can't take this anymore. I get one day of not throwing up under my belt and now we're trying to dethrone my mother and demolish the narrative of her that I've clung to my entire life?

"I have to go," I say quickly as I stand up and start to leave.

"Wait, Jennette, this is good work. Important work."

"I've gotta go," I repeat over my shoulder as I pull open the door and speed out as quickly as I can.

Tears fall down my cheeks while I drive home, trying desperately to process everything. Laura suggested that Mom was abusive. My whole life, my entire existence has been oriented to the narrative that Mom wants what's best for me, Mom does what's best for me, Mom knows what's best for me. Even in the past, when resentments started to creep in or wedges started to come between us, I have checked those resentments and wedges, I have curbed them so that I can move forward with this narrative intact, this narrative that feels essential to my survival.

If Mom really didn't want what was best for me, or do what was best for me, or know what was best for me, that means my entire life, my entire point of view, and my entire identity have been built on a false foundation. And if my entire life and point of view and identity have been built on a false foundation, confronting that false foundation would mean destroying it and rebuilding a new foundation from the ground up. I have no idea how to go about doing this. I have no idea how to go about life without doing it in the shadow of my mother, without my every move being dictated by her wants, her needs, her approval.

I pull up to my lonely house and sit in my car with the engine running. I pull out my phone and draft an email to Laura.

Laura, thanks for all your help this past month, but I will no longer be attending therapy. Thank you, Jennette.

My finger hovers over the send button for a few seconds before I tap it abruptly and click off my phone. I rush up my front steps and, once I'm inside, run to the bathroom. I make myself throw up repeatedly. I jam my fingers down my throat harder and harder and harder until I cough. Some blood comes up. I keep going. Vomit streaked with blood pours out of my mouth and into the bowl. It slides down my arm. Chunks of it get in my hair. I keep going. I need this.

I take a bath afterward, attempting to relax. By the time I get out, my body feels achy and feverish, the same way it feels after every purge.

I crawl into bed with my sore, tired body and curl into a ball. I swipe open my phone. Three missed calls from Laura and one voicemail. I delete Laura's number. I guess I won't have a plus-one for my next event.

73.

I'M STANDING BY THE DOOR, running my hands along my pants anxiously as Steven's taxi pulls up in front of my house. Steven got a project out here in LA—a six-month project—and he'll be staying at my place the entire time. We are living together. This is huge. And that part's great, it really is.

The part that isn't great, however, is the part where I have to tell Steven that I've quit therapy. I have no idea what his reaction will be, but I'm sure it won't be good since he's the one who instigated it in the first place.

He opens the cab door and spills out of it in his crewneck sweater and chinos. The cab peels away as Steven bounds up the steps with his canvas bag and rolling carry-on. He's got more energy than usual. Steven is not typically a bounder. Steven is typically a saunterer, a wanderer, a sidler. I figure the extra energy must be from how excited he is to see me, which compounds the guilt I already feel about telling him the news. Once he gets through the front door, he scoops me up into a big squeeze.

"*Jenny, Jenny bo Benny Banana fanna fo Fenny Fee fy mo Menny, Jenny!*" He sings while he flings me around.

I start to do the jingle back but bail halfway through because... it's a lot. Steven sets me down and I brace myself for what I'm about to do. I'm gonna tell him. I'm gonna do it.

"Steven..."

Before the words can come out of my mouth, Steven starts talking a mile a minute about how excited he is—but not about being in LA, not about the project he'll be working on, not about us living together. None of the things I expect him to be excited about. Steven says he is excited... to take me to church.

Church? I haven't been in a church since Mom's funeral, and I didn't plan on going back to one anytime soon (ever). I know Steven grew up Catholic, but supposedly his family never even went to service. I didn't think religion carried any sort of significant weight to him even in his youth, let alone nowadays. I'm confused. Steven explains.

"I don't know, I just feel like there's more to life. More depth, more meaning."

I don't understand the connection. How does Steven expect to achieve more depth through Catholicism? I don't want to tear him down while he's so lit up, so I throw on my best gentle tone and remind him of our early dating conversations, where he seemed to agree with me that religion is a thing that stunts growth, not a thing that promotes it.

"Right." He nods. "But I completely disagree with that now." Okaaaay. I ask him to elaborate.

"Well, I saw *God's Not Dead* on Netflix, and it really resonated with me. I just think there's a lot of truth to it, Jenny. A whole lot of truth. And I want us to try going to church. I want us to try finding some kind of religion."

"Hang on. You saw a shitty Christian movie on Netflix and now you want to abandon your whole life philosophy for Jesus?"

My tone hurts Steven; I can see it in his eyes. There's a moment of silence. I start to wonder if Steven's okay. He doesn't seem like himself. Then again, we're only a few months into our still very-new relationship. Maybe this shift is the natural shift that occurs when the honeymoon phase is over. Maybe this is who he truly is.

"Steven, I... quit therapy."

I can't believe the words just spilled out of my mouth like that, the words I was so nervous to say ten minutes ago. Maybe I just said them to say something, to fill the dead air. Or maybe I said them to take the focus away from church. Regardless of why, I said them and now they're out in the open. I wait for Steven's reaction. He stops rummaging through his bag to look at me.

"That's fine."

Really? It's fine? I can't believe it. This feels too good to be true. He opens his mouth to say more.

"You don't need therapy. Not if you have Jesus."

74.

STEVEN AND I ARE SITTING in one of the back pews of a Southern Baptist church in Glendale while a choir wails on a hymn. The hymn itself is whatever, but some of these women are downright stars.

Despite the talent of the choir, I'm sitting here with my eyes drooped half shut. This is the fourth church service Steven and I have gone to in a week. I didn't even resist it. I've just been grateful that he's not forcing therapy on me. Humoring what I imagine will be a very short-lived phase for Steven feels like a low price to pay in exchange for never having to see Laura or any other therapist hell-bent on ripping my narrative of Mom to shreds.

First we went to a Catholic church service, which Steven said didn't feel right to him. Then we went to a nondenominational service in Hollywood, which Steven felt was too Hollywood. Then we went to the Scientology center, which Steven was wary of from the get-go but wanted to try just in case. It's the Goldilocks and the Three Bears of churches, only GoldiSteven didn't find one that was "juuust right" in the first three, so now we're at church number four.

Steven seems genuinely engaged. He nods his head along with the sermon. He opens his notes tab in his iPhone to jot down scripture verses. He lifts his arms in praise during the hymns. Finally the service lets out. Hallelujah. This is the closest I've gotten to believing in God all day.

By the time we get home I'm ready for a glass of wine mixed with vodka, same as I've been doing for the past few months. Steven is going on about the service. I'm checked out until he says...

"And Jenny... I've prayed about it and I don't think we should have sex anymore. I'm taking a vow of celibacy."

"I'm... sorry? Excuse me?"

"Yeah, I just... don't think we should be sinning like that anymore."

My fingers clench into a death grip on my wineglass. Steven goes on.

"I prayed about it, and I really don't think we should be having sex anymore. It's a sin. I hope you're okay with that."

I'm... not. Our sex is the best sex I've had. I wouldn't want to give that up even if my life was soaring in all the other areas. But it isn't. My life is miserable right now. Sex is a reprieve. It's where I lose myself. I do not want to give up this shred of silver lining in my life.

"What if I'm not?" I finally choke out.

I gulp the last of my winodka down and set my glass on the table as seductively as I can manage, letting my fingers linger on the rim of the glass just so. Fucking Marion Cotillard over here, don't mind me. I lean over and start kissing Steven. He kisses me back, tentatively at first, and then passionately. Got him.

Pretty soon my hand's on his dick. It's hard. Real hard.

"Look how hard you are for me," I whisper in his ear.

"Jenny, stop," Steven says, his face flushed.

"You want me to stop?" I say in my best dirty-talking voice, which lands somewhere between curious toddler and whiney tween but still seems to work. I'm amazed at what a little horniness will forgive. I start to pull my hand away.

"No... no. Don't stop." Steven takes my hand and places it back on his dick. I unzip his pants, pull them off, and lean over to start giving Steven the blow job of a lifetime. I'm pulling out all the stops. I am living, I am giving, I am working it. There are blow jobs, and then there is this blow job. I'm sucking, I'm stroking, I'm whispering, I'm licking, I'm caressing, I'm giving it 150,000 percent. He cums in my mouth.

I pop up, proud and expectant, sure that Steven is going to announce that it will be impossible for him to not have sex with me. That he wants to, NEEDS to have it with me every second of every day. I'm just about to swallow with as much seduction as I can muster, when Steven starts to stroke his chin.

"Yeah, that didn't feel right, Jenny. We can't do that again. We really can't do that again."

There is such finality in Steven's eyes that I know I'm getting nowhere near that dick for the foreseeable future. The cum slides out of my mouth and down my chin. It dribbles onto my lap. Dead in the eyes, I stare at him. What have I done?

75.

"So was there ever a good phase of your relationship with Mom, or was it always... how I remember it?"

I'm familiar with Mom's side of the story, that Dad was "probably cheating" or "didn't do enough for the family" or whatever the qualm of the day was. "Your father is lazy and incompetent, no other way to slice it. He's a distant man with the emotional range of a potato."

As for how I remember it, I remember a few good things. I remember loving the way that Dad's flannels smelled—pinewood with a dab of fresh paint. Sometimes I would sleep in them for comfort. I remember him teaching me how to tie my baby-pink Winnie the Pooh shoes bunny-ears-style while I sat in a shopping cart in Sam's Club and Mom complained about how expensive toilet paper had gotten. I remember him inviting me to his work Christmas party at Home Depot. I couldn't believe he had chosen me to go to the party with him. Me! I didn't have to believe it for long because I quickly discovered it was Mom who wanted me to go with him, to collect intel on which co-workers he might potentially be having an affair with. "Don't rule out Don. I've always wondered if your father's secretly gay. Something about the way he sits, the way he crosses his legs." Regardless, I had a fun time at the party. There were red-and-green chiffon curtains hanging from the walls. Unsold Christmas trees lined the room. I learned how to play blackjack. I really felt loved by Dad that day.

But otherwise, the memories were less than fantastic. Mostly I remember Dad not being present. Seeming uninterested. I remember him trying to read *Stan the Hot Dog Man* to me and Scottie every night for what must have been a three- or four-week stretch until eventually we gave up on him reading it because he couldn't get through the children's book without falling asleep. I remember him forgetting dance recitals and falling asleep during the family watch parties Mom would have for my TV performances. I remember The Great Pornography

Debacle of '03. Mom caught Dad watching pornography—a major sin in Mormonism—and kicked him out of the house again, that time for a month. She insisted that I call him by his first name—"Mark"—after that. I did until she died.

Now, as I sit here opposite Dad and his new girlfriend, I'm not looking for Mom's side, and I'm not looking for how I remember things. I'm looking for Dad's side.

"You know, it was so long ago I hardly even remember," Dad finally answers, after a ten-second pause. He looks over to his girlfriend for approval.

Dad's girlfriend is Karen, Mom's high school best friend who stole her baby name. As I study Karen from across the room, I realize Mom tried to do her makeup like Karen does hers. Or maybe Karen tries to do her makeup like Mom did hers. I can't tell, but either way it makes me uncomfortable.

I want Dad to be happy but he's a little... *too* happy. It's been a year since Mom's death, and he's been seeing Karen since one week after she died. Dad seemed more concerned with getting Karen's phone number than he was with mourning his wife of thirty years at the funeral after-party. (Is that what they call the part after the funeral where everyone eats finger sandwiches and tells you how they can relate to your loss because they lost a cat a few years back?)

Dad moved quicker than my brothers and I expected, and it hasn't been easy on any of us. We struggle but still make efforts to connect with him. We already lost our mom, we don't want to lose our dad, too.

To be fair, Dad's been making efforts as well, a lot more than he made when Mom was alive. He's been calling us every so often to check in, and he had us make Amazon wish lists for Christmas so he'd know what to get us.

That's why when Dad called me up last week to say he wanted to meet in person to "talk about things," while I was slightly surprised by the framing, I assumed that this chat session set for today was just another one of those efforts.

But as I'm sitting here across from Dad and Karen, soaking in the lack of chemistry, I quickly realize that this is not one of Dad's efforts at all. There's something stiffer than usual in his body language. I figure this must be some sort of announcement.

Now my body stiffens. Shit. Dad and Karen are getting married. Oh God, am I gonna have to pretend to be supportive, excited even? I pick at my fingernails so I don't have to make eye contact while I prepare myself for what I'm about to ask.

"So... Why'd you want to meet up?"

"Oh, well, uh..." Dad looks to Karen. She gives him big "go on" eyes. Oh God, no, here it comes.

Here it comes...

"Dustin, Scottie, and you... are not... my biological children."

...

...

...

Huh?

I'm shocked. I feel the color drain from my face. I'm sure I'm about to pass out.

"Wha—?" my cottonmouth finally chokes out.

Dad just nods. Tears well in Karen's eyes.

"But he is your father," she says, her voice cracking with emotional strain. "This man's your father."

The dizziness starts to subside, but I still can't think straight. Tears fall down my cheeks even though I'm completely numb.

"I just thought you should know," Dad says, eyes looking down at his hands while he rubs them together. Mom always hated when Dad rubbed his hands together. "Get a hand cream, Mark."

I lean over and hug him. He hugs me back. Karen watches.

"Thank you for telling me," I say.

My head's buried in his flannel. I smell the familiar pinewood and paint. All I can see is the plaid chest pocket right in front of my eyes. I feel the fabric getting all wet from my tears.

Karen leans toward my hunched-over body and drapes her right arm over me in a sort of half hug. Why, whenever two people are hugging in a room of three, does the third person feel the need to get in on the hug? Hugs were meant as a two-person activity, not a three-person one. We don't need you, Number 3. Thank you.

"He told me, and I told him he had to tell you," Karen whisper-speaks into my hair. "I told him he just had to tell you. You deserve to know."

I finally break away from the thrug and look out the window so I don't have to look at Dad or Karen. There's something about inherently dramatic moments that makes eye contact during those moments feel even more weighty and dramatic. It's a hat on a hat. There's enough drama here as it is. We're good.

I'm looking out the window when I start to think about asking Dad who my biological father is. I want desperately to ask. I'm dying to know. Who is he? Do I have anything in common with him? Would he and I get along easier than Mark and I? Would there be a naturalness to our dynamic? I'm close to asking, but I stop myself. I don't want to offend Dad. Or "Dad," rather. For tonight, we'll just leave it at this. I've got time to ask all my questions later.

"So, should we go see a movie, or...?" "Dad" asks.

Potato.

76.

I'M SO NERVOUS TO TELL Steven the news that I've held off until as late as I possibly could—this exact moment. I'm supposed to leave for a press junket in Australia in an hour. Netflix is launching there, so they're sending a few cast members from various shows overseas to promote the launch. It'll be me, Daryl Hannah, Ellie Kemper, Aziz Ansari, and I've even heard rumblings of the goddess herself, Robin Wright. Fingers crossed.

"I have something big to tell you," I say to Steven while we sit across from each other at my dinner table.

It's been a week since Mark told me he's not my dad, and I've far from processed the information. Every day since has felt like a blur. I've been relying heavily on purging and alcohol to get me through the week.

I've had time to ask Mark some of my many questions. Did he know about Mom's affair as it was happening? (He says yes.) Do my brothers know about this whole fiasco? (He says no.) Is he absolutely 1,000 percent sure that this is the truth? (He says yes.) Does he know who my father is? (Yes.) But other than these basic, concrete answers that I've gotten, every other question I ask is brushed off with "I don't know" or some variation of it.

How did he stay with Mom for all those years when he knew she was having an affair that produced three children? ("I don't know...") Does my biological father know I exist? ("I'm not sure...") How did the affair finally end? ("Ummmm... dunno.")

The question that I most desperately want the answer to, by far, is why didn't Mom tell us? Why did Mom not tell us when she had the chance? How could Mom not tell us?

I've tried to justify her decision, to make sense of it. But the more I mull it over, the more I try to excuse her decision or even try to understand it, the angrier I become.

Regardless of *why* she didn't tell us, she didn't. That hurts me in and of itself.

This is the person who meant more to me than anyone or anything in the world. This is the person who was the center of my existence. Her dreams were my dreams, her happiness was my happiness. How could the person who I lived and breathed for have kept such a fundamental piece of my identity hidden from me?

I could pretend that she never had the chance to tell us, that she desperately wanted to tell us but that it was never the right time... but that's just not true. She had chances, times where she thought she was dying, where she was aware of her own mortality. I think of somebody's dying days as the perfect opportunity to tie up loose ends, get their affairs in order, tell their children who their real fathers are. So why did Mom not do that with hers? Why did she continue to avoid the truth?

The lack of answers, of any semblance of closure, is infuriating. The more questions I don't get answers to, the more questions I have. The more questions I have, the more questions I don't get answers to, and I'm driving myself crazy in the process of trying to find them. I need someone I can vent to, a sounding board, a voice of reason.

I intentionally haven't told Steven about the whole bio-dad situation for the past week because I was waiting for the whole religion situation to subside. I figured you can either have a bio-dad situation or a religion situation, not both at the same time. But now that I've gotta leave for my flight, I have no choice. It'd be weird to wait until I get back to tell the most significant person in my life.

"Okay..." Steven says as he takes in the introduction to my announcement. "And actually, I have something big to tell you too...."

"Okay..." I say, kind of puzzled. "Well, you go first, 'cuz mine's pretty big."

"No, you go first, mine's *really* big," Steven says confidently.

"Look, just go. Please."

"All right," Steven says with a weighted exhale. "I... am Jesus Christ reincarnated."

...

...

...

Huh?

My first instinct is to burst out laughing, the kind of uncomfortable laugh that's an automatic result of shock, sadness, anger, and disbelief combined. Steven thinks he's Jesus-Our-Lord-and-Savior-Christ? Come on. He's gotta be kidding me. The second I realize he's not, my second instinct hits me. I want to cry. I want to just crumple into myself and let it all out.

"You've gotta believe me, Jenny," Steven says with gravity. "I know it sounds crazy, but you've gotta believe me."

I shake myself off and go puke in the bathroom while I come up with a game plan. By the time I get back, I'm trying to figure out if there's anything I can do about my boyfriend thinking he's Jesus Christ in the minutes I have left before I need to head out.

It's clear Steven is unwell, but I have no one to tell that information to who would be helpful in any way. I don't have any of the phone numbers for his family members or friends—our relationship is too new for that. I try and discreetly ask for the phone number of one of his friends that lives nearby, but Steven bursts into tears, begging me to not tell anyone the secret I told him.

"It's just between me and you, Jenny," he cries.

"I think you should tell your family," I urge him, knowing that if he does, they'll see that something's up and likely fly down to take care of him.

"I can't," he says, shaking his head. "I just can't. They won't believe me. Only you'll believe me, Jenny."

I don't respond. There's nothing left in me to respond with. I am powerless. And distraught. Steven is my first real love. Up until ten minutes ago, the joy I've gotten from this relationship has been the only positive thing in my life recently. I'm not ready to let go. I wipe a tear away with my sleeve, and my eye catches the clock on the wall. I'm gonna be late. I have to leave.

I hug Steven. He hugs me back. I get a text from my manager on the way to the airport. Robin Wright has confirmed.

77.

THE FLIGHT TO SYDNEY IS fourteen hours of puking-in-an-airplane-bathroom hell. I eat two full in-flight meals and puke them both up, plus the near-constant stream of snacks that the flight attendant offers—gummy bears, graham crackers, Doritos. Every last snack is down, up, and out for me. It's chaos. There's not one moment of the flight where I'm not eating or throwing up or—in the time between the eating and the throwing up—planning how to get up for the fourteenth time without getting a weird stare from the businessman in the toupee sitting next to me.

By the last time I throw up, I feel like I'm about to pass out. My mouth feels sour from the vomit and sore from the act of vomiting. I shove my fingers down my throat, my eyes bulging as a by-product, and with the brown chunky fluid that pours out of my mouth and into the gray toilet bowl like an ugly waterfall, I spot a small, white, hard chunk. I run my tongue along my teeth and realize one of them is missing. The acidity from my stomach fluids has worn down my enamel to the point that I just lost a lower-left molar.

I taste pennies and spit into the sink. A stream of blood. I reluctantly cup my hand under the airplane bathroom sink and wash my mouth out with the questionable water. I do this four or five times before catching my reflection in the mirror. I try and avoid it, but I can't. Not in a space this small with a mirror this big. I look at myself for a long beat. I don't like what I see.

We touch down in Sydney. As I walk toward the Nissan Sentra that's waiting for me, I see on my phone that there's a voicemail from an unknown number. I swipe my phone open to check it. It's Steven's parents. They tell me that Steven called them, frantic, and they were so concerned that they flew out to visit him. They're with him now at a mental facility to run some tests because a psychiatrist there thinks that Steven might have schizophrenia. I finish the message and get into the back seat of the car.

"Hey, how's it going?" the upbeat Uber driver asks.

I look straight ahead, not answering the driver. How's it going? It's going fucking terribly. Mom lied my entire life about who my biological father was, I'm caught in the undertow of bulimia, I'm gonna have to do an entire press junket while missing a lower left molar, and my boyfriend's schizophrenic. It could not be going any worse.

"Ooh, I love this song. You mind if I turn it up?"

The Uber driver cranks up the volume knob before waiting for my answer. It's Ariana Grande's hit single "Focus on Me."

"It's even better than her last single, huh?" the driver asks. He bobs his head and hums along. Beats the dashboard with enthusiasm.

I look out the window and see the Sydney Opera House in the distance. I tongue my missing molar, deep in thought. Maybe Ariana's got a point. Maybe it's time to focus on me.

78.

"Hello, Jennette."

"Hi, Jeff."

"Why don't you go ahead and step on the scale?"

Ahem? Excuse me? Nowhere in my consultation paperwork was there a clause stating that I would have to weigh myself at the first session with this eating disorder specialist I found online. If I'd read that, I'm not sure I would have booked the appointment. And even if I had somehow managed to still book the appointment, I would have worn my "getting weighed in public" outfit, which I wear to every doctor's appointment I have, regardless of the weather—a poplin skirt and my thinnest tank top. (I want my clothes to add as little weight as possible.) I never would have worn jeans. Goddamned thick, heavy jeans. And a sweater. A lumpy, hefty, cable-knit sweater.

"Do I have to?"

"Yes. But you don't have to look at the number and I won't tell it to you. It's simply for my clinical purposes. I'll need to document your weight at the start of each session."

I wring my hands with agitation.

"You seem upset."

"I don't want to be weighed."

"This is just part of the process, and I totally understand how it might be upsetting. To be honest, your reaction is mild compared to a lot of what I see."

"What do you see?"

"People start sobbing, sometimes they yell, someone threw her purse across the room once. That was fun."

I laugh.

"Facing your emotional experience is going to be the most transformative part of your recovery. That starts with facing your emotional experience around food, eating, your body, and yes, getting weighed. I'll be here to help you through all of it, but if you want to get better, you're gonna need to face all of it."

"Doesn't sound like there's much wiggle room, Jeff."

He chuckles, and then his chuckle ends abruptly and he doesn't say anything. He just keeps looking at me.

Jeff is tall—six foot three, maybe—with kind blue eyes and a perfectly trimmed blond beard to match his perfectly styled blond hair, neatly swept to one side. He wears slacks, a checkered button-down with a tie, and a black belt with a silver buckle. His gestures are as exact as his phrasing—no uhhs or umms, in speech or in mannerisms. This is an umless man. I respect him. It takes a lot to be an umless man.

I get up and walk over to the scale. I shut my eyes and take a long inhale, then step on it. I hear him make a note on his clipboard.

"You can step off now."

I do. I return to the couch and sit on it. Jeff smiles at me—there's a little warmth to his smile, but it's more so the smile of someone who means business.

"Let's get to work."

79.

"I CAN'T BELIEVE I EVER thought I was Jesus," Steven says with a laugh, as he eats a fry.

We're sitting across from each other at a table at Laurel Tavern, a bar in Studio City. I'm nursing a mezcal mule and taking in Steven the way I used to take in my mother after any of her brushes with death that she survived. It's a pure way of taking somebody in. There's a grateful astonishment. They're here. They're still here.

I thought Steven's trip to the psychiatric ward might be the last I'd hear from him. But as soon as he had access to his phone again, he called. We both wept. He sounded like his usual self, sort of. There was more lethargy to his tone, a numbness that didn't used to be there. He told me this was due to the lithium he was taking and that, with time, he'd get back to his old pre-diagnosis self. I wanted desperately for that to be the case.

And now, sitting across from him two months later, I'm starting to think it might be. We're living together again, and he seems to be doing well. He's actively seeing a therapist and psychiatrist. He's on medication. His vow of celibacy is over and we're having great sex. He's making light of his schizophrenic episode the way you can only do when the thing you're making light of is truly a thing of the past.

"I can't believe it either," I agree.

Steven takes my hands in his from across the table. His fingers are greasy from the fries. I don't mind.

"That must've been so scary," he says.

"It was."

"I'm sorry I wasn't there for you."

"It's okay. I really couldn't be there for you either, honestly. With everything going on."

"I know. But we're both working on our stuff now. We're gonna be able to be there for each other. It's gonna be so good."

I nod. I believe him.

80.

I'M STARING AT THE PLATE of spaghetti in front of me. I've been staring at it for at least ten minutes while I process all the thoughts and emotions that are coming up for me before eating it.

I pick up my pencil and start filling out my worksheet.

Thoughts: I want this spaghetti, but I don't want this spaghetti. I'm terrified that this will make me heavy. I don't want to feel bogged down. I don't want to feel heaviness. I'm tired of feeling so much heaviness. I'm scared of eating. I don't want to throw this up.

Feelings: Dread—8/10. Anxiety—8/10. Fear—7/10. Lust—6/10.

I take a deep breath and then I take a bite. More thoughts. More feelings. Always more thoughts and feelings. Exhausting, constant thoughts and feelings. I go back to my worksheet to start writing them down.

Thoughts while eating: Mom always said sodium made my face puffy. I'm scared my face is gonna be puffy tomorrow. Mom would be mad if she saw me eating this. Mom would be disappointed. I'm a failure.

Feelings: Sadness—8/10. Disappointment—8/10.

I start to cry. I set my pencil down and let the tears fall, as instructed by Jeff.

I've been seeing Jeff for three months now, and the progress is slow but steady. We've done so much work it's hard to keep track of it at this point.

The work started with me throwing out all diet foods (Lean Cuisine frozen dinners, diet cranberry juice, diet teas, etc.), as well as all gym clothes. No working out during this phase of recovery. Stretching and reasonable walks are fine, but no half-marathons for me anymore. All indicators of diet had to go.

Then I was told to track my binges and purges for two weeks, as well as every single thing I ate and the time that I ate it. Tracking my purges made sense to me, that was a thing Laura had me do, so I expected it, but tracking my food intake confused me. Isn't tracking food a part of disordered eating? Isn't it a compulsive, unhealthy thing to do?

"Yes, tracking what you eat is going to be a behavior that we want to knock out with time. In fact, eventually I'll have you keep a tally on how often you track, so that we can work toward getting that number to zero."

"So, tracking... tracking."

Slight chuckle. Abrupt ending. "Correct."

"All right. So then why am I tracking my foods now if I'm supposed to work toward not tracking them?"

"I need to get a sense of your behaviors around food. Seeing what goes into your body and when will help me understand that."

After two weeks of tracking, Jeff reads over my worksheets while stroking his beard.

"Hmmm. Yes. Interesting. Hmm. Yes."

What? What, Jeff? What?

"Interesting..."

"What's interesting?" I ask finally, when I can't hold it in any longer.

"So you skip breakfast almost every day, and then you eat a late lunch, around two thirty or three p.m. But it's not really a lunch. It's not a full meal. I'm seeing eight bites of salmon on Tuesday—very specific—a protein bar on Wednesday, two eggs on Thursday. Why did you purge the eggs?"

I shrug.

"We'll get there. Okay, so you're having these very late, incomplete lunches, and then around eight p.m. it looks like you have dinner, which is also incomplete every night. Then, and here's where things start to really click, around eleven p.m. you have what you describe as a binge. An entire plate of pad Thai with fried rice, plus a burrito from Del Taco. And then it looks like you purge whatever you eat around that time, every night."

Yes, I know, Jeff. I wrote the list.

"Right," I say, pretending like I'm learning something.

"So here's the thing, Jennette. You're starving yourself for the first part of the day. You're not eating breakfast, you're having late and incomplete lunches and dinners, and then you're so famished by eleven p.m. that you're *eating* because your body is begging you for it. And it makes perfect sense the foods you're choosing to eat around this time. Because you're so famished you want something hearty, something that will sustain you. But then, of course, because of your judgments around those foods and because of your deeply entrenched destructive thought patterns, you purge them up. And then repeat the cycle the next day."

"Honestly, this was a good week," I explain. "I think because I want to 'do well' in therapy or whatever."

"That makes sense," Jeff assures me. "No need to overanalyze it. Just take it as it is. A step up." He nods politely, then lowers his chin and looks at me with determination. "But I think we're capable of more."

I believe him. He's so sure. And an umless man isn't sure of something for no reason. An umless man is sure of things that he is sure of.

"Here's what we're gonna do. We're gonna normalize your eating. Three full meals a day and two snacks, each at predetermined times. No negotiations. Before starting the eating normalization process, we need to identify your risky foods. Risky foods are the foods you have a lot of judgment around—the foods you feel more compelled to purge."

Don't have to tell me twice. I start rattling off a list.

"Cakes, pies, ice cream, sandwiches, french fries, bread, cheese, butter, chips, cookies, pasta…"

"Great, great," Jeff says as he takes rigorous notes but refuses to ask me to slow down. It's the achiever in him, I can tell. The pen flies. He's going for the gold. He crosses the *t* in "pasta" and looks up at me.

"So one of our ultimate goals here in therapy is to reduce judgment around food. All judgment. We want you to neutralize food. It's just a thing you eat, neither good nor bad. Regardless of whether it's pineapple or pancakes."

"I see both of those as bad, because they both have a lot of sugar."

Jeff blinks once.

"Right, so that's what we're gonna work on."

"Okay."

"And I'll warn you, Jennette, normalizing your eating patterns and mentally neutralizing food is not gonna be easy. At all. It's gonna be hard emotional work.

For so long, your eating has been so... fucked up."

Didn't expect that F-bomb, Jeff, but I appreciate the fervor.

"It's gonna be intense. But I'll help you through it."

* * *

I'm sitting here with my salty tears falling onto my plate of spaghetti, watering down the marinara sauce. Jeff was right. Normalizing my eating and neutralizing food is hard emotional work.

The crying gets heavier to where my chest starts heaving. I get mad at myself for crying. It makes me feel dramatic. Out of control.

Tears fall onto my worksheet and blur the ink. Fuck. I try to blow on the wet spot to dry it, but snot drips out of my nose and falls onto the page and makes it worse. I crumple the worksheet into a ball and throw it across the room toward the trash can. It doesn't land anywhere close. Jesus Christ.

Fuck it. I get up, hurry to the bathroom, and purge.

81.

"SLIPS ARE TOTALLY NORMAL. WHEN you have a slip, it's just that. A slip. It doesn't define you. It doesn't make you a failure. The most important thing is that you don't let that slip become a slide," Jeff tells me, and then he hands me a packet titled *Don't Let Slips Become Slides*. (I have a feeling he rehearsed this moment. "Say it, then hand them the packet. Yeah, that'll hit home.")

These packets are a weekly occurrence with Jeff. At the end of every session, he hands me a new one. Usually they include an article, maybe a quiz or two, and some worksheets. The topics have a wide range, everything from *How to Establish Healthy Relationships (And Take Stock of Your Current Ones)* to *Building an Identity without Your Eating Disorder* to *What Is Self-Care, Actually?*

I enjoy doing the packets. I like that I'm able to get myself on paper. It simplifies things for me. When everything's in my head, it feels chaotic and jumbled. But when I can look down at a sheet of paper and see myself reflected back in words and tallies and graphs, it's clarifying.

The packets always reiterate whatever our session was about, so I know today's session is going to be about slips.

"Jennette, this is going to be one of the most important parts of recovery. Accepting slips and moving on from them."

I nod.

"People with a propensity for eating disorders tend to be the types of people who get very caught up in their mistakes and struggle to move on from them. Perfectionists. Does that resonate?"

"Yeah…" (The label's a little annoying, but it resonates.)

"The problem with this is that if we beat ourselves up after a mistake, we add shame onto the guilt and frustration that we already feel about our mistake. That guilt and frustration can be helpful in moving us forward, but shame…

shame keeps us stuck. It's a paralyzing emotion. When we get caught in a shame spiral, we tend to make more of the same kinds of mistakes that caused us shame in the first place."

I nod, catching on.

"So it makes slips become slides."

Jeff points at me with pride.

"Bingo."

I could've done without the "bingo," but the point connects with me in a deep and powerful way. I'm realizing how much shame spirals have contributed to my issues. I'm so tired of swearing over and over again that "this time I'm done for real." Maybe this acceptance of slips is the missing piece. Maybe when I have a slip, I can acknowledge how disappointing and frustrating it is without getting caught in the shame spiral. Without letting that spiral lead to more slips, and more slips, and more slips, until they've become a slide. Maybe now a slip can be, as Jeff says, just that. A slip.

82.

Shit. I'm running late for a meeting. I grab my bag and hurry downstairs when I see him sitting there, looking out the window and twirling his hair with his index finger. His expression is catatonic, the way it often is lately. It scares me when I see him like this. The first time it happened, I thought maybe it was because he was on too high a dose of lithium. But the lithium dose has been adjusted a dozen times, and the catatonia hasn't stopped. That's when I realized it was something else.

"Hey boy," I say, trying to sound as casual as possible. "How's it going?"

He doesn't seem to hear me.

"Steven?"

Nothing. I bite my lip.

"Um, I have to go to a meeting. Do you wanna come along for the ride? You can maybe walk around while I'm in there? Shouldn't be more than an hour."

I've started inviting Steven to come along with me whenever I have appointments or work or meetings. I'm afraid he won't leave the house otherwise.

Steven has completely stopped working and seems opposed to ever returning to it. He claims "work is a waste of life." He has no hobbies and isn't interested in spending time with his friends. The only thing Steven does these days is smoke weed. He wakes up in the morning and smokes immediately, then continuously smokes throughout the day. He's high every minute he's awake. So high. Higher than I've ever seen anyone. Catatonia-level high.

At first I thought it was okay. It seemed like a reprieve for him from his schizophrenia diagnosis and all the overwhelm that came with it. I tried to be supportive. I even helped him find a dealer who could get him the amount he wanted, which seemed to be a lot.

But then it became this. And it's not that I don't understand this. I do. I very much understand the need to numb out everything in your life. But I'm not numbing out anymore. And maybe that's the problem here, for us at least. I'm making strides in my bulimia recovery. I'm no longer abusing my body to nearly the extent that I used to. I'm trying every day to face myself. The results vary, but the attempts are consistent.

The further into my recovery I get, the further into his drug of choice Steven gets. And the further away from each other we grow.

And so a few weeks ago I had the brilliant idea that I'd get us back on the same page, whatever it took. Steven tried to help me with my bulimia, so I'll try and help him with his marijuana addiction.

I printed out a bunch of articles about how to quit smoking weed. I looked up support groups. I suggested he try a new therapist who specialized in addiction. I planned activities for us so we'd be out and about and he'd be less likely to use. I invited him everywhere I went so I could monitor him. I pitched him on potential hobbies to take up. I threw away his weed.

Nothing has worked. He won't read the articles. He won't go to the support groups. He won't try a new therapist and even quit going to his current one. He doesn't want a hobby. He bought more weed.

I'm helpless. I'm powerless over him. But I love him. And I want us to be together. So I'll keep trying.

"So do you wanna come?" I ask him again.

"Oh, uh... nahhh, Jenny. I'm just gonna stay here. But thanks for inviting me," he says as he keeps twirling his hair.

83.

"BOB, DID YA HEAR HER?! She ran out of all her money!" Grandma wails, then throws her head on Grandpa's shoulder and weeps a tearless weep into it. Grandma's not even a weller.

"She didn't say anything like that, hun," Grandpa assures her with more patience than I understand.

I'm sitting with my grandparents in the living room of my Studio City home. I still have Grandma blocked, but she won't let Grandpa see me without her tagging along. I've just broken the news to them that I'll be selling my house. The news is not going over well.

"What am I gonna tell Linda? And Joanie? And Louise?!" Grandma yells with her arms flailing in confusion.

"I think you can just tell them the truth," I offer.

"That my granddaughter who I love more than anything on this entire planet decided willy-nilly to up and move out of her beautiful home and into a measly little one-bedroom apartment?!"

"Sure."

"No!"

"It's gonna be okay, hun," Grandpa tells Grandma with a pat on her hand.

The areas in my life that cause me stress is a topic I discuss often in therapy with Jeff. My house has come up enough that Jeff asked why I don't sell it.

"Well, I've wanted to sell it for a while, but I can't do that."

"Why not?" Jeff asks.

"Because it's... not smart."

"Why is it not smart?"

"Because a home is a good investment."

"Hmm. Tell me what's stressful about your home."

"Well it's constantly falling apart. There's always something to fix—a contractor comes by almost every day. I didn't realize homeownership was gonna be another job, a job I'm not interested in and don't have the time for."

"Anything else?"

"It feels lonely. And kinda scary. It's too big for me. And I don't like the neighborhood. And somebody leaked my address online so I've had a couple stalkers who show up sometimes and leave creepy notes, and one time one of them left a bouquet of roses dripping with blood..."

"That's a lot of stressful things."

"Yeah."

"And yet you're not selling it because it's a good investment?"

"Yeah."

"What about it makes it a good investment?"

"I'm not exactly sure. It's sorta just a thing I've heard. You know? Everybody says a home is a good investment."

"A good investment for one person might be a bad investment for another."

"Okay."

"What about your investment in your mental health? Feeling safe is important to mental health, and you mentioned that you don't feel safe."

"I don't, but... I don't know. I don't think I can sell it."

Jeff holds an unblinking stare at me.

"I could buy some plants." I shrug. The amount of times I've thought buying plants might make a difference in my life is staggering.

"Any other ideas?" Jeff asks.

"I could take more vacations."

"But that doesn't directly impact your main environment—your home. Which is the main environment that influences your mental health. So why don't we stay focused on the home?"

"But no plants?"

"Bigger than plants." Jeff nods.

"I could... hire an interior decorator?"

"Okay, and how would that reduce your stress?"

"Well, the house is kind of empty-looking. And feeling. It feels lonely."

"And some rugs are gonna help that?"

"They might," I say with a little sauce. Don't love that judge-y question, Jeff.

"All right," Jeff says simply. "Then why don't we start there?"

I get home and call my realtor to ask if he knows of any good interior decorators. He says he knows just the one.

* * *

Liz shows up at my place in a black flowy top and cheetah-print leggings. I should've known then. Shania Twain is the only person on earth who should be allowed to go anywhere near cheetah print.

"So how would you describe your home style?" Liz asks as she sits down at the dining table. She plops her big bucket bag on it and starts pulling out scraps of fabric, binders of materials, and thick home magazines.

"Uhhh…" I look around the empty room. "I have no clue. I was thinking I'd just go with whatever you were thinking."

"Oooh, excellent," Liz says excitedly. "I have lots of ideas. I think the front-runner is… glamor chic with animal-print accents."

I do everything in my power to avoid looking at her leggings.

"Not a huge fan of animal print."

"Oh," she says, slightly offended. "Well, it would just be subtle accents. We could do some cheetah print, or cow print, or zebra print, that's very in right now."

Why are you pushing zebras on me, Liz?! I don't want zebra print on my pillows or my blankets or my curtains. It's a thing I've never understood, why we have to go and try to make pillows and blankets and curtains "fun" with prints. These things aren't fun, they're functional. Give me some simple, solid-colored, coordinating furniture and let's call it a day.

"That's okay," I say as delicately as I can. "I just want simple stuff. I don't have an eye for it, but I know I want simple."

"But you're so young! And fun! Don't you want your space to reflect that?"

No.

"Uhh…"

"Why don't we just try it? Why don't we just start with this plan and then anything you don't like I can return, except for the things that are nonrefundable."

A pushover is a bad thing to be, but an opinionated pushover is a worse thing to be. A pushover is nice and goes along with it, whatever it is. An opinionated pushover acts nice and goes along with it, but while quietly brooding and resentful. I am an opinionated pushover.

"Okay," I say politely, brooding.

Three days later, mint-and-cream cheetah-print curtains show up at my doorstep with a receipt: $14,742. Liz is clearly used to working with clients who don't mind dropping fifteen grand to block the sun, but I am not one of those clients.

Prints and pricing aside, I'm starting to accept that it doesn't matter what kind of blankets or curtains or pillows I have, they won't make up for the constant construction and the loneliness and the stalkers with the bloody roses. I can't be in this house.

I call Liz to tell her I won't be needing her services anymore.

"Well, I am disappointed," she tells me. "But I totally understand and wish you the best of luck with decorating your home."

"Thanks, but actually I think I'm gonna sell it."

"Oh?"

"Yep."

"Well okay..."

"Yeah. So, anyway... let me know where you want me to drop off the cheetah curtains so you can return them."

"Oh, those are nonrefundable."

* * *

Now, days later, I'm trying to reason with Grandma.

"I don't understand why me selling this house is such a big deal to you."

"Because!" Grandma shouts.

I always forget that trying to reason with the unreasonable is... unreasonable.

"This is what's best for me. And I'd really appreciate if you'd support the decision."

"Well I don't. I just don't!" Grandma buries her head in Grandpa's armpit.

"It's all right, hun. It's gonna be all right," Grandpa tells her.

"Where are ya even gonna be movin' to, doll?" Grandma asks with a sniffle.

"I'm moving into an apartment above The Americana."

"The Americana?" Grandma turns to face me, sniffle-less. "That fancy shopping center with the fountain and the Frank Sinatra music?"

"That's the one."

She hesitates.

"I guess it won't be that bad. They do have an Ann Taylor Loft there…"

84.

"Is this trying too hard?" I ask Colton and Miranda. They're helping me pick out the outfit I'm gonna wear to the big event.

"I'd take off the skirt. It's a little... much," Colton tells me.

I appreciate his honesty and grab some jeans instead.

"Better." He nods.

"What if he doesn't like me?" I shout to them as I head into the bathroom to change.

"He's gonna like you," Miranda calls out to assure me.

I'm so jittery. I'm way more nervous than I've ever been to go on a first date. Maybe because the stakes are higher. This isn't just any first date. This is my first date with my biological dad.

We're in Miranda's Porsche on the 405 as we head down to Newport Beach to the hotel where the concert is happening.

"So your bio-dad plays the trumpet?" Colton asks as we get close to the destination.

"Trombone," I correct him.

"Same thing," Colton says with a shrug.

I know he's trying to keep the conversation going because the mood's gotten heavier the closer we've gotten to the hotel. With good reason. I'm showing up unannounced at the jazz concert performed by my biological father who I'm not sure even knows I exist.

Even though I wasn't able to find out much from Mark-Dad about the situation, I was able to get bio-dad's full name and occupation, which was enough for a quick online search to lead me to his official website. He had a list of credits that he's played on the soundtracks of—various *Star Wars* films, *Jurassic World*, *Lost*, and countless others—and a list of upcoming tour dates for his fun side passion project, a jazz band. I chose the latest possible LA area date to attend, because I wanted as much time as possible to emotionally prepare.

And now here I am, minutes away from this concert, and months since I'd first decided to come, and I still don't feel emotionally prepared.

Does Andrew know he's my father? Does he know he's Dustin and Scott's father? Was he ever around when I was little? Where did he and Mom leave off? Did he keep in touch with her? Does he know she's dead? Does he have a family now? Do they know about this situation?

I have so many questions, and the range of possibilities of answers is unsettling to me. I've considered the possibility that he has a family, that his kids might be at the show, and that they might not know. And I don't want to be the one to introduce this news into their lives. So I've decided that I'll approach him at the end of the concert, as soon as he's leaving the stage, and only if he's alone.

I've also considered that maybe he'll deny it. Maybe he'll say, "fuck off." Maybe he won't know. I have no idea what I'm in for.

Miranda pulls up to the valet and we all hop out of the car. Colton grabs my arm for comfort—Miranda doesn't. So many female friendships seem so rooted in physical contact—the clutching of hands, constant hugging, hair touching, whatever. Miranda and I have a friendship that is not entirely void of physical contact, but almost. Hugs between us are rare, and it feels right.

We walk through the hotel corridors, and I stop at the bathroom to pee. Miranda comes with me, I think to make sure I'm not vomiting. She's never told me this directly, but I can tell. She doesn't come with me every time. She's not the obvious type.

Typically I'd feel agitated, the way I would when Steven always tried to intercept a purge. But not this time, because this time I'm not planning on it. There's nothing in my body to purge. I've felt nauseous all day and unable to eat. I've made a mental note to bring this up in therapy tomorrow, but for today, I just want to get through.

I wash my hands for a long time, hoping this will rid them of their clamminess. I add more mascara and a little more blush. Why am I so concerned with how I look around my bio-dad? I've noticed this all day long. I stuff my mascara back into my bag and we head through the hotel and out to the courtyard, where the gig is happening. I hate the word gig but I'm pretty sure that's the proper term for this.

Colton, Miranda, and I sit at a table near the back a few minutes before the show starts. The crowd is mostly folks in their forties and fifties, wealthy-looking. Lotta Gucci.

"What brings you kids here?" the woman sitting next to me, wine-drunk and pearls-clad, asks.

I think about saying, "Well my biological father who I've never met plays the trombone in this band, so I was just gonna accost him after the show to try and find answers about my dysfunctional mess of a childhood," but I don't.

"We just like jazz," Colton says finally, after he realizes there's nothing more than a blank stare coming from my end.

"Oh, that's good. We need more young people like you. Cultured. Which jazz bands do you like?"

"Just all of 'em. The whole... all of 'em." Colton nods.

"Great, great," Pearls responds with a smile, seemingly satisfied by that non-answer. "Ooh, here they are!"

Pearls claps ecstatically, and the three of us turn to see the band walking out onto the stage. I laser in on my dad, carrying his trombone. I can't say I see a resemblance. Maybe I'm sitting too far back. Or maybe Mom's genes were stronger.

The band starts playing. Colton grabs my hand a few times. Miranda watches me out of the corner of her eye. I feel like I'm in a trance the whole time the band's playing.

An hour later, the saxophonist announces they're on their last song. My mouth goes dry. My hands are drenched. My heart is pounding.

"Okay, let's go," Colton says, taking my hand. The three of us get up from the table and head toward the stage exit.

"Where're you guys going?!"

Not now, Pearls.

The final song is coming to the final measures and we're not yet to the stage exit. We pick up the pace.

"You can't come here," a security guard tells us.

"Sorry, she has a quick thing she has to do," Colton says with the confidence of someone who's giving legitimate information.

The security guard is confused enough to let us pass. I look up and see him crossing off the stage—my biological dad.

"Hurry!" Miranda says.

I run the last thirty yards or so until I get to him just as he's walking down the stage steps. He feels me. We make eye contact. He looks puzzled, maybe a little alarmed.

"I think we have something in common" is what comes out of my mouth.

His eyes well with tears. Mine do too.

The next ten minutes are an informational exchange of a blur. I ask him if he knew about me, that I existed. He says yes. And my brothers. He says that he's been waiting for us to contact him. He didn't want to contact us because he wasn't sure if we knew. He asks how I found out. I tell him. He says things ended poorly with Mom and that there was a big custody battle when we were little—that Mom said he was physically abusive (he assures me he wasn't). She won. I ask him if he knew Mom died. He says yes, he saw it on *E! News*. I think about what a strange sentence that is.

Tech people start telling us we have to move. Bio-dad gives me his phone number and tells me to text him. We hug and say goodbye. Miranda and Colton come over to me. I'm having a lot of feelings and I can identify what they are. It feels like progress.

I'm glad he knew we existed. I'm relieved to have this event over with. I'm disappointed by the brevity of it. I'm confused and sad that he didn't reach out to me first. I will never know for sure if he wanted to meet me, or if he's just saying it because that's what you're supposed to say.

As far as first dates go, this has certainly been the most interesting one I've been on. I'm not sure if there will be a second.

85.

It's cold and heavy in my hands. I walk slowly with it because I'm stalling. I've gotten rid of it before, seven or eight times. But every time, I go right back out the next day and get a new one. So far I haven't been able to get through twenty-four hours without getting a new one, but I'm hopeful that this time might be different. Maybe this time, since I'm making it more of an occasion, since my getting rid of it is my gift to myself for my twenty-fourth birthday, I'll be able to get rid of it for good.

My scale has defined me for so long. The number it shows tells me whether I'm succeeding or failing, whether I'm trying hard enough or not, whether I'm good or bad. I know it's unhealthy for anything to have that much authority over my self-worth, but no matter how hard I've tried to fight it, I have always felt reduced to the number on the scale—maybe because, in a way, it's easier. Defining yourself is hard. Complicated. Messy. Letting the number on the scale do it for you is simple. Direct. Straightforward.

I am 95 pounds. Or 105 pounds. Or 115 pounds. Or 125 pounds. Whatever the scale reads, I am that and only that. That is who I am.

Or rather, who I was. I no longer want that number to be the entirety of who I am. To define me. I am ready to experience life beyond the scale.

It sounds ridiculous, "life beyond the scale." It's so dramatic but unfortunately true for me. I'm embarrassed that this is my reality. Maybe that's a good thing. Maybe that's growth, to be embarrassed.

I approach the trash room and pull down the latch to open the chute door. I drop the scale into the chute. I hear the scale slide down it, banging against the sides of it as it falls. It lands. I leave.

The next day comes and goes. I don't get a new scale.

86.

WE'RE SITTING IN A SWAN boat on Echo Park Lake. A goddamned hideous swan boat. Neither of us have said a word for the past five minutes, which feels like a lot more than five minutes when you're sitting in a goddamned swan boat.

I'm staring at Steven. He doesn't feel me staring. He's looking off into the distance half wistfully, half depressed. He's so contemplative these days, but in the way that gets you nowhere. It's the way that makes your wheels spin and your thoughts keep going in circles but there's no forward movement.

I tried for so long to help Steven. Or to control him. I'm not sure which since they're so closely related. But a few months ago, I gave up.

It started with Jeff giving me some materials to read on codependency. Everything I read resonated a little too much and forced me to accept that Steven and I were in a deeply codependent relationship. Jeff suggested I stay focused on trying to solve my own problems.

"But I'm here. I *am* trying to solve my problems."

"And you're doing a great job." Jeff nodded, affirming. "But I have a feeling you might be able to make more progress if you take all that energy you're spending trying to manage Steven's life and instead put it toward managing your own."

The shift happened quickly. Per Jeff's suggestion, I added group therapy to my weekly self-improvement regimen. I read more books on eating disorder recovery. The more time I spent focused on my issues, the less time I had to focus on Steven's. And the less I was focusing on Steven's, the further apart we grew.

It's been sad to recognize how much fixing has been the backbone of our relationship. Whether it was Steven trying to fix my bulimia or me trying to fix his marijuana addiction or pushing him to find the right cocktail of medication, it's been the glue of our relationship. Without that aspect of fixing the other, we don't have much to talk about. Like right now.

"Steven," I say finally. It jogs him out of his trance. He looks at me.

I don't have to say a word. He knows what's coming. He starts to cry. I do too. We cry and we hold each other and we pedal our giant fucking bird boat.

87.

"Jennette, I have the whole team for you," one of my agent's assistants tells me over the phone.

Whenever "the whole team" is on a call, it's one of two things: very good news or very bad news. "The whole team" only jumps on a call to celebrate or handhold, nothing in between. One by one each member of "the whole team" clicks into the conference call. I wait to find out which kind of news it is.

"Is everybody on?" a voice asks.

"Yeah, we're all here," another voice says.

"So, Jennette..."

Bad news. A pause is always bad news.

"... your Netflix show got cancelled."

Silence. It might be bad news in my agents' minds, but it doesn't sound bad to me. It sounds... fine.

"Okay."

"Okay?" one of the voices asks, confused.

"Okay," I repeat. "Thanks for telling me."

"Okay," another voice says, sounding relieved. "Well, all right then. Uh, yeah, so... good news is, we can start submitting you for other roles now since you're not on hold for Netflix anymore."

"Actually..."

A tense beat while they all wait to hear what's coming next. I can almost feel their fears through the phone. *Is she gonna cry? Please don't let the actress cry. God help me.*

"Actually, I've been thinking about this for a while, since we've been waiting to hear if the show got picked up for a third season. And I decided that if we got picked up, I'd do it. But if we didn't, I'd take a break from acting."

Silence.

"Oh," a voice finally chimes in. "All right then, um... huh. Are you sure?"

"Yeah, I'm sure."

"Like, for sure for sure?" one of them asks.

"Yes, double for sure."

"All right. Well... let us know if you change your mind. We'd love to keep sending you out for roles."

"I'll let you know."

A few awkward goodbyes are exchanged and then the call's over. It's as simple as that. An eighteen-year career ended in a two-minute phone call.

I feel at peace with the decision. Finally. I didn't at first. It's taken me over a year of mulling and back-and-forth with Jeff in order to get here. I've known for so long that my relationship with acting is a complicated one. Not dissimilar to my relationship with food and my body.

Both of them feel like constant pulling, yearning, begging, fighting. I'm trying desperately to get their approval, their affection, and I never quite seem to. I'm never quite good enough.

I'm resentful of the fight, and exhausted with it.

I've finally started to take some control of my relationship with food, and the healthier that relationship becomes, the more unhealthy a career in acting seems for me. I understand that many aspects of any job are out of the control of the person doing it, but in acting that's especially the case.

As an actor, you can't control which agents want to represent you, what roles your agent submits you for, which auditions you get, what callbacks you get, what roles you get, what the lines are for your role, how you look for your role, how the director directs your performance, how the editor edits your performance, whether the show gets picked up or the movie does well, whether critics like your performance, whether you get famous, how the media portrays you, and so on. God bless the souls who can tolerate that much up-in-the-airness in their lives, but I can't anymore.

So much of my life has felt so out of my control for so long. And I'm done with that being my reality.

I want my life to be in my hands. Not an eating disorder's or a casting director's or an agent's or my mom's. Mine.

88.

"I LOVE IT," I SAY, and I'm not lying the way I did when I turned six and opened my Rugrats pajamas. I really do love it.

I've had my backpack for three years and it's gotten pretty beat-up-looking. I've complained about it for months but haven't been able to find a decent replacement. But Miranda did. She found a beautiful black Tumi backpack with gold details. It's perfect.

The only thing that beats Miranda's presents are her cards. I pull hers out to read it. Her handwriting is meticulous. Her phrases are kind and simple. She always squeezes in a couple of well-placed jokes. And she always signs her cards to me as Alec Baldwin. I don't even remember where this joke came from anymore but it still makes me laugh every time.

"Should we go into Disneyland first or should we get dinner?" Miranda asks.

It's my twenty-sixth birthday. Even though Grandpa no longer works at Disney, because he worked there for fifteen years he gets an honorary lifetime supply of park sign-in passes and employee discounts. He used his discount to get me 40 percent off this courtyard-view room we're staying at in the Grand Californian Hotel. Thanks, Grandpa.

"Let's go into Disneyland."

Of course I choose Disneyland. And not just because it's Disneyland. If there's ever the choice between dinner and another thing, I'll choose the other thing.

I'm a few years into my eating disorder recovery but the road is still bumpy. Some weeks I don't purge. Some weeks I do. The diagnostic criteria for bulimia stipulate that there must be a binging and purging sequence at least once a week for three months. So even though I exceed the weekly criteria sometimes, the purging is inconsistent enough that, according to Jeff, I'm no longer considered a bulimic. I'm just a "person who sometimes exhibits bulimic behavior." Which still doesn't sound great to me.

I'm glad at least that when I do have a slip, that slip no longer spirals into a slide. That's huge progress, I know. But I keep telling Jeff that I don't want to be a "person who sometimes exhibits bulimic behavior." I want to be better. Sturdier. More confident in my recovery. I want to feel like I've outgrown eating disorders and they're a thing of my past. But so far, that time hasn't come.

Food—the lack of it, the want of it, the lust for it, the fear of it—still takes up so much of my energy. Any mention of a meal, any reminder of one, still causes a rush of anxiety throughout my entire body.

That's why if there's a choice between dinner and another thing, I always choose the other thing. I want to postpone the chaos of a meal for as long as possible.

I grab my choppy auburn wig and sunglasses from the nightstand. I've started using this disguise when I go places to avoid getting recognized. Miranda and I walk to Disneyland and hop on Space Mountain, then on Matterhorn since it's close, even though neither of us likes it very much. We walk to the partner theme park California Adventure. We ride the Guardians of the Galaxy ride and walk through the Animation Academy building, where we learn how to draw Simba. We're folding up our drawings when the inevitable happens. My stomach growls. We both laugh and agree to get dinner.

Miranda knows all about my food issues. She's known for a while—since early on in my recovery when it was suggested that I tell a few trusted friends. Since then, Miranda's been very supportive.

I appreciate her support but it's also difficult at times. Before Miranda knew about this stuff, when bulimia was my secret, I could get through the ups and downs on my own. I was the only person I had to be accountable to, the only person I would disappoint. But now that she's in on the secret, I can tell she's hyperaware of my eating tendencies. She's constantly observing. I'm not just disappointing myself with my slips, but her too.

"Where do you wanna go?" Miranda asks.

"Wherever there isn't a line."

I just wanna get the eating over with so I can brace myself for the onslaught of emotions and will my way through their intensity until they pass and I haven't purged. Hopefully.

We walk to Downtown Disney, the shopping district attached to the theme parks, and head for Tortilla Joe's since they usually have the shortest line. We're seated in a corner booth and we order right away—chips and guacamole for the table, Miranda gets some tacos, I get salmon with salad. I always think if I order the healthy thing, I have a better chance of not throwing it up after. Less shame in salmon than in a hamburger, I suppose. Or I would suppose if it worked every time. But it doesn't.

I'm so hungry by this point that I can't stop myself with the chips and guacamole. I tell myself just one, just two, just four, just six, but I don't stop at just one, or two, or four, or six. I keep going. I think I'm selling casualness despite what's going on in my mind.

It's so annoying, eating-disorder brain. Anytime I'm having a conversation with someone over a meal, there's another conversation happening internally—judgments and criticisms and self-loathing that press on me with such severity. They're a brutal distraction. I can never be present with whoever I'm with. My focus is always more on the food than the person.

I'm told that this narrative, this way of thinking, this "eating-disorder brain," will lessen with time. I guess we'll see.

The main courses come. I can tell by the way Miranda's watching me that she knows I'm anxious. I remind myself to chew slowly, look calm, act normal. Then I excuse myself and say that I have to pee.

I get to the bathroom and check under the stalls to make sure they're all empty. I started doing this after a Disneyland trip three years ago when I got off Jungle Cruise and beelined for the Adventureland restroom to throw up my clam chowder. I was right in the middle of purging when a little hand poked out from under the stall next to me with her Mickey & Friends autograph book, asking me to sign it. I couldn't because I'm right-handed, and since I'd just purged, regurgitated bits of clam chowder were trickling down my arm. If those bits got on her autograph booklet, Little Bailey would be forever changed.

Luckily this time the stalls are all empty. I have to be quick so no one catches me. I hurry into the biggest one. I shove my fingers down my throat and purge repeatedly until nothing comes up anymore. I wipe the puke off my arm with toilet paper. I hate the toilet paper on Disney property because it's very thin so it crumples up around the vomit every time and I have to scrub the little puke-toilet-paper-dingleberries off my arm with more thin toilet paper and then there are more puke-toilet-paper dingleberries and then there's more scrubbing and so on.

I'm bent over the toilet bowl when I remember something Jeff told me.

"You don't wanna be forty-five at the office Christmas party, with three kids and a mortgage, sneaking into the bathroom to puke up the artichoke dip," he'd said.

Sure, I'm not forty-five. And I don't even like artichoke dip. But it is my twenty-sixth birthday. I am getting older.

I think of Mom. I don't want to become her. I don't want to live off Chewy granola bars and steamed vegetables. I don't want to spend my life restricting and dog-earing *Woman's World* fad diet pages. Mom didn't get better. But I will.

89.

I'M STANDING ON AN EXCRUCIATINGLY rich Brentwood homeowner's slanted lawn. My stilettos have sunk into the grass. I should've never worn stilettos to a party on a lawn, but I don't know how to dress myself and I no longer have Nickelodeon stylists who prepare me for events.

It's dark out and there are twinkly lights and celebrities all around me. I'm at some sort of holiday industry gathering my new manager invited me to, the manager that represents me for writing. (My agents dropped me after they realized my break from acting was not gonna be short-lived.)

I yank my heels up from the grass and make my way to the buffet table when what to my wondering eyes should appear but some miniature cheeseburgers... but I don't feel like something meaty and cheesy right now. I feel like something sweet. And these days I pay attention to what I feel. I spot a dense, warm chocolate chip cookie. Perfect.

As I chew, I realize that this is a chocolate chip cookie that I never would've allowed myself to eat in my anorexic days, and never would have allowed myself to keep down in my bulimic ones. A chocolate chip cookie that I haven't counted the calories in or had anxiety about eating. I think about how it's been over a year since I've purged and several months that I've actually been able to find enjoyment in the food I eat.

Recovery so far is, in some ways, as difficult as the bulimic/alcohol-ridden years, but difficult in a different way because I'm facing my issues for the first time instead of burying them with eating disorders and substances. I'm processing not only the grief of my mom's death, but the grief of a childhood, adolescence, and young adulthood that I feel I had never truly been able to live for myself. It's difficult, but it's the kind of difficult I have pride in.

I hear over my shoulder a booming voice that sounds familiar. I turn and see Dwayne "The Rock" Johnson. He looks so nice and Dwayne Johnson–like with his big smile. The man oozes charisma.

I think about going up to him and introducing myself, reminding him of that awards show years ago. Could Dwayne Johnson tell how miserable I was last time we met? Would he sense a difference now? Does he understand all the obstacles and accomplishments that this cookie represents? Is Dwayne Johnson God?

I'm trying to think of something funny or witty or charming to say, but I can't. My mind freezes in social settings, especially if those settings include The Rock/God. I miss my chance. He wanders off into the crowd. I go back to eating my cookie. Enjoying my cookie.

90.

I'M EATING DINNER AT MY apartment when my phone rings. It's Miranda. Typically I wouldn't expect a call from her these days. We've drifted apart. It's a sad reality for me in my late twenties. At the beginning of the decade, the people I was close to seemed like friends for life, people I could never imagine not seeing every day. But life happens. Love happens. Loss happens. Change and growth happen at different paces for different people, and sometimes the paces just don't line up. It's devastating if I think too much about it, so I usually don't.

But I know why she's calling today. I've been expecting this call and just didn't know when exactly it would come.

"Hello?" I say, while I get up from the table and throw on some sneakers.

"Hey."

We both start laughing. I can't remember the last time we spoke, yet the second we get on the phone with each other we start laughing.

I head out the front door so I can walk around the neighborhood while we chat. We fill each other in on our dysfunctional family updates and major life events and then there's the pause, the little lull before the reason for the conversation is about to be brought up.

"Miranda, I'm not doing the reboot. There's nothing you can say to convince me."

"Well I'm still gonna try!" She laughs. I laugh too.

She tells me she thinks the reboot could be an opportunity for all of us in the cast to "get back out there," maybe get some other opportunities from it. It's the same spiel I already heard from a network executive a few months back when I first learned about the *iCarly* reboot.

I know both the executive and Miranda mean well in saying these things. But I disagree. I don't think a reboot could realistically lead to other opportunities because, if the performer in the reboot hasn't done significant work in between, the reboot just serves as a reminder of that. It further entrenches the performer in the role that they initially got known for at least a decade prior, a role which likely keeps their career stuck—not flourishing.

This business is tough. And this business doesn't view a role in a reboot as a career revival—it's viewed as a career ender.

"But it's really good money," Miranda tells me. "I asked if they'd give you the amount I'm making, and they said yes."

Miranda's right—the network was generous in their offer—and it was kind of her to encourage that offer.

"I know," I say to Miranda. "But there are things more important than money. And my mental health and happiness fall under that category."

There's a moment of silence. It's one of those rare moments where I feel like I didn't say too much, or too little. I feel like I represented myself accurately and there's nothing I would change about the way I said it. I feel proud. We wrap up our conversation, promising to keep in touch, and hang up. I head back home to finish my dinner.

91.

"Hi, Mom," I almost say out loud, but I stop myself because I don't wanna look crazy to the other mourners around me. Mourner, singular actually. There's only one, and it's the same guy I see here every time. He sits in a lawn chair with a sun umbrella over him, playing soft rock from a stereo and staring at the headstone of who I assume to be his former wife.

I look at Mom's headstone. There are about twenty adjectives on it because everyone in the family had adjective pitches and nobody was willing to forsake theirs.

"We've gotta include 'playful,'" Grandpa insisted.

"Why does nobody like 'brave'? 'Brave' is a good word!" Grandma wailed.

So we just crammed all the words on there. Even Mom's place of death is cluttered.

This is my first time visiting Mom's grave since her birthday, last July. My visits have become less frequent through the years, even though I promised Mom, per her request, that I would visit her grave every day. In the beginning, I visited once a week and felt guilty about it, like it wasn't enough. But with time and with reality, the visits have become less and less, and so has the guilt.

I sit cross-legged in front of her grave. I take a longer look at the words on her headstone.

Brave, kind, loyal, sweet, loving, graceful, strong, thoughtful, funny, genuine, hopeful, playful, insightful, and on and on...

Was she, though? Was she any of those things? The words make me angry. I can't look at them any longer.

Why do we romanticize the dead? Why can't we be honest about them? Especially moms. They're the most romanticized of anyone.

Moms are saints. Angels by merely existing. NO ONE could possibly understand what it's like to be a mom. Men will never understand. Women with no children will never understand. No one but moms know the hardship of motherhood, and we non-moms must heap nothing but praise upon moms because we lowly, pitiful non-moms are mere peasants compared to the goddesses we call mothers.

Maybe I feel this way now because I viewed my mom that way for so long. I had her up on a pedestal, and I know how detrimental that pedestal was to my well-being and life. That pedestal kept me stuck, emotionally stunted, living in fear, dependent, in a near constant state of emotional pain and without the tools to even identify that pain let alone deal with it.

My mom didn't deserve her pedestal. She was a narcissist. She refused to admit she had any problems, despite how destructive those problems were to our entire family. My mom emotionally, mentally, and physically abused me in ways that will forever impact me.

She gave me breast and vaginal exams until I was seventeen years old. These "exams" made my body stiff with discomfort. I felt violated, yet I had no voice, no ability to express that. I was conditioned to believe any boundary I wanted was a betrayal of her, so I stayed silent. Cooperative.

When I was six years old, she pushed me into a career I didn't want. I'm grateful for the financial stability that career has provided me, but not much else. I was not equipped to handle the entertainment industry and all of its competitiveness, rejection, stakes, harsh realities, fame. I needed that time, those years, to develop as a child. To form my identity. To grow. I can never get those years back.

She taught me an eating disorder when I was eleven years old—an eating disorder that robbed me of my joy and any amount of free-spiritedness that I had.

She never told me my father was not my father.

Her death left me with more questions than answers, more pain than healing, and many layers of grief—the initial grief from her passing, then the grief of accepting her abuse and exploitation of me, and finally, the grief that surfaces now when I miss her and start to cry—because I do still miss her and start to cry.

I miss her pep talks. Mom had a knack for finding just the right thing in a person to get them to light up and believe in themselves.

I miss her childlike spirit. Mom had an energy that could at times be so endearing. Even captivating.

And I miss when she was happy. It didn't happen as often as I would've liked, it didn't happen as often as I tried to force it to happen, but when she was happy it was infectious.

Sometimes when I miss her I start to fantasize about what life would be like if she were still alive and I imagine that maybe she'd have apologized, and we'd have wept in each other's arms and promised each other we'd start fresh. Maybe she'd support me having my own identity, my own hopes and dreams and pursuits.

But then I realize I'm just romanticizing the dead in the same way I wish everyone else wouldn't.

Mom made it very clear she had no interest in changing. If she were still alive, she'd still be trying her best to manipulate me into being who she wants me to be. I'd still be purging or restricting or binging or some combination of the three and she'd still be endorsing it. I'd still be forcing myself to act, miserably going through the motions of performing on shiny sitcoms. How many times can you pratfall over a carpet or sell a line you don't believe in before your soul dies? There's a good chance I would've had a complete and public mental breakdown by this point. I'd still be deeply unhappy and severely mentally unhealthy.

I look at the words again. *Brave, kind, loyal, sweet, loving, graceful...*

I shake my head. I don't cry. The Doobie Brothers' "What a Fool Believes" starts playing from the sad man's stereo. I stand up, wipe the dirt off my jeans, and walk away. I know I'm not coming back.

Acknowledgments

Thank you to my editor, Sean Manning, for your impact on this book. For understanding my voice and making it so much stronger.

To my manager, Norm Aladjem, your early support and encouragement means so much to me. Thank you for your wisdom, strategy, thoughtfulness, and unshakeable calm.

To Peter McGuigan and Mahdi Salehi—thank you for your talent and humor, and for helping to make this happen.

To Jill Fritzo and everyone at Jill Fritzo PR, thank you for your brilliance and expertise.

To Erin Mason and Jamie C. Farquhar—for the transformative guidance and tools you have provided me.

And finally, thank you, Ari, for your endless love, support, and encouragement. I love you so much. You're my best friend. I'm so happy we're a team. <harmonizing> *We are here for uuuussss.*

Made in the USA
Middletown, DE
19 September 2022